A
New Energy
Frontier

The **Institute of Southeast Asian Studies (ISEAS)** was established as an autonomous organization in 1968. It is a regional centre dedicated to the study of socio-political, security and economic trends and developments in Southeast Asia and its wider geostrategic and economic environment. The Institute's research programmes are the Regional Economic Studies (RES, including ASEAN and APEC), Regional Strategic and Political Studies (RSPS), and Regional Social and Cultural Studies (RSCS).

ISEAS Publishing, an established academic press, has issued almost 2,000 books and journals. It is the largest scholarly publisher of research about Southeast Asia from within the region. ISEAS Publishing works with many other academic and trade publishers and distributors to disseminate important research and analyses from and about Southeast Asia to the rest of the world.

ISEAS SERIES ON ENERGY

A New Energy Frontier

The Bay of Bengal Region

EDITED BY
SUDHIR T. DEVARE

INSTITUTE OF SOUTHEAST ASIAN STUDIES
Singapore

MANOHAR
2010

First published in Singapore in 2008
by ISEAS Publishing, Institute of Southeast Asian Studies

First Indian edition 2010

ISBN 978-81-7304-870-8

Published by
Ajay Kumar Jain *for*
Manohar Publishers & Distributors
4753/23 Ansari Road, Daryaganj
New Delhi 110 002

Printed at
Salasar Imaging Systems
Delhi 110 035

Contents

Foreword

This volume is of special relevance for a number of very pertinent reasons. Firstly, the nations of South and Southeast Asia are going through rapid economic change, particularly with India having registered very healthy rates of growth over the last five years or so. At the same time the Asian economic crisis of a decade ago has now become history, and the countries of the region are now making rapid progress in every sector of their economies. But one important area, which could influence economic growth and development in either direction is the issue of energy which, given the dependence of the region on oil imports and prevailing high prices of oil, does introduce an element of uncertainty about the future.

The editor is particularly well qualified to write on the subject of energy and related issues in the Bay of Bengal region. While the countries of the region have clear opportunities for mutually beneficial cooperation in the field of energy, the success of any effort in this direction would hinge on diplomatic initiatives and the history of relationships between the countries of the region. There are also compelling domestic factors that would influence cooperation in the future, such as the ability of Myanmar to open up its hydrocarbon sector to foreign investments and trade. Similarly, in the case of Bangladesh, the possibility of export of natural gas to India or even the provision of a transit pipeline to allow gas from Myanmar to be supplied to India became an emotional issue several years ago. Diplomacy has to take political realities into account if progress has to be achieved with regional initiatives in areas such as energy. The BIMSTEC region has been grappling with possibilities of closer cooperation in energy trade in recent years but without notable success. Hence the need for some "out of the box" thinking and action.

The book effectively makes the point that the Bay of Bengal region holds a total population of 1.5 billion people, which in a relatively small area of land contains one quarter of humanity. While hydrocarbons are produced in the countries of this grouping, it is not a major oil and natural gas producing region of the world. However, there is no doubt of significant potential for enhancing production, particularly with larger investments flowing in. There are also opportunities for cooperation in power supply. Integration of electricity grids in the region would have major benefits for all the stakeholders. Essentially, trading in energy of all forms would provide benefits to suppliers as well as importers in the region. There would also be significant benefits in the flow of technology and perhaps establishment of production facilities such as in the case of renewable energy devices, where economies of scale would benefit all the countries of this grouping.

The book by virtue of the innovative approach that it takes clearly establishes a case for some fresh thinking on energy policies within all the nations of the Bay of Bengal region. It brings out the benefits of coordination and cooperation rather than isolated plans and strategies based on narrow national perspectives. To that extent, the book serves an extremely important purpose, which is to open new pathways in the field of energy decision-making, with benefits for this region as a whole. If it succeeds, it would also act as a model, for other regions of the world to emulate.

R. K. Pachauri
Director General, The Energy and Resources Institute (TERI)
New Delhi, India;
*Chairman, Intergovernmental Panel on Climate Change (IPCC)**

Message from the Director

I would like to congratulate Ambassador Sudhir T. Devare for his energy and enterprise in organizing the Conference on Energy in the Bay of Bengal on 28–29 September 2006 at the Institute of Southeast Asian Studies, Singapore. I would also like to thank my colleague, Mr Mark Hong, Energy Programme Coordinator, for his ideas and input into the process of assisting to conceptualize the conference and publishing the book.

It is only recently that people have begun to realize the many linkages between the countries surrounding the Bay of Bengal, which are usually perceived as merely the foyer to the vital Straits of Malacca. This dismissive view began to change when major oil discoveries were made onshore as well as off-shore along the littoral states. Gradually, energy experts realized that this region could be one of the last great oil and gas provinces left relatively unexplored.

Thus this book serves as a useful eye-opener to the great energy potential of this region, even as oil and gas demand are ever increasing. In addition, the Bay occupies a strategic position squarely across the energy SLOC's connecting the Middle East and African energy producers with the great Asian markets in Southeast Asia and Northeast Asia. China and others have realized the vulnerability of the choke-points along the Malacca Straits and have devised various by-passes, such as pipelines from Myanmar to Yunnan and across northern Malaya.

This book thus discusses these strategic implications as well as the various national energy potential of the littoral states, the potential for regional cooperation. In doing so, the chapter writers shed light on a little-studied region, and thus add to our store of knowledge and understanding. ISEAS has launched an ISEAS Energy Series of books devoted to building knowledge on Southeast Asian and Asian energy issues. We hope that this book, the third in the series, will help to add to international understanding of a vital resource.

Ambassador K. Kesavapany
Director
Institute of Southeast Asian Studies
16 May 2007

Preface

This book is the outcome of the Conference held at the Institute of Southeast Asian Studies (ISEAS) in Singapore in September 2006 to discuss energy and energy-related issues in the Bay of Bengal region. The region can be described as comprising the countries around and in the proximity of the Bay of Bengal. With a combined population exceeding 1.5 billion, the energy requirements of this region are enormous and are expected to grow exponentially. While the potential for energy resource availability is high, the investments for their exploration or extraction had so far been marginal. Prospects for renewable and sustainable energy also needs to be fully examined. There are other issues as well, such as transportation security, role and responsibility of the private sector including multinationals. The energy scene in the Bay of Bengal region therefore merits extensive study.

Energy is a principal concern and preoccupation today. In fact, most discourses on international relations these days touch upon energy security. While there is competition among many nations to acquire assets of energy, there is also interest to initiate dialogues with energy as the main focus. Pipeline diplomacy has assumed increasing importance. Energy, especially the hydrocarbons, appears to be leading to a sense of interdependence in the world.

Besides discussing the overall energy position in the region and its potential, the book features perspectives on a few countries of the region with regard to energy availability, energy security or energy trading capacity.

While energy-related issues are marked by their universal relevance and importance, it is instructive to see how they apply in the regional or sub-regional context, including in the Bay of Bengal region. The book analyses some of these issues, such as renewable energy, "corporate social responsibility", or maritime security of energy transportation, both in their basic concept as well as the contextual importance to the region.

I am thankful to all the contributors who spared their time and shared thoughts and suggestions on a relatively unexplored topic. It is hoped that the information and analyses they provided on the subject would be a useful basis for the study and practical application on the issue of energy in the Bay of Bengal region.

It is a privilege to have the Foreword penned by Dr Rajendra K. Pachauri, Director General, The Energy and Resources Institute (TERI) in New Delhi, which I acknowledge with deep thanks. In spite of his commitments around the world as the Chairman of the United Nations Intergovernmental Panel on Climate Change (IPCC), he was gracious enough to find the time to share his invaluable insights and advice on the subject. I was delighted that the IPCC was declared the co-winner of the Nobel Peace Prize in 2007.

I am grateful to Ambassador K. Kesavapany, Director of ISEAS, for his keen interest and full support for the conceptualization of the theme, organization of the conference and publication of this volume. Dr Chin Kin Wah, Deputy Director of the Institute was a constant source of encouragement and ideas for which I am deeply appreciative.

It is to my colleague and friend, Ambassador Mark Hong, from ISEAS that I owe much gratitude. Be it in the crystallization of the topic, or for his enthusiastic participation in the conference or for various suggestions on the manuscript, his has been an enormous support at every stage of this publication.

My sincere thanks are also due to Ms Betty Kwan from ISEAS without whose efficient and competent assistance from the time of the conference to completing the manuscript, this book could not have been completed.

Mrs Y.L. Lee, Head of Administration, and Mrs Triena Ong, Managing Editor of the Publications Unit, were supportive and cooperative, as they had been at the time of publication of my earlier book.

I am also thankful to Mr Deepak Nair, Research Associate from ISEAS for the assistance he provided during and after the conference.

I would like to express my sincere appreciation to Dr Vijay Kelkar, a renowned economist and former Finance and Petroleum Secretary, Government of India and currently Chairman, Finance Commission of India for giving valuable comments on this book. Similarly, my deep thanks to Mr Tariq Karim, former Bangladesh Ambassador to the U.S. and presently Harrison Fellow at Maryland University for his encouraging remarks on the subject.

I am grateful to my former colleagues from the Indian Missions in the Bay of Bengal region who were very helpful with their suggestions/assistance with regard to speakers at the conference.

Finally, a word of special thanks for my wife and family for their encouragement and support for my undertaking. It related to a region which all of us have for years found so vibrant and full of energy.

Sudhir T. Devare
Singapore
December 2007

The Contributors

Talmiz Ahmad has been the Indian Ambassador to the United Arab Emirates since August 2007. After obtaining his Master's degree in History, Ahmad joined the Indian diplomatic service in 1974, and served in the countries of the Arabian Peninsula, including Kuwait, Iraq, Yemen and Saudi Arabia. He also served in the Indian diplomatic missions in New York, London and Pretoria. He headed the Gulf/Haj Division in the Ministry of External Affairs between 1998–2000. He was the Indian Ambassador to Saudi Arabia (2000–2003) and Oman (2003–2004). He was Additional Secretary in the Ministry of Petroleum and Natural Gas (2004–2006) and was responsible for handling India's diplomatic effort in the area of energy security. In April 2006, he became the Director-General of India's premier foreign policy think-tank, the Delhi-based Indian Council of World Affairs (ICWA). His book, *Reform in the Arab World*, was published in July 2005. He has also delivered lectures and published articles and papers on resurgent Islam, the situation in West Asia and India's energy security issues.

Debapriya Bhattacharya is Ambassador and Permanent Representative of Bangladesh in Geneva. Prior to this, he was the Executive Director of the Centre for Policy Dialogue (CPD), Bangladesh. He is a macro-economist and public policy analyst. He holds an M.Sc. (Economics) with distinction and Ph.D. (Economics) from the Plekhanov Institute of National Economy, Moscow. He was a Post-doctoral Fellow at the Queen Elizabeth House, University of Oxford. He was a Senior Fulbright Fellow at the Centre for Global Development (CGD), Washington D.C. He was a member of the Macro-economic Policy Advisory Committee, Ministry of Finance; Banking Sector Reform Committee; Advisory Committee of the Securities and Exchange Commission; Panel of Economists, Fifth Five Year Plan (1997–2002), Ministry of Planning; Member, National Committee on Utilization of Gas Resources, Ministry of Energy and Mineral Resources. Bhattacharya was also a member of the Bangladesh delegation to the WTO Fourth Ministerial Meeting held in Doha (November 2001). Currently he is a member of the Advisory Committee on WTO Affairs, Ministry of Commerce. He is a faculty member of the WTO Trade Policy Course. He is associated with various national, regional, and international professional organizations. He has more than one hundred publications to his credit including chapters in books, monographs, journals, articles and research reports. He is currently the Regional Editor of the *Oxford Development Studies*, member of the Editorial Board, *South Asian Studies*, Colombo and Chairperson of the *EU-LDC Network*, the Netherlands. He is a member of the Board of Trustees of the *South Asia Centre for Policy Studies* (SACEPS).

Christophe Bongars is Founder and Executive Director of SustainAsia. He has twenty-two years of experience in the field of consulting, business development, large-scale industrial, infrastructure and clean technologies project development and management. He has successfully created, developed and managed projects and businesses in diverse countries in Asia, Europe and Africa. Based in Asia since 1995, he was Project Director for Air Liquide group until the end of 2001, developing and managing industrial gas and utility projects. He then joined the Suez — a leading global industrial and services group providing electricity, gas, energy services, water and waste management — as Vice-President Asia Pacific, pioneering innovative business solutions in water and environmental services in Asia, before founding SustainAsia in March 2004. Mr Bongars is Managing Partner at Cleantech Asia Capital Management Ltd, a specialized private equity investment fund in Hong Kong and sits on the advisory board of Cleantech China. He also serves as Vice-Chairman of the Sustainable Development committee of the French Chamber of Commerce and Industry in Hong Kong and chairs the Sustainable Development working group of the Business Environment Council, Hong Kong. He is also a frequent speaker on issues of sustainable development, clean technologies and renewable energy.

Ong Eng Tong holds a B.Sc. Engineering from London, and Diploma in Business Administration from Singapore. He has worked for forty years in the oil industry principally in marketing distribution and trading and logistics. He represented Singapore at the ASEAN Meetings for Energy Ministers from 1985 to 1999. He is a Consultant on Oil Matters to Electrical Power

Generation Company and City Gas Company. He is the Far Eastern Representative of a German downstream company in the Far East.

Vijay Sakhuja has been Visiting Senior Research Fellow at the Institute of Southeast Asian Studies since 2006. Prior to that, he was a Senior Fellow at the Observer Research Foundation, New Delhi, India. A former Indian Navy officer, Sakhuja received his doctorate from the Jawaharlal Nehru University, New Delhi. Earlier, he completed his M.Phil. studies from the same university. He was Research Fellow at the Institute for Defence Studies and Analyses, New Delhi, and United Service Institution of India New Delhi. He has authored a book titled *Confidence Building from the Sea: An Indian Initiative* and is the recipient of Vice-Admiral S. L. Sethi Maritime Media Award, 2002. His research areas include Asia-Pacific security, regional maritime and naval developments and maritime risk analyses.

P. K. Singh, an Indian national, holds an engineering degree from India and did his MBA in Italy in 1980. He has over thirty years of project management experience in both lump sum turnkey and reimbursable contracts in the fields of fertilizers, refining and gas processing projects in Middle East, Africa, India and Southeast Asia, with wide international travelling. He has interacted with international engineering companies like M.W. Kellog, Foster Wheeler, John Brown, Parsons (all in the United States), Snamprogetti, Haldor Topsoe, Tecnicas Reunidas, Linde (all in Europe), JGC, Toyo, Chiyoda, Marubeni (all in Japan), Hyundai, Daelim and LG (all in Korea), EIL and PDIL from India and leading international manufacturers. His biggest assignment so far is the current US$2 billion lump-sum turnkey contract for a grassroot refinery project in Vietnam being executed by a Joint Venture of Technip France (Leader), JGC and Toyo of Japan and Tecnicas Reunidas of Spain, with operating centres spread in Central America, Europe, India, Southeast Asia and East Asia involving over twenty different nationalities. He is employed as Executive Project Director with Technip France and is currently based at Kuala Lumpur in connection with a Vietnam project.

Andrew Symon is Managing Director of Menas Asia in Singapore, a subsidiary of U.K.-based political and strategic risk consultants, Menas Associates. An Australian citizen, he has been living in Asia since 1992 and has been employed as a consultant/researcher for both business planning and public sector/public policy projects, and as a journalist managing and writing for various publications. A focus of his work is the energy, mining/natural resources and infrastructure sectors as well as analysis of more general political, economic and social issues and conditions in Asia concerning and affecting both business planning and government policy. He was a Visiting Research Fellow at the Institute of Southeast Asian Studies, Singapore from 2004 to 2005. He is completing a book about energy sector development, *Fuelling Southeast Asia's Growth: The Energy Challenge.* He is currently also an associate of the South Australian Centre for Economic Studies, a joint research and consultancy arm of the University of Adelaide and Flinders University in South Australia. In Australia, he has worked in journalism, government at state and federal levels, and in the national parliament in Canberra. He is also a Bahasa Indonesia/Malay speaker.

Tazeen Tahsina is Research Associate at the Centre for Policy Dialogue (CPD). She holds a B.A. in Economics from the North South University, Dhaka. She has been working in the areas of trade and investment policies.

U Than Tun has served in the Ministry of Foreign Affairs of Myanmar, Yangon and in various overseas posts of embassies and the permanent mission of Myanmar. He is the Joint Secretary at the think-tank organization, Myanmar Institute of Strategic and International Studies (Myanmar-ISIS) as well as Advisor at the Ministry of Foreign Affairs. He retired as Director, ASEAN Affairs Department, Ministry of Foreign Affairs, Myanmar. He attended Australia Foreign Service Training at the Department of Foreign Affairs, Canberra, A.C.T, in 1980. He has a Master's degree in Public Policy (MIPP), from the School of Advanced International Studies (SAIS), Johns Hopkins University, Washington D.C., in 1988.

Elspeth Thomson is a Fellow at the Energy Studies Institute of the National University of Singapore. She is co-editor of East Asia Institute's journal, *China: An International Journal.* She received her Ph.D. in Chinese Economic History from the School of Oriental and African Studies, University of London. Her main research interests are Asian energy and transport. Her book, *The Chinese Coal Industry: An Economic History,* was published by RoutledgeCurzon in 2003 and an edited volume, *Energy Conservation in East Asia: Towards Greater Energy Security,* will appear in 2007. She has published articles concerning various aspects of Asia's energy sector in *The China Quarterly, Pacific and Asian Journal of Energy, Journal of Applied Statistics, China Review, East Asia: An International Quarterly,* and *Perspectives.* Through the 1990s she taught at Simon Fraser University in Vancouver and Lingnan University in Hong Kong.

Sugiarta Wirasantosa is the Director of Research Centre for Maritime Territory and Non-living Resources, Agency for Marine and Fisheries Research, the Ministry of Marine Affairs and Fisheries. He studied Geological Engineering at the Bandung Institute of Technology and has an M.Sc. in Marine Geology and Geophysics, University of Hawaii in 1983. He obtained his Ph.D. in Oceanography, focusing on Marine Geology and Geophysics from Texas A&M in 1991. He was a Researcher with the Research Centre for Geotechnology, Indonesia Institute of Sciences from 1976 to 2000 and has held various positions with the Ministry of Marine Affairs and Fisheries, Republic Indonesia. Since 1995, he has held important posts such as Chief Scientist of "Doang Borderland" Marine Geology & Geophysics Expedition in the Banda Sea; Guest Lecturer for a presentation at the Institute of Oceanography, National Taiwan University Taipei, ROC; Director of Surveillance of Marine Non-Biological Resources, Ministry of Marine Affairs & Fisheries; Director, Surveillance of Marine Ecosystem, Ministry of Marine Affairs and Fisheries; and Director, Project Management for Preparation of Independent Oil Spill Response Organization.

The Editor

Sudhir T. Devare is currently Associate Senior Fellow at the Institute of Southeast Asian Studies, Singapore and a Fellow, Weatherhead Center for International Affairs, Harvard University, U.S.A. He was a member of the Indian Foreign Service and served as India's Ambassador to the Republic of Korea (1985–89); Ukraine, Georgia and Armenia (1992–94; the first Indian Ambassador to these newly independent countries) and Indonesia (1994–98). From 1998–2001, he was Secretary in the Ministry of External Affairs, Government of India in New Delhi. As Secretary, he dealt with India's multilateral economic relations and was closely associated with India's "Look-East" policy and the evolving relationship with the Asia-Pacific. He was a Member of the National Security Advisory Board of India in 2002–03; a Visiting Professor at the Jawaharlal Nehru University, New Delhi in 2002; and Vice-Chairman of the Research and Information System of Developing Countries (RIS), New Delhi. He had been a Visiting Senior Research Fellow at ISEAS in 2003–06. His book, *India and Southeast Asia: Towards Security Convergence*, was published by the Institute of Southeast Asian Studies, Singapore and by Capital Publishing, New Delhi in 2006.

1

An Overview of the Energy Scene in the Bay of Bengal Region

Sudhir T. Devare

The world is going through an uncertain energy situation. A number of circumstances not directly related to oil and gas production had been driving the prices to a record high. The sharp rise of oil prices which had reached US$70 per barrel in 2006 had thrown markets in a dizzy. And the price which crossed US$135 per barrel in May 2008 shook the economies around the world. Clearly this price is too high for most of the non-oil-producing countries to sustain.

In Asia, it is a coincidence that most of the major economies, namely, Japan, China, India and ASEAN (there are only a couple of ASEAN countries such as Malaysia and Brunei which export oil; the rest including the largest country Indonesia are net importers) are dependent on oil and natural gas imports. With the Indian and Chinese economies projected to grow by 8 to 10 per cent in the coming decade or so, their requirements for energy are expected to rise exponentially. Both are oil importers. India currently depends on imports for over 70 per cent of its oil needs, and that dependence is likely to go up to 85 per cent by 2015. By 2010, China also is estimated to depend on imports for more than 60 per cent of its oil requirements. As in the case of oil, these rapidly growing economies would require very large and regular supplies of natural gas in years to come.

Oil and Natural Gas in the Bay of Bengal Region

Today, Asia's influence on the world's energy landscape is considerable. Asia is the leading producer and a major consumer. Consumption of energy in the fast-emerging economies of Asia is growing rapidly. By 2010, the Asian oil demand will be higher than that of North America. Today, Asian cooperation is vital for both consuming and supplier nations of the world. Looking at different parts of Asia, the Middle East and Central Asia are some of the principal oil and gas producing countries in the world; Northeast Asia with the industrialized economies of Japan, China and Korea, is a large consumer, while South and Southeast Asia are rapidly growing economies with a high level of consumer demand. The Bay of Bengal and the adjoining seas like the Andaman Sea and the Malacca Straits are the link between Southeast and South Asia. This region, comprising these seas and the countries on their rim or in the proximity of, has not been known so far as a major oil and natural gas producing area. It is in fact one of the least explored or extracted offshore or onshore regions. Nevertheless it is home to a number of highly populous countries like India, Indonesia, Bangladesh, Thailand, Myanmar and Sri Lanka (with a total population exceeding 1.5 billion). In terms of foreign investment in the energy sector, this region (barring Malaysia and Indonesia) appears to have been neglected in the past. Perhaps the Cold War political affiliations had something to do with this. During that period, Western oil multinationals had not made any significant investments in the oil and natural gas sectors in countries like India, Bangladesh, Myanmar or Sri Lanka. Lately, however, there is a growing number of multinational investments, both from outside as well as from within the region.

In recent years, there have been discoveries of natural gas in the offshore areas of Myanmar (in the Gulf of Martaban and off Rekhine coast), inland and offshore areas of Bangladesh and the Kaveri, Godavari and Krishna basins on the east coast of India. According to the Reliance Group from India, which discovered 7 trillion cubic feet (tcf) of gas off Visakhapatnam on the Andhra Pradesh coast in October 2002, "this large gas find would completely change the basic energy equation in India in the coming years". These discoveries led the former Indian Petroleum Minister Mani Shankar Aiyar to project a hope that the Bay of Bengal might turn out to be Asia's North Sea.

The Bay of Bengal can be described as a hub for oil and natural gas for the countries of South and Southeast Asia, as well as Northeast Asia. In the

Malacca Straits, connecting the Bay of Bengal with the South China Sea, Malaysia is a major oil and gas producing country and Singapore at the end of the Malacca Straits is a principal international centre for oil storage and refining. The well-established Arun gas field in Aceh, Indonesia is at the northern end of the Malacca Straits. The oil-rich Riau Province in Indonesia also lies off the Malacca Straits. For China, Japan and Korea, the main sea lanes of communication through which their oil supplies pass on the way from the Persian Gulf are in the Bay of Bengal. China is also exploring possible avenues to tap energy sources in the Bay of Bengal region and is engaged in exploring/extracting gas off the Rekhine coast of Myanmar. China has also shown interest in building gas and oil pipelines from the Myanmar coast to its southwestern Yunnan province.

For India, the Bay of Bengal is of vital strategic and economic importance. Nearly half of India's coastline and its major islands, the Andamans and Nicobars, lie here. Five of India's ASEAN neighbours, namely, Myanmar, Thailand, Malaysia, Indonesia and Singapore, are situated across the Bay of Bengal. India has maritime boundaries with Myanmar, Thailand and Indonesia. Nearly 50 per cent of India's trade goes through the Bay of Bengal. India is also exploring the possibilities of finding hydrocarbons in its Exclusive Economic Zone in the Bay of Bengal and recently had promising discoveries off the Andhra and Orissa coasts. India is engaged in gas exploration/extraction off the Rekhine coast of Myanmar.

The eastern Indian Ocean is believed to be intrinsically rich in hydrocarbons and minerals. Several major rivers of Asia such as Ganga, Bramhaputra, Mahanadi, Godavari, Krishna, Cauvery, Irrawaddy, Salween empty in the Bay of Bengal and the adjoining seas creating vast sedimentary basins which can be potential deposits for hydrocarbons. Only six of twenty-six sedimentary basins of India have been explored. Similarly, at present, only small sections of the Bay of Bengal are under exploration for oil and natural gas. There are also difficulties due to overlapping claims over the maritime boundaries and exclusive economic zones of some of the Bay of Bengal countries. Considerable work therefore needs to be undertaken in the offshore areas for which large investments of capital and advanced technology will be required.

Linkage between Energy and Strategic Policies

With the importance of energy in foreign policy calculations increasing rapidly, countries of the Bay of Bengal region may leverage their energy endowment on political relationship with each other as well as with major

Asian neighbours like China and India in the realm of energy security. India-Bangladesh relationship in the field of energy or Myanmar's relations with India or China in the oil and gas sector could get linked to their overall political relationship. Equally, countries of the region are expected to take the view that they are not regarded as mere suppliers of energy, but are treated as partners in the strategic relationship with their large neighbours. The criticality of the input of energy gives these countries a new opportunity in the strategic game that is being played out in the region and beyond.

Energy Scenario in Individual Bay of Bengal Countries: Present Situation and Future Prospects

A survey of the present energy consumption and future requirements of the individual countries of the Bay of Bengal region, the availability of resources and the capital and technology estimated to tap them would provide a broad picture where this region stands today on the energy scene. Growth prospects can then be analysed based on possible investments, both national as well as from oil multinationals or through regional or sub-regional cooperation. The areas of energy would include hydrocarbons as well as coal, hydro and nuclear, besides renewables such as solar, wind or bio-fuels.

A discussion on the possible role of nuclear energy could also be important for the countries of the Bay of Bengal region. In Southeast Asia, as of now, there is practically no nuclear power generation. Thailand, Malaysia, Indonesia and the Philippines have had plans to build nuclear power facilities. Vietnam has small research reactors. If the price of oil were to rise further and coal, though abundantly available in Indonesia and Vietnam, is found increasingly unsuitable as a high environmental risk, Southeast Asia might also choose to widen its choices and go for a small-scale nuclear power production, mainly to supplement its overall energy needs.

In India nuclear power accounts for about 3 per cent of total power generation but at the end of 2007 it had seven reactors under construction. India plans an eight-fold increase by 2022 to 10 per cent of the electricity supply. India and the United States have been engaged for the past two to three years on a civilian nuclear cooperation agreement. There are no nuclear power plants in operation in Bangladesh, Sri Lanka, Nepal or Bhutan.

Politics of Energy Security

Energy is a major concern around the world these days. The realization that economic development and prosperity cannot come about without energy availability is driving countries towards acquiring or creating energy assets, ensuring safe transportation, and building storage facilities. In doing so, sovereign political or economic interests of nations may overlap or occasionally clash with that of their neighbours or with the countries in the region and even beyond. Management of the politics of energy security is therefore becoming a key preoccupation even as countries are engaged in regional or sub-regional cooperation. It will be instructive to see how the competitive issue of energy is being addressed by ASEAN+3 (China, Japan and Korea) or in the Bay of Bengal region.

Regional and Bilateral Cooperation in Energy

In ASEAN+3, energy cooperation is increasingly being institutionalized. At the ASEAN+3 Energy Ministers' meeting at Vientiane in July 2006, key energy concerns to achieve the goals of greater energy stability, security and sustainability through ASEAN+3 Energy Partnership had been noted and several measures to fulfil them were identified. An Energy Charter Treaty and ASEAN+3 Energy Security Communication System have been proposed. As an oil consuming region, these countries have also suggested a dialogue with oil-producing countries in the Middle East.

In the Bay of Bengal region, too, regional energy cooperation agreements/ arrangements are being considered. These come under the South Asian Association for Regional Cooperation (SAARC) or ASEAN's activities in this regard. As noted above, ASEAN+3 have already taken some useful steps in this direction. Cooperation in energy under the purview of the SAARC Integrated Programme of Action has been undertaken since 2000. In January 2004, a South Asia Energy Ring concept was mooted and in July 2004 a plan of action proposing a South Asia Energy Forum and a South Asian Energy Centre was put forward. In March 2007, a South Asia Energy Dialogue was held in New Delhi which commissioned a study on possibilities of trade in energy in the region. While some useful ground has been covered under these programmes, bilateral differences among member states on several energy issues remain unresolved. There are a number of such examples, both from SAARC as well as ASEAN. Nepal's enormous hydroelectric power potential has remained largely untapped due to the lack of progress on this subject between India and Nepal. Bangladesh has differences with India with regard to the latter's proposal to link its major rivers. However, energy can also be a major area of cooperation between India and Nepal or Bangladesh. The hydroelectric power projects, Chukha and Tala in Bhutan, which supply power to India are good examples of a win-win situation for both. India is also considering importing power across the Palk Straits from Sri Lanka.

In ASEAN too, bilateral differences have come in the way of energy cooperation. Indonesia and Malaysia nearly came to a fight in March 2005 over the issue of sovereignty in the oil-rich Ambalat part of Sulawesi Sea. There are conflicting claims among four Southeast Asian states over the oil rich Spratlys' Islands in South China Sea. On the other hand, ASEAN states have formed an ASEAN Centre for Energy and their energy ministers meet regularly. Thailand and Malaysia are working on a product sharing arrangement in an area in the Gulf of Thailand which is not demarcated between the two. This could be a useful example for other countries in ASEAN and SAARC which have outstanding bilateral problems with neighbours.

Transregional Cooperation

In the Bay of Bengal region, various avenues, bilateral, sub-regional or regional, are being explored to develop or promote cooperation in energy. In BIMSTEC (Bay of Bengal Initiative for Multi-Sectoral Technical and Economic Cooperation) a transregional grouping connecting South and Southeast Asia, energy has been identified as an important area for sub-regional cooperation. Myanmar volunteered to be the coordinator for energy under this forum. An Action Plan for Energy Cooperation for BIMSTEC was drawn up in October 2005. Under this, power exchanges and development projects are being planned. It is also proposed to consider an Energy Charter for BIMSTEC where there is good potential for sub-regional energy trade. A power transmission network has been agreed to. BIMSTEC nations are also considering transregional gas pipelines. The proposal of a Myanmar-Bangladesh-India gas pipeline, if acceptable to all parties, could be a concrete case of transregional cooperation in the Bay of Bengal region.

Maritime Security in Bay of Bengal

Safety of transportation of oil and liquefied natural gas (LNG) through the Arabian Sea and the Bay of Bengal is a matter that Asian countries continue to remain concerned with. It has been estimated that countries of Northeast, Southeast and South Asia will primarily depend on the oil and gas from the Persian Gulf for next two to three decades. Political stability and peace in the Persian Gulf will therefore remain a major concern for them. Moreover, how to ensure maritime safety of oil through the sea lanes of communication in the northern Indian Ocean is a priority issue for all. There is also the need to enhance dialogue with Islamic countries of the Persian Gulf and the Middle East, which have seen considerable political turmoil and violence after the events of 11 September

2001. There has been a sharp reaction in a number of countries in the Bay of Bengal region to the events in Iraq and Afghanistan.

India's geostrategic location in the Indian Ocean lends a certain advantage and responsibility. The main choke points lie in the vicinity of India's Laccadive and Minicoy; and Andaman and Nicobar Islands. The entrance to the Malacca Straits is barely 160 kilometres from India's southernmost islands. In assessing energy transportation security, this geographical factor assumes importance.

Naval Strategies of Major Powers in the Bay of Bengal Region

In the discussion on energy, especially its maritime transportation in the Indian Ocean, naval strategies pursued by major powers such as the United States, Japan, China or India, as well as by the states in the region would have a direct or indirect bearing.

It can be stated that there is a strategic continuum of the whole Bay of Bengal region with its maritime connection extending from India to Southeast Asia and beyond. In an unprecedented tragic manner, the oneness of the vast Indian Ocean, especially the Bay of Bengal region was drawn home when the tsunami waves dealt a blow to Indonesia, Thailand, India, Sri Lanka and the Maldives.

The major influence and presence of the preponderant naval power, the United States continue to be significant in the western Pacific as well as in the northern Indian Ocean, especially with the Iraq War, and the politico-security situations in Afghanistan and Pakistan. China and India are also expanding and modernizing their navies. China's naval projection as well as strategic interest in the Indian Ocean seems to be served through the countries with which China has close ties. China has been engaged in assisting Pakistan to build a major port at Gwadar near the Pakistan-Iran border. According to various studies, China has also been engaged with Myanmar for over a decade, modernizing or constructing port facilities at Kyapku, Sittwe, Hangyi, Yangon and Mergui. Russia continues to be a naval power in the Asia-Pacific besides emerging in recent years as a leading global power in the field of energy. Japan's Self Defence Forces are deployed for the first time in the post-Cold War period and they are in the Indian Ocean region. In September 2007, the naval forces of India, the United States, Japan, Australia and Singapore conducted a major exercise, "Malabar", in the Bay of Bengal.

Southeast Asian countries appear anxious that they could be affected by a rivalry among the major Asian naval powers. They are equally sensitive to any "interference" by extra-regional powers in their waters. In 2004, Malaysia and Indonesia reacted sharply to any suggestion that the U.S. navy might start patrolling the Malacca Straits regularly, and along with Singapore decided to set up "Malsindo", a joint task force which will patrol the Straits. Malaysia has since established a Coast Guard organization.

Energy Independence as against Energy Security

With energy independence being increasingly unattainable, countries seem to seek reduced dependence on imported oil and natural gas. In his State of the Union Address of 2006, President Bush had spoken of his concern over the "U.S. addiction to oil" and the need to lessen U.S. oil imports. Large consumers of oil such as China, Japan, India, too, would, no doubt, seek to reduce their dependence on imported oil and natural gas. However, it is apparent that with respect to transportation fuel, there may not be any credible or available alternative to oil or gasoline for several years to come. Since economies of these countries, as indeed that of most other countries, are transportation related, dependence on oil is not likely to reduce substantially.

Energy independence for power generation may perhaps be within the realm of possibility. By using sources like coal or nuclear, or the renewable sources like hydro, solar, wind, or biomass, power generation may be enhanced in a self-sufficient manner. Even with respect to these sources, fuels may not always be available locally and require imports. This also applies to technologies. For example, coal imports and clean coal technology are necessary for several countries. For nuclear power, too, import of appropriate fuel and technology is a requirement for many countries.

It can be thus argued that while energy independence is almost an impossible goal, energy security is a more attainable objective. How countries of the Bay of Bengal region look at issues of energy security as against energy independence in their policy framework as well as in their interaction with the outside world constitutes an important element of this study.

Energy Trading

It is interesting to note that while a number of Bay of Bengal countries are deficient in oil and natural gas, some of them have developed excellent capacities for storage as well as refining. The need for value addition through refining and processing different fractions of crude oil, namely, naphtha, gasoline, kerosene, aviation fuel, and fuel oil, has been recognized by these countries. Singapore is a well-known example in this regard which for some time now is a major international hub, both for crude oil handling and storing as well as for refining. Thailand has also made considerable strides in refining and downstream processing. Malaysia, a producer of crude oil and refined products, has extensive trade in these items with Singapore and India, countries in the Bay of Bengal region as well as with China. Indonesia is a major producer of LNG. It also has a number of refineries and is planning to expand its refining capacity in a major way with foreign investment. India has built large refineries and petroleum processing complexes and is currently engaged in expanding its capacity substantially.

There is a growing trade between China, India, and Singapore in products such as naphtha, kerosene, aviation oil and other petroleum products. With China and India expanding their refining capacities, it is possible that they could take some share of Singapore's exports to countries in the South Pacific or the Bay of Bengal region respectively. A certain amount of competition in the processed oil and petroleum products between China, India, Singapore, Malaysia and Thailand can also be visualized. For example, India may be in a position to supply processed crude oil products to Indonesia, Myanmar or Bangladesh competitively. This could be done in smaller vessels capable of delivering oil and petroleum products at medium or small size ports in the Bay of Bengal countries. An Indian company, the Indian Oil Operation, is running several retail outlets in Sri Lanka. China is planning to set up a large refinery in Singapore. Besides meeting its requirements from this facility, China could export refined products in the region.

Environment and Energy Consumption

The countries in the Bay of Bengal region are all developing countries where the effect of their growing energy consumption on environment is being witnessed. Climate change is a major concern which is equally affecting developed countries of North America and Europe as well as the developing countries of the Asia-Pacific. The connection between global warming or climate change and energy consumption is now generally accepted. However, this places developing countries in a big dilemma. Can they reduce energy use significantly which would also lead to deceleration of their socio-economic development? How can they find the means including technology to utilize energy in an environment-friendly and cost-effective manner? For example, clean coal technology is the major need for all since thermal power from coal is the principal source for electricity in most developing countries. Abundant and relatively cheap supply of coal available from several sources makes it a ready and popular energy material. However, at the same time, coal happens to be a major polluter which contributes to CO_2 emissions. How to strike an optimum balance between the environment-polluting and clean forms of energy in the context of availability and cost is the major challenge that the countries of the Bay of Bengal region as indeed elsewhere in the world are confronted with today.

Sources of Environmentally Clean Energy

Hydroelectric, natural gas, nuclear as well as the renewable sources like wind, solar, and biomass are among the various sources of clean energy. While the hydroelectric power is cheap and can be abundantly produced, its gestation period is long and initial cost of construction is high. Moreover, building dams on rivers is also connected to environmental and social issues relating to inundation of forests and irrigable lands as well as rehabilitation of displaced people.

Natural gas can be a good source for generating clean power and is currently extensively employed. It is being recognized as the fuel of the twenty-first century. However, using natural gas for power production alone also leads to wastage of gas (which is rich in petrochemicals) which developing countries can ill-afford.

As discussed earlier, nuclear energy assumes importance and priority as the energy crunch becomes imminent with dwindling oil supplies and its escalating price. The nuclear source is clean, abundantly available and has proved suitable as quality power. It has, no doubt, strong opponents on the grounds of problems of disposal of waste material, safety of radioactive leakage and the fear of proliferation for weapon purposes. Moreover, the costs of constructing a nuclear power plant are high and the time required for construction is also quite long. However, in a number of countries, especially developed ones, nuclear power has already become an important source of electric power.

Renewable sources like wind, solar, biomass, and ethanol hold considerable promise in the countries of the Bay of Bengal region. They have large and almost unlimited supplies of these items. Investments in these forms of power are relatively small. As the search for renewable energy sources intensifies in Western countries, could the countries of the Bay of Bengal region afford to lag behind in this important area of technological innovation?

Research and experimentation on new sources like hydrogen are nowadays actively being pursued. In the Bay of Bengal region, Singapore has taken the lead in this direction where a few cars running on hydrogen are demonstrated. Similarly, hybrid cars are also being tried out in Singapore for which the

Japanese technology is constantly trying out innovative ways. Ethanol use as an alternative or supplementary fuel can have immense possibilities in the region since several countries are producers of sugar from sugarcane. Brazil's example in this direction is before them.

Energy Conservation and Energy Intensity

The test of success in the energy field will lie in addressing the question of conservation of energy, especially with respect to the finite and exhaustible sources like the hydrocarbons. In developing countries, the energy intensity in transportation, power generation or manufacturing processes is high which leads to considerable wastage. As long as this is not reduced, optimum utilization of energy would not be possible. For the countries of this region reducing energy intensity would be a major challenge.

An Asian Energy Market for Consumers as well as Producers

While the geopolitics and geoeconomics of oil have a global dimension and cannot be considered in the context of a region or a continent alone, it is becoming evident that the growing impact of Asia on the world oil scene cannot be missed. On one hand, demand for oil from the rapidly developing economies of the Asia-Pacific is on a constant increase. Over the next twenty years, Asian demand is likely to be the primary growth engine accounting for 38 per cent of global oil demand, 14 per cent of global gas demand and 60 per cent of global coal demand in 2025. On the other hand, much of Asia's oil and gas production is being consumed within the region, driven by the economic logic. In 2003, 55 per cent of crude oil was consumed within the region. This inter-dependence between consumers and producers in Asia is driven by the geographical setting and economic fundamentals of demand and supply factored by favourable transportation costs. Can the principal buyers and sellers of oil from Asia come on one platform to determine their respective needs and concerns? China, India and the countries of Bay of Bengal region are major consumers of hydrocarbons and their demands are expected to grow exponentially. Energy can therefore become a potential cause for rivalry among them. However, as of now, there is little coordination among these consumer nations when dealing with major producer nations of Asia, especially in the Persian Gulf. The latter are aware of the strength of the market forces spurred by the increasing demand in India and East Asian countries. At the same time, they are also concerned over the reduction in foreign investment in their own countries in the oil and natural gas sector. The events of 9/11 and the war in Iraq have further exacerbated their wariness.

It may still be premature and perhaps unrealistic to visualize a common energy supplier-consumer platform emerging in Asia. However, an important beginning was made when at the invitation of the former Indian Minister for Petroleum, Ministers and high-level representatives from China, Japan, Korea and ASEAN countries on the one hand and Saudi Arabia, Iran, Kuwait, the United Arab Emirates (UAE) and Central Asian states on the other gathered in New Delhi in January 2005 to discuss the demand and supply, pricing, and exploration opportunities. Their interaction has subsequently continued at technical level.

Looking Ahead

In the discussion on energy issues of environment or climate change are acquiring a central place. For the developing countries of the Bay of Bengal region, they are of particular urgency considering how vulnerable some of the countries are to the effects of degradation of environment or impact of glbal warming or climate change. It is encouraging that climate change has rapidly become a top priority global agenda. At a historic conference in Bali in December 2007, a Bali Roadmap was agreed upon, which calls for a global, comprehensive agreement to address climate change. The Bali decision sets out an agenda for a deadline of 2009 to complete the negotiations.

With rapid economic progress in several Asian countries, their dependence on the driving engine of their growth, namely, energy, has increased manifold. Consequently, Asia is on the way to become a dominant consumer in the global energy industry. The countries of the Bay of Bengal region have a sizeable share in this development. Moreover, a new interdependent relationship between the consumers and producers is beginning to emerge. This will, no doubt, be influenced by considerations of transportation costs, maritime safety and basically, by economic fundamentals of supply and demand of energy. Inter-dependence could prove useful for economic development of the countries of the region and the Asia-Pacific as a whole.

In analysing the emerging energy scenario in this strategically vital region what is aimed to be emphasized is that despite the differences including the "politics of energy security" that divide the countries of this broad region, the imperative of mutual benefit through regional or sub-regional cooperation should increasingly lead to a dialogue and closer interaction among the energy industry, civil society as well as policy-making bodies in these countries which would augur well for the future of the region and beyond.

Briefly, this book attempts to present a broad picture of the energy situation in the Bay of Bengal region, a highly populated and developing area where demand for energy is growing rapidly. Though relatively an unexplored region as far as hydrocarbons are concerned, it offers a promising potential with regard to oil and natural gas, as well as coal and renewable forms of energy. The chapters in this book cover a wide range of subjects and issues related to the energy situation in the Bay of Bengal region. There are country perspectives on India, Bangladesh, Myanmar, Indonesia and Singapore; and a synopsis of the energy scene, both consumption and production-wise in the ten countries of the region. Other chapters deal with such issues as the maritime security of energy transporation, corporate social responsibility, sustainable and renewable energy as well as possible areas for holistic regional cooperation.

Elspeth Thomson has made a detailed survey of the energy resource endowment in the highly diverse region covering the countries around and in the proximity of the Bay of Bengal. She discusses current energy production and consumption and analyses the prospects over the next two decades.

Talmiz Ahmad highlights the energy salience which the Bay of Bengal region has acquired following the recent oil and natural gas discoveries and the promise of vast potential for gas. He discusses at length the implications of this development for India's energy security as well as for possible regional engagement and cooperation.

Debapriya Bhattacharya and Tazeen Tahsina identify energy shortages as one of the main bottlenecks affecting the economic development of Bangladesh. In the study, the authors locate the major macroeconomic challenges constraining the growth of the energy sector. The chapter goes on to give possible immediate and long-term solutions to the problems caused by shortages in energy and power supply.

U Than Tun analyses Myanmar's energy needs, present production from various sources and the future potential. He highlights Myanmar's energy cooperation projects with neighbouring countries and regional cooperation in the energy field in the context of BIMSTEC.

From the Indonesian perspective, Sugiarta Wirasantosa discusses energy resources in the eastern Indian Ocean, particularly in Indonesia, in terms of energy potential, demands and alternative sources. Describing alternative sources as critical to an archipelagic country like Indonesia, Sugiarta projects alternative energy sources to be mainly marine-related.

Due to its strategic location straddled between West and East Asia, Singapore is a major hub for oil and its products. Ong Eng Tong analyses Singapore's role as a major oil trading place and a leading refining centre with its refineries serving as "swing" refinery. He also describes Singapore's position as a top bunkering port with financial services and laboratory testing facilities.

P. K. Singh takes the view that any discussion on energy in the Bay of Bengal region will have to be viewed as part of the overall picture which would include areas such as trade, maritime security, infrastructure, tourism, higher education and research, particularly in the cutting edge technologies and goes on to discuss the cooperation potential in these fields among the countries of the region.

Vijay Sakhuja describes energy infrastructure as a "soft" target which exposes the energy transportation security system to terrorist attacks. In his study, Sakhuja highlights the vulnerability of energy-related infrastructure in the Bay of Bengal. In doing so, he analyses the concept of energy supply chains and underlines the economic impact of disruptions and its immediate global consequences.

According to Andrew Symon, one of the most important but sometimes overlooked concerns over energy supply and security is the issue how best to manage the social and environmental aspects of petroleum development. The role of governments and private corporations becomes important in this regard. He calls for a strong case for a partnership between the central and local governments, corporate sector and local communities to deal with social and environmental dimensions of energy development.

Christophe Bongars highlights the importance of renewable energy in the light of two major challenges: climate change and human development goals. Touching briefly on various forms of renewable energy, he analyses renewable energy policies followed in Asia, including the Bay of Bengal region. According to Bongars, education and capacity building is the key in embracing the full extent of the rapid changes in the global energy landscape.

REFERENCES

Alexander's Gas and Oil Connection. "News and Trends: E & SE Asia", Vol. 10, no. 20, 26 October 2005.

ASEAN Secretariat. "Chairman's Statement" at the Third ASEAN+3 Ministers on Energy Meeting, Vientiane, 27 July 2006.

Garver, John. *Protracted Contest: Sino-Indian Rivalry in the Twentieth Century*. Seattle and London: University of Washington Press, 2001.

International Energy Outlook. IEA, 2001.

Khosla, I. P., ed. *Energy and Diplomacy*. New Delhi: Konark Publishers, 2005.

Muni, S. D. and Girijesh Pant. *India's Energy Security: Prospects for Cooperation with Extended Neighbourhood*. New Delhi: Rupa & Co. and Observers' Research Foundation, 2005.

Munk, Bernard E. "Energy independence is not energy security". Foreign Policy Research Institute, <www.fpi.org>.

Nuclear Power Worldwide. "Status and Outlook". A report of the International Atomic Energy Agency (IAEA), 23 October 2007.

SAARC Energy Ministers' Meeting. "South Asia Energy Dialogue". Press Information Bureau (PIB), New Delhi, 7 March 2007.

Selth, Andrew. "Burma's China Connection and the Indian Ocean Region". Paper presented at Conference of Asia-Pacific Center for Security Studies, Honolulu, August 2003.

Tuli, Vipul. "Regional Cooperation for Asian Energy Security". RIS Discussion Papers, RIS-DP no. 112, RIS New Delhi, August 2006.

Yahoo! India News, Indo Asian News Service, 31 March 2005.

2

Current and Expected Energy Production and Consumption within the Bay of Bengal Region: A Synopsis

Elspeth Thomson

The Bay of Bengal region is extremely diverse in its energy resource endowment.[1] At one extreme there is Singapore, an island city state with no hydrocarbon or hydropower resources whatsoever. At the other extreme are India, Myanmar and Bangladesh with considerable hydrocarbon and hydropower resources.

This chapter summarizes the current energy situation — production, consumption, imports and exports — within the Bay of Bengal region and discusses the outlook over the next twenty-five years. Most of the data is for 2004, the latest available at the time of writing from the Energy Information Administration (EIA) and International Energy Agency (IEA).[2] Though fragments of later data were coming available, for the sake of comparability, the author opted generally to employ 2004 data throughout.

Total Energy Consumption and Economic Growth

The greatly different geographical scale and resource endowment of these countries, in combination with historical and political factors, have meant that they differ considerably in terms of economic development. Several are pre-industrial. For example, in Myanmar, Nepal and Bhutan, the agricultural sector accounts for over a third of GDP (see Table 2.1). On the other hand, in Singapore, Sri Lanka, Bangladesh and India, the service sector accounts for over half of GDP. It must be noted, however, that these are merely generalizations because most of these economies have large informal sectors which are not captured in national data.

Over time, it can be expected that the agricultural sector in all of these economies will reduce in size while the manufacturing and service sectors will expand. Fewer people will live in rural areas and grow crops. Many of the young people from the existing rural households will seek in the urban areas of their countries higher paying and less physically demanding employment, as well as better schooling and facilities, in turn, for their children. This is related to Engel's Law, that is, as income increases, the proportion spent on food decreases. As this occurs, there is a trend towards greater provision of services. People living in urban areas need to create employment, tend to earn more money and can afford to spend it on an increasingly wide variety of services ranging from healthcare to travel.

Of the economies comprising the Bay of Bengal region, Singapore is the only one that might be considered "mature". As an island state, its economic structure and development options are rather unique. The other economies are either already into their economic "take-off" stage or will, barring some political or natural catastrophe, enter theirs soon.

Many of these countries have large populations. Indeed, this group of countries as a whole accounts for over one-quarter of humanity (see Table 2.1). The speed at which economic take-off occurs in any country is a function of many geographical, historical, cultural and political factors. Regrettably, several of this region's member states are afflicted by inter-regional rivalries. These tend to slow national economic progress.

A country's energy consumption is very much related to its state of economic development. Per capita energy consumption (of commercial fuels only) ranges from 2.3 million British thermal units (mBtu) in Nepal to 444.6 in Singapore. In several of these countries, per capita energy consumption is far below the world average of 70.1 mBtu. However, it must be mentioned that these particular figures in Table 2.1 are somewhat misleading in that

Table 2.1
Bay of Bengal Region Energy and Economy Indicators

	Total Primary Energy Consumption 2004 (quadrillion Btu)	Population 2004 (million)	Population Growth 1994–2004 (%)	Per Capita Energy Consumption 2004 (million Btu)	Per Capita Energy Consumption Growth 1994–2004 (%)	Agricultural Share of GDP (%) 2003	Industrial Share of GDP (%) 2003	Service Share of GDP (%) 2003	Per Capita GNI (US$) 2002
India	15.417	1,065.07	1.65	14.5	3.16	22.4	26.5	51.1	442
Bangladesh	0.658	141.34	1.86	4.7	5.22	21.0	25.3	53.7	337
Myanmar	0.202	46.52	0.96	4.4	6.20	57.2	10.5	32.4	
Thailand	3.423	63.73	0.92	53.7	5.87	9.8	44.0	46.3	1,838
Malaysia	2.519	23.52	2.06	107.1	4.26	9.5	48.6	45.5	3,312
Indonesia	4.686	238.45	1.63	19.7	2.82	16.6	43.6	39.9	599
Singapore	1.936	4.35	2.40	444.6	2.95	0.1	32.7	66.4	20,066
Sri Lanka	0.197	19.91	1.01	9.9	3.12	19.0	26.3	54.7	818
Nepal	0.063	27.07	2.40	2.3	7.38	39.2	20.9	39.9	211
Bhutan	0.020	2.19	2.27	9.0	0.71	33.2	39.5	28.8	237
World	446.442 (total)	6,372.70 (total)	1.30 (average)	70.1 (average)	0.85 (average)				5,737 (average)

Note: Shares of GDP are for 2003 except for Myanmar (2001).

Sources: EIA website at <http://www.eia.doe.gov/emeu/international/contents.html> (31 October 2006); Asian Development Bank, *Key Indicators 2004* (Manila: ADB, 2004); United Nations, *Statistical Yearbook 2004* (New York: Economic and Social Commission for Asia and the Pacific, 2005); *CIA World Factbook* and Nationmaster at <http://www.nationmaster.com/red/graph/eco_gro_nat_inc_percap-gross-national-income-per-capita&nofb=1> (31 October 2006).

Table 2.2
Electrification Rates (%)

India	55.5
Bangladesh	32.0
Myanmar	11.3
Thailand	99.0
Malaysia	97.8
Indonesia	54.0
Singapore	100.0
Sri Lanka	66.0
Nepal	33.0
Bhutan	NA
Africa	37.8
Latin America	90.0
Middle East	78.1
World	75.6

Source: IEA. *World Energy Outlook 2006* (Paris: OECD/IEA, 2006), pp. 567 and 570.

many of these countries, such as Singapore, have significant oil refining industries which consume large amounts of energy.

Per capita energy consumption growth in many of the Bay of Bengal countries, on the other hand, from 1994 to 2004 has generally been far higher than the world average of 0.85 per cent. This ravenous appetite for energy is expected to continue for several decades (discussed further below).

The electrification rate for the world as a whole in 2005 was 75.6 per cent (90.4 per cent for urban areas and 61.7 per cent for rural). In the Bay of Bengal region, it ranged from 11.3 per cent in Myanmar to 100 per cent in Singapore (see Table 2.2).

Breakdown of Total Energy Consumption

Several of these countries presently depend heavily on combustible renewables and wastes (mainly biomass: crop residues, twigs, grasses, bark, dung, etc.) to meet their energy requirements. For example, it is estimated that such energy accounts for 87 per cent of total energy consumption in Nepal, 79 per cent in Myanmar, 58 per cent in Sri Lanka, 53 per cent in India, 45 per cent in Bangladesh and 35 per cent in Indonesia (see Table 2.3).

All countries in the world have at one point relied heavily on such materials to burn for cooking and heating. For example, such was the case in the early 1960s in Japan and Korea. However, within the space of a generation,

Table 2.3
Energy Consumption Breakdown, 2004 (%)

	Coal	Crude Oil	Oil Products	Natural Gas	Geothermal et al.	Combustibles	Electricity	Heat
India	9.0		26.5	2.1		52.9	9.5	
Bangladesh	1.9		19.8	24.2		45.3	8.7	
Myanmar	0.7		14.3	3.1		78.6	3.3	
Thailand	8.7	4.1	52.1	3.3		16.5	15.3	
Malaysia	2.6		59.1	16.8		4.4	17.2	
Indonesia	6.3		40.3	11.9		35.0	6.6	
Singapore			80.2	0.7			19.0	
Sri Lanka	0.8		34.8			57.7	6.6	
Nepal	2.0		9.1			87.2	1.6	
World	8.4	0.1	42.1	16.0	0.1	13.7	16.2	3.3

Note: "Geothermal et al." denotes electricity generated from geothermal, solar, wind, wood and waste sources.
Source: Calculated from IEA Energy Statistics @ OECD/IEA, 2007, at <http://www.iea.org/Textbase/stats/index.asp> (15 January 2007).

these fuels were almost completely substituted by oil, gas, hydropower and nuclear power.

Though it is not possible to predict how quickly or how uniformly the adoption of commercial energy will take in the Bay of Bengal region, it can be said with certainty that it will take place in the coming years. The process is well underway in Malaysia and Thailand. The particular types of commercial energy and the relative ratios of each that are adopted in each country depend on resource endowment and government policy. It is universally recognized that the greater the energy diversification, the greater the energy security.

All of these countries, except Singapore, have natural energy resources of one or more types. The relative magnitudes of the various forms of discovered energy in the region are discussed in the next section.

Coal Production and Consumption

India is by far the largest coal producer and consumer in the region (see Table 2.4). It is the third largest producer in the world after China and the United States and has the fourth largest reserves in the world (see Table 2.5). Most of this coal is used for thermal power generation — 69 per cent of India's electricity is generated from coal (see Table 2.6) — with most of the rest used for heavy industries.

Though abundant, India's coal reserves have high ash and sulphur contents. Thus, the government must introduce clean coal technologies because use of this coal is highly polluting. The steel industry relies on imports of coking

Table 2.4
Coal Production and Consumption (million short tonnes)

	Production in 2004	% growth 1994–2004	Consumption in 2004	% growth 1994–2004
India	443.72	4.0	478.16	4.3
Bangladesh	0	0	0.77	64.4
Myanmar	1.44	56.1	0.14	10.3
Thailand	22.09	2.0	30.41	4.4
Malaysia	0.32	18.7	7.30	1.4
Indonesia	142.31	15.1	23.94	7.6
Singapore	0	0	0.01	negligible
Sri Lanka	0	0	0.005	21.3
Nepal	0.01	negligible	0.32	18.1
Bhutan	0.06	negligible	0.07	negligible
World	6,078.58	2.10	6,098.78	1.95

Sources: EIA website at <http://www.eia.doe.gov/pub/international/iealf/table25.xls> and <http://www.eia.doe.gov/pub/international/iealf/table14.xls>.

Table 2.5
Hydrocarbon Reserves

	Crude Oil Reserves, 2006 (billion barrels)	Natural Gas Reserves, 2006 (trillion cubic feet)	Coal Reserves, 2003 (million short tonnes)
India	5.848	38.880	101,903
Bangladesh	0.028	5.000	0
Myanmar	0.050	10.000	2
Thailand	0.291	14.754	1,493
Malaysia	3.000	75.000	4
Indonesia	4.301	97.786	5,476
Singapore	0	0	0
Sri Lanka	0	0	—
Nepal	0	0	1
Bhutan	0	0	—
World	1,292.936	6,124.016	997,506

Sources: EIA website at <http://www.eia.doe.gov/emeu/international/reserves.xls> and <http://www.eia.doe.gov/pub/international/iea2004/table82.xls> (15 November 2006) quoting *Oil and Gas Journal*, 1 January 2006.

Table 2.6
Breakdown of Electricity Generation, 2004 (%)

	Coal	Oil	Gas	Biomass	Waste	Nuclear	Hydro	Geo-thermal
India	69.1	5.4	9.5	0.3		2.5	12.7	
Bangladesh	0	6.7	87.5				5.7	
Myanmar	0	6.8	57.0				36.2	
Thailand	15.9	6.2	71.0	2.2			4.8	
Malaysia	27.9	3.3	61.8				7.0	
Indonesia	40.1	30.2	16.1				8.1	5.5
Singapore	0	31.2	68.8					
Sri Lanka		63.2					36.8	
Nepal								
Bhutan	NA							
World	39.6	6.7	19.5	0.9	0.4	15.6	16.5	0.3

Note: Two other categories are given on the website, namely solar PV and solar thermal, but were not included here because the quantities were too small.
Source: Calculated from IEA Energy Statistics @ OECD/IEA, 2007, <http://www.iea.org/Textbase/stats/index.asp> (15 January 2007).

coal to meet about a quarter of its requirements. Of India's steam coal imports from the region, about 66 per cent come from Indonesia (equivalent to about 19 per cent of Indonesia's total exports of steam coal). Of India's exports of coal in the region, 83 per cent go to Bangladesh, 16 per cent to Nepal, 1 per cent to Bhutan and a very small quantity to Sri Lanka.

The next largest coal producer in the region is Indonesia, though its reserves are only a fraction of India's (see Table 2.5). Indonesia is the world's second largest coal exporter after China. Within the region, it exports large quantities to Malaysia as well as India. As can be seen from Table 2.6, over 40 per cent of Indonesia's electricity is generated from coal, while the proportion is about 28 per cent in Malaysia and 16 per cent in Thailand.

Several countries in the region are planning to use more coal for thermal power production to free up their gas and oil for other purposes. For example, Bangladesh would like to reduce its reliance on gas for electricity generation. It completed its first coal-fired plant in 2006. The country has only small coal reserves, and commercial coal production did not begin until 2003. The same is true of Sri Lanka which plans to build a coal-fired plant and import coal as it has minimal coal resources of its own.

Crude Oil Production and Consumption

Table 2.7 gives total production and consumption of crude oil in 2004 as well as the average annual growth rates from 1994. The region as a whole presently

Table 2.7
Crude Oil Production and Consumption, 1994–2004
(thousand barrels per day)

	Production in 2004	% growth 1994–2004	Consumption in 2004	% growth 1994–2004
India	844.0	2.8	2,450.0	5.7
Bangladesh	6.8	18.8	85.0	6.5
Myanmar	20.7	6.7	37.0	5.5
Thailand	257.7	12.7	900.0	4.3
Malaysia	861.2	2.5	515.0	3.2
Indonesia	1,181.0	–2.9	1,200.0	4.5
Singapore	0.0	0	763.0	4.3
Sri Lanka	Negligible	Negligible	80.0	6.1
Nepal	0	0	16.0	9.5
Bhutan	0	0	1.2	5.9
World	83,004.7	1.9	82,594.7	1.9

Sources: EIA website at <http://www.eia.doe.gov/pub/international/iealf/tableg2.xls> and <http://www.eia.doe.gov/pub/international/iealf/table12.xls>.

depends heavily on imports of oil from the Middle East. India has the highest reserves in the region (see Table 2.5). At present, India imports about 65 per cent of its oil requirements, and over 60 per cent of these come from four countries: Saudi Arabia, Nigeria, Kuwait and Iran. This percentage is likely to rise considerably as no large oil fields have been discovered on or offshore since the Bombay High fields in the late 1960s.

Indonesia has the second largest reserves in the region. It is currently the largest producer in the region, followed by Malaysia and India (see Table 2.7). Though a member of the Organization of Petroleum Exporting Countries (OPEC) and still exporting oil, Indonesia became a net importer in 2004 due to declining production since 1996. In 2004, Indonesia was the largest exporter of crude oil in the region, followed by Malaysia and Thailand (see Table 2.8).

Within the region, Indonesia exports to Thailand (5.4 per cent of Indonesia's total crude oil exports), to Singapore (4.4 per cent) and to Malaysia (1 per cent). Of Indonesia's imports of crude oil, nearly 30 per cent come from the Middle East, another 6 per cent from Malaysia and 4 per cent from Thailand. Malaysia's oil resources are dwindling. At present, of Malaysia's exports of crude oil within the region, 20 per cent go to India, 18 per cent to Thailand, 8 per cent each to Singapore and Indonesia and 2 per cent to Sri

Table 2.8
Crude Oil and Oil Products Trade, 2003
(thousand barrels per day)

	Crude Oil Imports	Oil Products Imports	Crude Oil Exports	Oil Products Exports
India	1,788.7	166.7	0	325.2
Bangladesh	26.7	53.5	0	1.0
Myanmar	4.9	14.5	0	0
Thailand	775.8	19.4	61.5	134.4
Malaysia	138.1	154.1	426.1	189.9
Indonesia	370.5	280.5	518.1	189.3
Singapore	750.0	883.0	0	977.3
Sri Lanka	39.9	35.0	0	0
Nepal	0	15.7	0	0
Bhutan	0	1.1	0	0
World	41,507.8	18,283.4	39,965.9	19,418.7

Sources: EIA website at <http://www.eia.doe.gov/pub/international/iea2004/table31.xls>, <http://www.eia.doe.gov/pub/international/iea2004/table33.xls> and <http://www.eia.doe.gov/pub/international/iea2004/table34.xls> (15 November 2004).

Lanka. Of Malaysia's imports of crude oil, about 77 per cent are from the Middle East and 5 per cent from Indonesia.

Nearly 40 per cent of Thailand's production of crude oil, which has expanded since the early 1980s, is exported to Indonesia. Several deposits have recently been discovered in the Gulf of Thailand. Of Thailand's imports of crude, about 88 per cent come from the Middle East.

Bangladesh has oil, but more attention is given to the gas reserves. It is a net oil importer. Myanmar has sizeable oil reserves. However, the government has neither the capital nor the expertise to extract the oil. Both India and China would like to buy large quantities of Myanmar's oil. Sri Lanka passed the Petroleum Resources Act in 2003 which permitted private investment in oil and gas exploration. Unlike Bangladesh, Sri Lanka is allowing Indian and Chinese companies to carry out exploration activities.

Refined Oil Products Production and Consumption

India has greatly increased its refining capacity in recent years. By 2008, Jamnagar in Gujarat will become the world's largest refining city. The second largest producer of oil products in the region in 2003 was Indonesia (see Table 2.9). The government of Thailand is aiming to make the country an oil distribution, refining and trading hub. Singapore is the world's third largest oil product trading centre. At the same time it is the world's largest fuel oil storage location and bunkering port. In 2003 it exported about 980,000 barrels of oil products per day (see Table 2.8). Within the region, Singapore

Table 2.9
Total Output of Refined Petroleum Products, 2003

	Thousand barrels/day
India	2,461.1
Bangladesh	30.2
Myanmar	19.7
Thailand	908.9
Malaysia	511.2
Indonesia	1,040.9
Singapore	756.5
Sri Lanka	40.8
Nepal	0
Bhutan	0
World	78,080.0

Source: EIA website at <http://www.eia.doe.gov/pub/international/iea2004/table32.xls> (15 November 2006).

exports about 13 per cent to Malaysia, 10 per cent to Indonesia, 2 per cent to Thailand, 1 per cent to Myanmar and less than 1 per cent to each of India, Bangladesh and Sri Lanka.

Natural Gas Production and Consumption

In 2004, Indonesia and Malaysia were the largest producers and exporters of natural gas in the region (see Tables 2.10 and 2.11). Singapore imports about 20 per cent of its natural gas from Malaysia (accounting for all of Malaysia's exports) and 80 per cent from Indonesia (accounting for about 16 per cent of Indonesia's total exports of natural gas). Malaysia exports liquefied natural gas (LNG), but almost entirely to Northeast Asia.

Indonesia has large natural gas reserves (see Table 2.5). In 2002, Indonesia accounted for about 21 per cent of the world's total LNG exports. The country has two LNG ports. However, the gas exports are falling. As its reserves are declining, it has informed Japan and other large importers that it will soon be reducing gas exports because it wants to use the gas for electricity production.[3]

Bangladesh lacks the necessary equipment to carry out detailed surveys. According to Table 2.5, Bangladesh has 5 trillion cubic feet of gas reserves. This is the official figure. Many oil companies, however, believe the

Table 2.10
Natural Gas Production and Consumption, 1994–2004

	Production in 2004 (trillion cubic feet)	% growth 1994–2004	Consumption in 2004 (billion cubic feet)	% growth 1994–2004
India	0.996	5.3	1,089	6.3
Bangladesh	0.463	7.1	463	7.1
Myanmar	0.363	26.3	95	6.8
Thailand	0.790	8.9	1,055	12.1
Malaysia	2.205	9.2	1,164	9.4
Indonesia	2.663	2.9	1,309	3.3
Singapore	0	0	233	35.9
Sri Lanka	0	0	0	0
Nepal	0	0	0	0
Bhutan	0	0	0	0
World	98.620	2.5	99,665	2.5

Sources: EIA website at <http://www.eia.doe.gov/pub/international/iealf/tablef24.xls> and <http://www.eia.doe.gov/pub/international/iealf/tablee3.xls> (15 November 2004).

Table 2.11
Natural Gas Trade, 2004 (billion cubic feet)

	Exports	Imports
India		93
Bangladesh		
Myanmar	265	
Thailand		265
Malaysia	1,040	
Indonesia	1,353	
Singapore		233
Sri Lanka		
Nepal		
Bhutan		
World	28,519	29,215

Sources: EIA website at <http://www.eia.doe.gov/pub/international/iealf/table44.xls> and <http://www.eia.doe.gov/pub/international/iealf/table43.xls> (15 November 2006).

quantities available are much higher. Until the exact dimensions of the deposits are known, the government is reluctant to export gas, preferring to use it domestically. Also complicating matters are maritime border disputes with India and Myanmar.

Myanmar also has substantial reserves of gas, and both China and India are extremely keen to import. Myanmar presently exports gas to Thailand.

Promising gas fields were discovered in India in 2002 (the Krishna-Godavari Basin) and 2004 (the Bay of Bengal). Without doubt, demand for gas will rise exponentially in the coming years. A goal has been set to raise the share of gas in the total energy mix from 8 per cent in 2003 to 16 per cent by 2020. The country hopes to import large quantities of LNG and to build several pipelines: from Oman (a deep-water pipeline), from Iran via Pakistan, from Turkmenistan via Afghanistan and Pakistan, from Qatar via Pakistan and from Myanmar via Bangladesh. India currently sources most of its LNG from Qatar and smaller quantities from Oman and Australia. (India has two LNG ports.) India imports no LNG from Indonesia or Malaysia.

A number of pipelines have been built in the region: two from Indonesia to Singapore, two from Myanmar to Thailand, one from Indonesia to Malaysia and one from Malaysia to Singapore. There are plans to build a gas pipeline from the Malaysia-Thailand Joint Development Area to Thailand and Malaysia as well as from the Commercial Agreement Area between Malaysia and

Vietnam to Malaysia. The Trans-ASEAN Gas Pipeline project, which envisions many more cross-border lines, was launched in 1998.[4]

Renewable Energy

As noted at the outset, several of the Bay of Bengal countries rely heavily at present on combustible renewables and wastes for energy. The manner in which this energy is procured and used at this time is such that it could never power modern industrial, commercial and civilian sectors.

Some analysts believe that there is tremendous potential for the development of renewable energy in the Bay of Bengal and hope that some of the governments will have the determination to build their economies on the basis of various forms of renewable energy and avoid becoming dependent on imports of fossil fuels. They argue this would lead not only to much higher energy self-sufficiency and security, but also far less environmental degradation and global warming.

As far as hydropower potential is concerned, the region does indeed have considerable potential. India is presently the largest generator of hydroelectricity (see Table 2.12). About 13 per cent of the total electricity generated there is from hydropower plants (see Table 2.6).

The next largest producers of hydropower are Indonesia, Malaysia and Thailand. It is hoped that a Memorandum of Understanding on construction of the ASEAN Power Grid will be signed at the 25th ASEAN Ministers on

Table 2.12
Hydropower Production (billion kilowatt-hours)

	Production 2004	% growth 1994–2004
India	83.76	2.26
Bangladesh	1.14	7.37
Myanmar	2.25	6.11
Thailand	5.98	8.41
Malaysia	6.18	4.78
Indonesia	9.37	4.67
Singapore	0	—
Sri Lanka	2.93	–1.04
Nepal	2.35	9.90
Bhutan	2.05	2.34
World	2,746.88	1.56

Source: EIA website at <http://www.eia.doe.gov/pub/international/iealf/table26.xls>.

Table 2.13
Electricity Trade, 2004 (billion kilowatt-hours)

	Exports	Imports
India	0.060	1.500
Bangladesh		
Myanmar		
Thailand	0.372	3.388
Malaysia	0.050	
Indonesia		
Singapore		
Sri Lanka		
Nepal	0.220	0.206
Bhutan	1.400	0.020
World	553.283	552.520

Source: EIA website at <http://www.eia.doe.gov/pub/international/iealf/tables1.xls> and <http://www.eia.doe.gov/pub/international/iealf/tables3.xls> (8 December 2006).

Energy Meeting to be held in Singapore in 2007.[5] Malaysia presently exports electric power to Thailand and Indonesia. Myanmar aspires to export hydropower to Thailand and China.

Of the total electricity generated in Bangladesh, 6 per cent is from hydropower plants (see Table 2.6). There is some potential, though limited, for further hydropower development. However, both Nepal and Bhutan have enormous hydropower capacity and would like to expand production and create a grid connecting their two countries with India and Bangladesh. In 2001, sales of hydropower to India accounted for 45 per cent of Bhutan's total government revenues and 11.6 per cent of GDP.[6]

Nuclear Power Production and Consumption

Within the Bay of Bengal region, India is presently the only country that has nuclear power. In 2004, it generated 15.04 kilowatt-hours of power, equivalent to about 3 per cent of the country's total electricity generation (see Table 2.6). India has minimal uranium reserves and these are of low quality. However, there are plans to develop the rich thorium reserves which could potentially enable India to become self-sufficient in electricity production. The Indian Prime Minister visited the United States in 2005 and signed a civil nuclear cooperation deal. In November 2006, it was approved by the U.S. Congress.

Indonesia has three research reactors and has formally announced plans to have a nuclear power plant operating by 2016. Thailand has one research reactor.

One Set of Forecasts

Table 2.14 provides energy consumption growth, population and carbon dioxide emission projections to the year 2030 from the EIA. The EIA analysts take into account the countries' GDP per capita, structure of the economy, expected population growth, among others.[7] The "Reference Case" is used here. The EIA also generates "High Economic Growth" and "Low Economic Growth" scenarios.

Unfortunately, apart from India, data for each individual country is not provided. As the "Asia" category here includes many more Asian countries than this study covers (though it excludes China, Japan, South Korea and India), it is far from ideal. However, the general trends are at least apparent. It is not the purpose of this synopsis to provide precision.

It is apparent the total energy consumption, population and carbon dioxide emissions growth for India and Asia are expected to be much higher than for the Organization for Economic Co-operation and Development (OECD) countries and the world. Consumption of natural gas, nuclear power and hydropower are expected to see the most growth in Asia, relative

Table 2.14
EIA's Energy Consumption Growth, Population and Carbon Dioxide Emission Projections, Reference Case (average annual growth, %, 2003–2030)

	India	Asia	OECD	World
Oil	2.4	2.3	0.8	1.4
Natural gas	5.9	4.4	1.5	2.4
Coal	2.7	1.7	1.2	2.5
Nuclear power	7.4	3.1	0.3	1.0
Hydropower and other renewable energy	4.2	4.5	1.5	2.4
Net electricity consumption	4.6	4.4	1.5	2.7
Total energy consumption	3.2	3.0	1.0	2.0
Population	1.1	1.3	0.4	1.0
Carbon dioxide emissions	2.9	2.7	1.1	2.1

Note: "Asia" in this table means all of Asia excluding Japan, South Korea, China and India.
Source: EIA website at <http://www.eia.doe.gov/oiaf/ieo/ieorefcase.html> (7 October 2006).

to the developed world. However, India's and Asia's shares of energy consumption (total and by type) and carbon dioxide emissions in 2030 will remain a fraction of what they are in the OECD (see Table 2.15).

Over the next twenty-five years there may be two key changes in energy use in the world. One is how electricity is generated and the other is what the fuel(s) of choice is for fuelling transport vehicles. With respect to electricity generation, the construction of nuclear power plants is of course highly political. Some countries such as France depend very heavily on nuclear power (78 per cent) whereas in other European countries such as Germany, governments are being forced to shut down existing nuclear plants.

In other parts of Asia, for example, Korea and Japan, nuclear power currently accounts for about 38 and 23 per cent of total electricity generated, respectively. Both Korea and Japan plan to greatly expand nuclear power production: in Japan to over 30 per cent of total electricity production by 2011, and in Korea to about 60 per cent by 2035.[8] Nuclear power presently contributes only 2.3 per cent to China's total electricity production but over the next fourteen years, plans are in place to build about two new plants per year. (Nonetheless, due to the scale of total electricity production in the country, the share of nuclear power will remain less than 5 per cent.) As mentioned above, nuclear power accounts for about 3 per cent of India's total electricity generation.

Table 2.15
Percentage of Global Consumption and Total Carbon Dioxide Emissions

	India		Asia		OECD	
	1990	2030	1990	2030	1990	2030
Oil	1.8	3.8	4.7	8.7	62.0	50.6
Natural gas	0.5	2.5	2.7	9.5	50.1	40.8
Coal	4.9	8.4	2.4	3.1	48.4	32.5
Nuclear power	0.3	3.4	1.7	2.7	85.6	69.9
Hydropower and other renewable energy	2.7	3.5	3.4	7.9	60.5	41.2
Net electricity consumption	2.4	5.7	3.2	7.7	64.1	43.9
Total energy consumption	2.3	4.5	3.6	7.2	56.8	42.8
Population	16.1	17.7	14.1	16.3	19.9	15.8
Carbon dioxide emissions	2.7	5.0	3.8	7.0	53.6	40.1

Note: "Asia" in this table means all of Asia excluding Japan, South Korea, China and India.
Source: Calculated from EIA website at <http://www.eia.doe.gov/oiaf/ieo/ieorefcase.html> (7 October 2006).

By 2030, governments around the world may believe that all the drawbacks of this form of energy (the well-known waste-disposal and safety issues, as well as the high capital costs and long construction times) have been sufficiently overcome and therefore nuclear energy is the best option for providing electricity. Or, due to another nuclear power plant accident or to sabotage, they could all resolutely dismiss the nuclear energy option.[9]

As for transport fuels, given the fact that the planet's oil and gas resources are finite and that electricity can be generated from a variety of means, it could be argued that ideally, oil resources in particular, ought to be saved exclusively for transport use. However, much can happen over the next twenty-odd years. Perhaps by then, electric cars will in fact be perceived as the most efficient and economical. Or, perhaps as a result of the feverish biofuel experimentation being carried out now, one particular concoction will emerge unquestionably as a perfect substitute for hydrocarbon fuels.

What is used for transport fuels in twenty-five years' time is pivotal in estimating future energy requirements. There is no doubt that as incomes rise in the Bay of Bengal region, so will the demand for cars and air travel.

Conclusion

There is presently considerable energy trading among the ASEAN members but relatively little within the Bay of Bengal region as a whole.[10] For historical and political reasons, several governments have found it more practicable to import from outside the region. Many of the countries are in the very early stages of developing their energy resources for their own use. It is imperative that they do so as quickly as possible. Ideally, too, the political questions obstructing the export of surplus energy, especially natural gas and hydroelectric power, within the region be resolved without delay.

India, due to its sheer geographical and demographic scale as well as its historical economic development, dominates the region in all ways including energy production and consumption. Within the next thirty years, it will overtake China as the most populous country in the world. Since the economic reforms were launched in the early 1990s, annual economic growth has averaged around 7 per cent. It is currently the sixth largest energy consumer in the world and relies on imports to meet nearly 30 per cent of its energy needs.

The countries of this region are all competing for foreign oil supplies. Without question, the major economies of the region, namely, India, Singapore, Malaysia and Thailand, have sophisticated outreach and negotiating power vis-à-vis the currently known and expected large oil exporting countries in the

Middle East, Russia, the Caspian region and Africa, as well as with Australia which aspires to export coal and natural gas to the region.

In the short run, it would seem that oil security is a zero-sum game, that is, one country's consumption means less available oil for another country.[11] International oil analysts' predictions about the scale and ease of exploitation of the world's remaining oil reserves vary widely. Much pivots on the price of oil. If it is high, innumerable deposits hitherto deemed hopeless become viable.

Many specialists believe there are many different ways to generate energy that do not involve the use of oil or fossil fuels at all. They claim that if the oil/gas reserves did indeed "run out", the world would not grind to a halt. However, most countries at this point in history, including many in the Bay of Bengal region have infrastructure designed for the use of fossil fuels. This infrastructure cannot be converted to use other fuels either easily or quickly. Doing so is also highly capital intensive. On the other hand, other member countries of the region are so young in their development, that if it was economically and practically doable, they could possibly take a fresh approach to modernization and opt to become non-fossil fuel economies.

It appears that the Bay of Bengal countries have no choice at this point in history but to fuel their economies mainly with fossil fuels, as has most of the Western world since the Industrial Revolution. Depending on the price of oil — which determines global supply — the Bay of Bengal region, especially India, may feel it is competing with the world's largest oil consumers, namely, China, the United States and Europe for energy, particularly oil security.

Given this ostensible global race to secure oil supplies, the countries comprising the Bay of Bengal region ought ideally to cooperate rather than compete with each other in their quest for energy security. However, some member states suffer various political and economic tensions that have simmered for decades, if not centuries. Tenaciously competing for energy could potentially exacerbate these tensions. On the other hand, the joint, successful resolution of energy supply problems could also serve as the basis upon which other problems could be resolved. Indeed, the formation of the European Union was premised on the need to share coal, coke, iron ore, steel and scrap metal following World War II.[12]

Through cooperation, the Bay of Bengal region could significantly reduce its vulnerability to oil supply or price disruptions. The governments all ought to work towards making the best use of the energy resources — both renewable and non-renewable — available within the region. They could also consider cooperating with respect to buying and conveying fossil fuels from outside the region. Instead of competing with each other, and other large consumers such as China, these countries could negotiate as a group with the large supplying countries of the Middle East, Latin America, Russia, etc., and also together agree on the most cost-effective energy transport routes, that is, sea lanes, ports and pipelines.

The region may also wish to consider building a shared network of strategic petroleum reserves which can serve as a buffer during supply or price disruptions. In 2004, the Indian government decided to establish strategic petroleum reserves equivalent to fifteen days of consumption. These are comprised of both crude oil and oil products. With the price of oil falling, the other countries could begin to consider when and how they too could build up reserves.

Another area of potential cooperation is the building and maintaining of oil refineries. These require enormous amounts of capital investment. Instead of all individually constructing refineries, the governments could decide to share the operation of these plants and the oil product distribution infrastructure therefrom.

However, it must be recognized that in order to attract foreign investment for the construction of pipelines, ports, and plants, the governments must take the difficult, but critical steps towards liberalizing and harmonizing their energy markets and pricing. Removing energy price subsidies and raising energy prices to international levels is fundamental to energy cooperation.

Commensurate with increasing energy supplies and phasing out energy price subsidies is the equally important imperative to raise energy consumption efficiencies to the highest possible degree. Many of these new economies have an opportunity to avoid the gross wastage and consequences therefrom, in terms of air pollution, that the Western world experienced in the early decades of the last century.

NOTES

1 The Bay of Bengal region is defined here as the following ten countries: Bangladesh, Bhutan, India, Indonesia, Malaysia, Myanmar, Nepal, Thailand, Singapore and Sri Lanka.

2 The EIA data is available at <http://www.eia.doe.gov/emeu/international/contents.html> (1 December 2006). Other key sources were IEA. *Energy Balances of Non-OECD Countries* (Paris: OECD/IEA, 2005); and *World Trade Atlas* (for more information see <http://www.gtis.com/product.cfm?level=1&type=W>).

3 "Indonesia to Reduce Rather than Halt Gas Exports", AFP, 29 March 2006 at <http://www.bkpm.go.id/en/news.php?mode=baca&info_id=3445> (10 August 2006]; "Indonesia to Halve LNG to Japan", *The Daily Yomiuri,* 29 September 2006.

4 Full details of the plans for the Trans ASEAN Gas Pipeline project are available at the ASEAN website at <http://www.aseanenergy.org/ace/work_programme.htm> (23 September 2006).

5 Joint Media Statement of ASEAN Ministers on Energy Meeting held in Vientiane, 27 July 2006 at <http://www.aseansec.org/18582.htm> (9 August 2006).

6 EIA, South Asia Overview (Country Report) at <http://www.eia.doe.gov/emeu/cabs/South_Asia/Electricity.html> (30 November 2006).

7 Discussion of the methodology used for generating the forecasts is available at EIA's website <http://www.eia.doe.gov/oiaf/analysispaper/forecasteval/forecast_eval.html> (24 September 2006).

8 See World Nuclear Association website at <http://www.world-nuclear.org> (16 September 2006).

9 For example, the catastrophes which occurred at Three-Mile Island in 1979 and Chernobyl in 1986.

10 For more details about energy flows within ASEAN, see Elspeth Thomson, "ASEAN and Northeast Asian Energy Security: Cooperation or Competition?", *East Asia: An International Quarterly* 23, no. 3 (Winter 2006).

11 This is highly debated. Oil is a fungible commodity, that is, it is replaceable or exchangeable in whole or part and is sold on one global market. For discussion, see for example this exchange on *Oil Drum*: <http://www.theoildrum.com/story/2005/8/25/122557/149> and *Grist*: <http://gristmill.grist.org/story/2006/2/19/143944/139> (15 January 2007).

12 For a discussion of the EU's progress and problems with energy integration and the relevance for East Asia, see Elspeth Thomson, "ASEAN-China Energy Cooperation", in *ASEAN-China Economic Relations*, edited by Saw Swee-Hock (Singapore: Institute of Southeast Asian Studies, 2007).

3

Gas Potential at the Bay of Bengal: Implications for India's Energy Security

Talmiz Ahmad

The *India Hydrocarbon Vision 2025* report, published by the Indian government in February 2000, painted a rather alarming picture of the Indian energy security situation.[1] It pointed out that India's requirements of oil and gas would increase significantly over the next twenty-five years to sustain the high growth rates of 8 to 10 per cent per annum to which the country was committed. It said that the country's domestic resources would not be able to meet these high demands, and that India's dependence on imported oil would increase from 65 per cent in 2000 to 85 per cent in 2025. Again, India's gas requirements would also increase significantly to fuel the needs of the power, fertilizer and industrial sectors and for domestic usage. The electric power sector was projected to account for 71 per cent of the total incremental growth in India's natural gas demand from 2000 to 2025.

The report highlighted the importance of boosting domestic production through a vigorous national effort, which would include further liberalizing the upstream hydrocarbon sector and encouraging Indian and foreign companies to participate in exploration and development activity by bringing in their rich experience and the latest technology.

One significant impact of this new focus on energy security has been the enthusiasm with which exploration activity is now taking place in India and discoveries are being announced in areas that had been largely unexplored till recently. The recent discoveries of oil and gas in the Krishna-Godavari basin of the Bay of Bengal indicate that this newly explored region has very rich potential. Even before these discoveries, earlier discoveries in the offshore areas of Bangladesh and Myanmar had already indicated that the Bay of Bengal could emerge, in the words of former Indian Petroleum Minister Mani Shankar Aiyar, as the "North Sea of South Asia".

The Bay of Bengal, which already had great significance in terms of India's strategic interests as the link between South Asia and Southeast Asia, has now acquired a new energy salience as well, with hectic exploration activity being undertaken both by India and Myanmar, and indications that Bangladesh and Sri Lanka are also anxious to expand exploration in their littoral. These discoveries have not just contributed to India's energy security interests; they have also given a new importance and urgency to regional cooperation, bringing together producer and consumer nations in an energy-related partnership for mutual benefit. Not surprisingly, given its substantial hydrocarbon requirements, India is at the centre of this emerging regional engagement.

Global Gas Scenario

Natural gas, being a "clean" fuel, is increasingly seen as the fuel of the twenty-first century. Between 1980 and 2003, the share of gas in the world energy mix rose from 18 per cent to 22 per cent. The demand for gas is expected to increase at 2.3 per cent per annum till 2025, when it will constitute 25 per cent of the world energy mix and consolidate its position as the number two fuel in the global mix.

On the supply side, the prognosis relating to gas is quite comfortable: present resources can meet current demand for sixty years. With new discoveries, reserves could meet demand for 150 years at present rate of consumption. Between 2002 and 2025, gas consumption will increase by nearly 70 per cent. The electric power sector will account for almost one-half of the total incremental growth in worldwide natural gas demand over the forecast period.

Both pipelines and liquefied natural gas (LNG) have a role to play in transporting gas. Pipelines are best for shorter hauls and thus should dominate local and regional trade: generally, LNG is cost-competitive with pipelines only over distances in excess of 4,000 kilometres.

Today, out of the total global gas production of 2,691 billion cubic metres (bcm), only 25 per cent is internationally traded, 19 per cent being transported through transnational pipelines and 6 per cent as LNG. Europe is the principal importer of gas by pipeline (320 bcm per annum), followed by the United States (102 bcm, from Canada). Japan is the principal importer of LNG (76.95 bcm), followed by Europe (40 bcm), Republic of Korea (30 bcm) and the United States (19 bcm). According to industry forecasts, international trade in natural gas is expected to increase significantly in coming years, accounting for one-third of world output, by 2020. This increased trade will cover both LNG and piped gas. International trade in LNG is expected to grow by 7 per cent per annum till it becomes 38 per cent of gas trade by 2020.[2]

Transnational Gas Pipelines

While oil pipelines have been in existence in different parts of the world since the early part of the twentieth century, transnational gas pipelines are of recent origin. The setting up of pipelines from the former Soviet Union to Germany and later to other parts of Western Europe in the 1970s and 1980s at the height of the Cold War, was a political, financial and commercial challenge. The increase in oil prices in the early 1970s encouraged Germany and other European countries to look for alternative forms of energy, particularly gas. In 1973, Federal Republic of Germany (FRG) received its first gas deliveries from the Soviet Union. Over the years, German imports continued to increase, with supplies to Federal Republic of Germany and German Democratic Republic reaching 17.2 bcm in 1980. In the 1980s, Soviet gas supplies were extended to France and other major European countries.

These supplies from the Soviet Union took place amidst strong U.S. opposition, which included extra-territorial sanctions on supply of equipment and technology. The United States had concerns that the gas trade would not only provide the Soviet Union with additional hard currency but could also reduce European resolve to confront in the "evil empire" in the Cold War. However, the European countries remained firm in their resolve to import Soviet gas and, by 1989, the Union of Soviet Socialist Republics met 30 per cent of FRG gas demand. It is important to note that, throughout the Cold War when Soviet gas was reaching the FRG, as also West Berlin, never once were the supplies disrupted.

Since the end of the Cold War, Russian supplies of gas by pipeline to Europe have increased, going further eastwards to the United Kingdom, Belgium and the Netherlands, in the early of part of this century.

Asian Gas Demand

Today, while the world's gas map depicts numerous gas pipelines moving across thousands of kilometers from Russia, Central Asia and the North Sea to Western Europe, there are hardly any pipelines in Asia that move eastwards and southwards. This is now set to change due to two important factors:

(i) the increasing Asian demand for gas; and
(ii) the ability of Asia to transport gas economically from producers to consuming centres.

Over the next twenty-five years, the energy requirements of Asia are expected to increase 2.5 times, an increase of an additional 2–2.5 billion tonnes oil equivalent (toe). Gas will have a significant place in this scenario. At present, Asia has much less share in gas demand than the world average (6 per cent versus 12 per cent). Hence, to meet Asia's rapidly increasing energy requirements, consumption of gas will have to increase; the expectation is that it will do so from 210 million toe in 1997, through 600 million toe in 2020, to 800–900 million toe in 2030.

The principal sources of global gas lie in Asia. The Asian area of Russia has 27 per cent of the world's proven reserves, followed by Iran (15 per cent) and Qatar (14 per cent). In fact, North and Central Asia and the Gulf between them have over 70 per cent of world reserves. As against this, the principal consumers of Asia — China, Japan, Republic of Korea and India — together have less than 2 per cent of global reserves, with Japan and Korea having no reserves at all. At the same time, in 2004, the latter two countries imported just over 100 bcm of gas as LNG as against a total global LNG trade of 178 bcm.

The Indian Hydrocarbon Scene

The *Indian Hydrocarbon Vision 2025* report had only looked at the hydrocarbon (oil and gas) scenario, and did not touch upon the other sources of energy required for national development. In the years following the publication of the *Vision* document, a number of energy institutions, Indian and foreign, prepared projections relating to India's gas demand.[3] These findings can be found in Appendix 3.1.

The International Gas Union (IGU)'s report on India's gas needs in the power sector has explained the different gas demand projections thus:

> It is noticeable that most studies result in considerably lower demand projections than the **Hydrocarbon Vision**. Partly, his is the result of the

> benefit of hind-sight whereby changes to the policy framework, actual versus planned capacity demand additions and supply side developments could be taken into consideration. But partly *the more conservative estimates of recent studies reflect recognition that the key determinant for future gas-based capacity additions is price sensitivity of end-consumers* and not solely the country's fast growing appetite for energy and electricity in particular.
>
> The major reasons behind the differences in projected gas demand for power generation are a result of the extent to which sensitivity to gas pricing, domestic gas availability and total gas supply stability were taken into consideration.[4] (Emphasis added)

Thankfully, this deficiency has now been made up by the Integrated Energy Policy document prepared by the Planning Commission, in August 2006, under the chairmanship of Mr Kirit Parikh. This report takes a holistic view of India's requirements to meet a minimum growth rate of 8 per cent per annum up to 2031–32, that is, the end of the 15th Five-Year Plan. The report postulates that, in order to reach growth rates of 8 per cent per annum up to 2031–32, the country:

(i) needs to increase primary energy supply by three to four times; and
(ii) electricity generation capacity has to be expanded five to six times from 2003–04 levels, that is, power generation capacity must increase from the current 160,000 megawatts (MW) to nearly 800,000 MW by 2031–32.[5]

Taking into account power and other commercial requirements, the report suggests that India's primary commercial energy requirement (in million toe) would be as follows:[6]

Year	Coal	Oil	Gas	Nuclear
2011–12	257	166	44	17
2021–22	464	278	97	45
2031–32	835	486	197	98

Source: "Integrated Energy Policy: Report of the Expert Committee", Planning Commission, New Delhi, p. 28.

The gas requirement in the average fuel mix adopted as a standard by the committee for growth rates of 8 and 9 per cent is as follows:[7]

Year	8% GDP growth rate	9% GDP growth rate
2006–07	12 bcm	14 bcm
2021–22	52 bcm	59 bcm
2031–32	119 bcm	134 bcm

Source: "Integrated Energy Policy: Report of the Expert Committee", Planning Commission, New Delhi, p. 22.

The place of gas in the energy mix between 2003–04 and 2031–32 is projected as follows:[8]

Energy source	2003–04 (%)	2031–32 (%)
Coal	51	50.5
Oil	36	30
Gas	9	12
Nuclear	1.5	6
Hydro	2.14	2.12

Source: "Integrated Energy Policy: Report of the Expert Committee", Planning Commission, New Delhi, p. 29.

The committee has recognized that fuel requirements for power generation can be met from various alternative fuels. The report states:

> to the extent that gas, hydro or nuclear capacity cannot be realized as projected in the scenario, coal-based generation will need to fill the gap. In reality, the choice between coal and gas will be guided by economic and commercial considerations including any policy prescriptions for pricing-in certain environmental externalities.[9]

The report takes account of a number of different scenarios in which domestic resources would be boosted through technological inputs to augment domestic production and enhance conservation and efficiency, besides expansion in the use of alternative fuels and unconventional and non-conventional energy, all of which taken together would yield an import dependence for energy in 2031–32 that could be as low as 29 per cent or as high as 59 per cent.[10]

To reach its growth targets, India would need to pursue all available fuel options and energy sources, conventional and non-conventional. However, the factual position in respect of specific energy resources has to be noted. Today, India's energy mix is: coal 50 per cent; oil and gas 45 per cent; hydropower 2 per cent, and nuclear 1.5 per cent. In 2022, fossil fuels will continue to dominate India's energy mix to the extent of 75 per cent, with hydropower providing 14 per cent, and nuclear power 6.5 per cent. Even robust votaries of nuclear power have noted that, most optimistically, nuclear energy will provide only 8.8 per cent in India's energy mix in 2032, as against 76 per cent for fossil fuels, and 12 per cent for hydropower. In 2052, when nuclear energy is likely to be 16.4 per cent of our energy mix, coal is expected to be 40 per cent; hydrocarbons 35 per cent and hydropower 5.1 per cent.[11]

The Kirit Parikh Report has looked at different international price scenarios pertaining to coal and gas; its conclusion is unambiguous:

> Any supply strategy over the coming decades will have to emphasise India's major resource, i.e. coal. Coal is the most abundant domestically available primary energy resource other than thorium and solar isolation. In the "coal-based development" scenario, the total demand for coal increases from 172 Mtoe in 2004-05 to 1022 Mtoe in 2031–32. Measured in [million tonnes] of Indian coal with 4000 kcal/kg, the requirement of coal will thus increase from 406 Mt in 2004–05 to 2555 Mt in 2031–32.[12]

The report recognizes that requirements of coal of this magnitude would not be easily met from domestic sources. Indeed, with increasing deterioration in the quality of domestic coal, India's needs would increase to 2,689 million tonnes by 2031–32, which would further increase the country's import dependency.[13] Obviously, the stage is set for a major national effort to revamp the coal industry by expanding private mining, state-of-the-art technological input upgradation and expansion of the national infrastructure such as ports and railways.

Even then, in order to meet the power generation requirements of the country set out in the Kirit Parikh Report, domestic coal would not be sufficient and India would have to depend on imported coal. The comparative economics of importing coal and obtaining gas through transnational pipelines and as liquefied natural gas (LNG) have not been examined in the report, nor has it been noted that prices of imported coal move in tandem with those of imported gas. The conclusion is unavoidable that gas will have a much larger share in the country's energy mix, particularly for its power requirements, than has been projected in the report, given the abundance of natural gas reserves in India's neighbourhood and also the domestic potential that is being explored and developed today.

The fact that import of natural gas is price-sensitive is self-evident and is, indeed, applicable to all commercial transactions. However, if India is to meet the targeted growth rates, we have to keep an open mind with regard to the utilization of different energy sources, and accept that different aspects of the national energy economy such as coal, gas and nuclear power, are a part of a globalized economy and cannot be immune from price trends in the international markets.

Gas Potential of the Bay of Bengal

Let us now take a look at the gas potential of the Bay of Bengal, both in the Indian economic zone and in that of its neighbours to evaluate the reserves position of the region and obtain an idea of recent developments in India's pursuit of its energy security interests in its eastern littoral.

INDIA

The gas potential of the Indian zone of the Bay of Bengal, known to geologists through the 1970s and 1980s, came in for commercial exploitation only in the 1990s. Today, the prognosticated hydrocarbon resources of the Bay of Bengal (oil and oil equivalent) are estimated at between 1,100–1,300 million metric tonnes (mmt). If the deep-water areas beyond 200 metres Iso-bath are taken into account, the area extends to about 1 million square metres and has prognosticated resources of about 4,000 mmt oil and oil equivalent.[14]

The Bay of Bengal comprises five sedimentary basins. These basins, with their prognosticated resources, are shown below:[15]

Basin	Offshore Basinal Area (sq. km)	Prognosticated resources (mmt of O+OEG)
Krishna Godavari	24,000	555
Cauvery	30,000	270
Mahanadi-NEC	14,000	100
Bengal	32,000	30
Andaman Nicobar	41,000	180
Total	1,41,000	1,135

Source: Directorate General of Hydrocarbon, New Delhi.

At present, commercial production is taking place in two areas: Krishna-Godavari (KG) and Cauvery. The Ravva field in the KG basin today produces 6,749 tonnes of oil per day and 2.3 million metric standard cubic metres per day (mmscmd) of gas, while the Cauvery is producing 721 tonnes oil and 0.19 mmscmd of gas.[16]

Besides this ongoing commercial production, oil and gas discoveries made so far in the Bay of Bengal indicate in-place gas reserves of 100 mmt in the deep waters of the KG basin and 12 mmt of gas in the shallow waters of the Mahanadi basin. In a number of fields, the in-place reserves have yet to be firmed up.[17] However, hectic exploration and production (E&P) activity is taking place at present all along the Indian zone of the Bay of Bengal:[18]

	No. of blocks	Area under exploration (sq. m)
i) KG basin	15	90,000
ii) Cauvery basin	9	70,000
iii) Andaman basin	4	46,000
iv) Mahanadi basin	12	128,000
v) West Bengal	1	6,700
Total	41	3,60,700

Source: Directorate General of Hydrocarbon, New Delhi.

Besides this ongoing activity, a number of blocks in the Bay of Bengal have been included in the latest exploration round, New Exploration Licensing Policy-VI (NELP-VI), for which bids closed on 30 September 2006; these are:[19]

	No. of blocks	Area (sq. m)
i) Cauvery	6	60,000
ii) Krishna Godavari	8	75,000
iii) Mahanadi	7	60,000
iv) Andaman and Nicobar	1	12,000
v) Palar	1	10,000

Source: Directorate General of Hydrocarbon, New Delhi.

Companies participating in E&P activities in the Bay of Bengal have been regularly reporting their understanding of the potential of their fields, though these have not been confirmed by the upstream regulator, the Directorate General of Hydrocarbons (DGH). Thus, in June 2005, the Gujarat State Petroleum Corporation (GSPC)) announced that it would begin commercial production in its blocks in the KG basin by December 2007. It stated that its initial production would be 10 mmscmd, which would increase to 80 mmscmd. It also announced that it had stuck 20 tcf of gas resources in a well in one of its blocks within KG basin.[20]

In February 2005, Oil and Natural Gas Commission (ONGC) announced that its block off West Bengal, where it would commence drilling of four wells from mid-March 2005, could yield 5–10 million tonnes of in-place reserves of oil and oil equivalent. The press note issued by the ONGC quoted unnamed American oil and gas experts as saying that the block off West Bengal "could have one of the world's largest oil and gas reserves stretching all the way to Andaman and Nicobar islands."[21]

In December 2006, the ONGC announced a huge gas find in the Krishna-Godavari Basin.[22] The company said that it had struck a 28 metre net gas pay zone when the deep-sea drill-ship, *Belford Dolphin*, reached 5,300 metres depth. Pointing out that drilling has not reached its target depth of 6,500 metres, the ONGC said that preliminary estimates put in-place reserves at 600 billion cubic metres (over 21 tcf), and that the second net pay zone could be in excess of 80 metres, along with traces of oil.

Earlier, in mid-2003, the former Director General of Hydrocarbons had stated that the Andaman and Nicobar area in the Bay of Bengal contained "vast unexplored natural gas reserves estimated at around 610 million tonnes".[23] He had added that seven gas hydrates had been mapped, which could yield "free gas reserves in the region in the order of 23 billion cubic metres".

These remarks echoed the findings of Indian experts who, in September 2004, had reported at a Petroleum Conference in Vancouver that, while the presence of gas hydrates in the Andaman area had been known since 1984, a National Gas Hydrate Programme (NGHP) had been set up in 1997, and that a "roadmap was in place to achieve the commercial production of gas from gas hydrates beyond 2008".[24] The explorers had concluded: "Integration of geophysical, geological, geo-chemical and microbiological data results suggest that the KG basin is highly conducive for gas hydrate occurrence."

In mid-September 2006, there were reports in some sections of the Indian media that India was giving final touches to its proposal to the United Nations Commission on the Limits of the Continental Shelf (UNCLOS) which would enable it to extend its exclusive economic zone up to 560 kilometres (from the present 320 kilometres).[25] There are estimates that the extended economic zone could have 2 billion barrels of equivalent gas hydrate. Four-fifths of the claim is expected to be in the Bay of Bengal, the remainder in the Arabian Sea.[26]

BANGLADESH

The present land area of Bangladesh has been the scene of considerable hydrocarbon exploration activity from 1910. From the 1960s onwards, there has been some success in discovery of gas reserves. Bangladesh's principal gas fields are as follows:[27]

Gas in Place and Reserves of Major Gas Fields (in bcf)

Fields	Year of Discovery	Recoverable (proven + probable)	Cumulative Production (December 2000)	Net Recoverable
Rashidpur	1960	1,309	194.920	1,114.080
Kailashtilia	1962	2,529	231.820	2,297.180
Titas	1962	2,100	1,783.400	316.600
Habibganj	1963	1,895	818.315	1,076.685
Sangu	1996	848	91.026	756.974
Total (with other fields)		15,507	4,083.52	11,423.48

Source: Monzur Hossain, "Bangladesh: Natural Gas Export", *South Asian Journal*, July–September 2005; downloaded from <www.southasianmedia.net/magazine/journal>.

Bangladesh has recoverable reserves of 15.51 tcf, of which 4.07 tcf has been already produced; thus the remaining reserves are about 11.42 tcf. At

7.5 per cent annual extraction, it is believed that Bangladesh's reserves would perhaps be exhausted by 2011.[28]

The development of Bangladesh's gas potential and gas exports has been a contentious issue in Bangladesh politics where broad opinion is that the export option should be considered "only after ensuring the reserves for long-term domestic gas consumption".[29] In 2002, the then Bangladeshi State Minister for Energy and Minerals had estimated that by 2030 US$20–40 billion would be required to supply gas to the local people.[30] At that time, the head of Unocal Bangladesh, had said: "There is a significant number of high quality and creditworthy customers in Delhi, who have the ability to pay better prices for surplus gas of Bangladesh."[31] He had added that a clear-cut policy decision to allow export of gas through pipeline was required in order to attract more investments into the sector. The irony is that, in spite of having such substantial gas reserves, Bangladesh continues to suffer from gas shortages of up to 100 mcf per day.[32]

Even as Bangladesh has been grappling with how to develop its potential most effectively and monetize its reserves, over the last two months, a controversy relating to "oil poaching" in the Bay of Bengal has emerged. Briefly, Bangladesh news reports had claimed that certain blocks included in the Indian NELP-VI round had encroached on Bangladesh territory. The Bangladeshi energy advisor was quoted as saying that India and Myanmar had encroached 19,000 square kilometres and 18,000 square kilometres, respectively, on Bangladeshi territorial waters extending up to 200 nautical miles (370 kilometres) in the Bay of Bengal and had floated international tenders for hydrocarbon exploration.[33] The reports also announced that Bangladesh would shortly be announcing its own third exploration round.

It is true that the Indo-Bangladeshi maritime boundary has not been delineated. However, according to Indian sources, the boundaries of the blocks of concern to Bangladesh had already been modified before NELP-VI was officially publicized, and that today there was no reason for any dispute in this regard. In this context, it may be noted that Bangladesh news reports have themselves quoted Bangladeshi officials as saying: "We do not have any clear marking of deep sea borders with India and Myanmar. This creates another serious uncertainty for potential bidders."[34]

While reporting on the Bangladeshi proposal to go in for a third exploration bid round, the Bangladesh media has pointed out that even basic seismic data is not available for inspection by potential bidders. An official has been quoted as saying: "We know very little about the Bay. When oil companies will seek existing data, we have little to offer them."[35]

In August 2006, there were media reports that Bangladesh's coastal waters could have oolite carbonate rocks, which usually promise a prime underground reservoir of oil. Oolites are believed to have been discovered accidentally by a German geo-scientific and national resources institution that was primarily studying sedimentation in the Bay of Bengal in June and July 2006.[36]

SRI LANKA

It has been reported that Sri Lanka has decided to permit India and China to explore for oil and gas along the northwestern sea belt. The first phase of exploration was scheduled to begin in the Gulf of Mannar, in August 2007. According to the Petroleum Resources Development Minister, A.H.M. Fowzie, two of the six blocks earmarked for exploration in the northwestern sea waters would be entrusted to India and China for hydrocarbon exploration. Sri Lanka might allow these countries to explore in other blocks as well for which it is conducting seismic surveys.[37]

MYANMAR

Myanmar has a long tradition of oil production from the mid-nineteenth century, with a pioneering role in the early development being played, first by the Rangoon Oil Company set up in 1871 and, later by the Burmah Oil Company set up in 1886; this company dominated the country's oil industry till 1962.

Natural gas production started in 1974 at the Aphyauk gas field near Taikkyi Township in the lower delta of the Irrawaddy River. Gas produced by the wells at this field was piped to Yangon for power generation at Thaketa and at Shwedaung near Prome, as well as for industrial use at the Sittaung paper mill in Yangon.

In 1975, gas production reached 4,575 million cubic feet (mcf), rising to some 40,000 mcf in 1990, dropping to 31,782 mcf in 1991–92, and rising again to 58,575 mcf in 1996–97.[38]

The Myanmar offshore area has been divided into twenty-five blocks covering an area of about 270,000 square kilometres. To the west of the Rakhine coast along the Bay of Bengal, in the north are situated seven blocks, A-1 through A-7. Eleven blocks, M-1 to M-11, are located in the Gulf of Martaban (as known as Gulf of Moattama), in the northern sector of the Andaman Sea, and seven blocks from M-12 to M-18 are by the Tanintharyi coastline, in the south, west of the Mergui Archipelago.

Deep-water areas are both within the western margins of blocks in the Rakhine (A-2 through A-7), Moattama (M-2, M-5, M-6, M-8 and M-11) and Tanintharyi (M-12, M-14, M-15, M-16, M-17 and M-18) zones, and westward of these permits in what Myanmar considers its Exclusive Economic Zone.[39]

In the early 1990s, the Myanmar government invited foreign bids for offshore exploration in eighteen concession blocks, thirteen in the Gulf of Martaban and five off the coast of Arakan state. Oil companies such as Texaco, Premier Oil, Total and Unocal were among the successful bidders. Two major offshore gas fields, Yadana and Yetagun, were discovered in the Gulf of Martaban. The Yadana field has estimated gas reserves of more than 5.3 trillion cubic feet, or 150 billion cubic metres, with an expected field life of thirty years. The Yetagun field has estimated reserves of 48 billion cubic metres.[40] Production from the Yadana field started in 1998, while production from Yetagun started in 2000.

The Yadana project was developed by a consortium consisting of Total (31 per cent), Unocal (28 per cent), PTT-EP of Thailand (26 per cent) and Myanmar's own organization, the Myanma Oil and Gas Enterprise (MOGE) (15 per cent).[41] It is operated by Total. Gas from Yadana is transported via a 346-kilometre subsea pipeline and a 63-kilometre onshore pipeline from the Yadana field to the border between Myanmar and Thailand at Ban I Thong. At the border, the Yadana pipeline connects with a pipeline built by Thailand, which carries the gas to its destination area near Bangkok, providing fuel to the Rathcaburi and Wang Noi power plants. Gas from the Yadana field covers an estimated 15–20 per cent of Thailand's demand for natural gas.

The Yetagun gas field was developed by a joint venture of Texaco (50 per cent), the British oil company Premier Oil (30 per cent) and Nippon Oil (20 per cent). Following Texaco's withdrawal in 1997 and Premier Oil's in 2002, Yetagun is operated by Petronas, in partnership with MOGE (20 per cent), Nippon Oil (19 per cent) and PTT-EP (19 per cent). The gas is transported by 210 kilometres of subsea pipeline and 67 kilometres of onshore pipeline, linking up onshore to the Yadana pipeline.[42]

Daewoo International partnered with MOGE to explore and develop offshore natural gas deposits off the coast of Arakan. Partners in the project's international consortium are Daewoo (60 per cent), the state-owned Korean Gas Corporation (10 per cent), and India's ONGC (20 per cent) and GAIL (10 per cent). In 2004, Daewoo announced the discovery of the Shwe field, off the coast of Sittwe, the capital of Arakan state. The A-1 block is the largest and estimated to contain between 2.88 and 3.56 tcf of natural gas.[43]

GAIL feels the Myanmar exploration blocks A1 and A3 could hold more than the 5.7 tcf gas estimated earlier by the reserves consultants, and both blocks would produce 16 mmscmd from the existing discoveries: Shwe (3.4 tcf), Shwe Phyu (0.5 tcf) and Mya (1.8 tcf); the resource certification indicates the total estimated gas initially in-place as between 5.7 tcf to 10 tcf. According to GAIL, there is a 50 per cent chance of the reserves figures exceeding the lower figure and a 10 per cent chance of meeting the upper limit.[44]

Myanmar has now emerged as the sixteenth largest natural gas exporter in the world and new discoveries indicate that it may have some major high-yielding basins. Gas is now the most important source of income for Myanmar: one-third of foreign direct investment (FDI) in the country is in the oil and gas sector.[45] The combined FDI in Myanmar oil and gas since 1988 is approximately US$2.5 billion, 33 per cent of all of Myanmar's FDI. From the newly discovered Shwe field alone, the Korean Daewoo International has predicted at least US$86 million in net profit annually for twenty years from 2010, while Myanmar is projected to earn a minimum of US$800 million a year, and potentially up to US$3 billion.

The Myanmar-India Gas Pipeline

In January 2005, the Petroleum Ministers of India, Bangladesh and Myanmar approved, in Yangon, a trilateral joint press statement to transport gas from the Sittwe gas fields by pipeline through Bangladesh to India. It was agreed that officials from the three countries would prepare a tripartite MOU, to be approved by the three ministers, after which a Techno-economic Committee would pursue the implementation of the pipeline project.

The overland route of the pipeline passing through Bangladesh had two variations:

(a) a shorter route from Sittwe to Dhaka via Cox's Bazaar and Chittagong, and then to Kolkatta via Khulna and Basirhat;
(b) a longer overland route from Sittwe to Dhaka via the Indian State of Tripura, moving on to Dhaka through Comilla and then on to Kolkatta via Khulna.

The advantage of alternative (b) was that it would enable India to monetize its gas reserves in Tripura which have remained undeveloped for over twenty years. A variation of the routing proposed was to pursue the shorter version with a short spur pipeline linking Tripura gas to the pipeline.

The proposed pipeline was seen as a win-win-win proposition since:

(a) it enabled the transportation of Myanmar gas to India through the most economical transnational pipeline route;
(b) it enabled Bangladesh to obtain transit fees for the length of the pipeline within its territory as also to transport its own gas from the east of the country where it is located to the west where it is required, at no cost to itself; and,
(c) it enabled India to exploit its Tripura gas reserves besides meeting to the power and industrial needs of east India.

Unfortunately, the trilateral government-to-government Memorandum of Understanding (MOU) could not be signed as Bangladesh insisted on the inclusion of certain bilateral India-Bangladesh issues in the MOU. These items were:

(i) India should facilitate power transmission from Nepal and Bhutan to Bangladesh when the former had surplus power;
(ii) India should facilitate the transit of Bangladesh goods to Nepal and Bhutan; and
(iii) India should take action to bridge the yawning trade gap between India and Bangladesh.

India objected to this approach on the grounds that:

(i) these issues had nothing to do with the trilateral pipeline project;
(ii) they involved other countries (Nepal and Bhutan) which were not a party to the pipeline project and, indeed, had not been consulted in respect of the issues raised by Bangladesh; and
(iii) the bilateral issues were, in any case, being pursued by the two countries at other fora.

Separately, perhaps concerned about the delay in finalizing the MOU for the pipeline via Bangladesh, Myanmar entered into an MOU with PetroChina in December 2005. The MOU was worded in general terms; however, news reports referred to the possible sale of gas from A-1 and A-3 blocks to China besides setting up of oil and gas pipelines from Sittwe to Kunming in the Yunnan province in southeast China, bordering Myanmar. The Myanmar press has recently quoted an unnamed Myanmar official as saying: "At present we have not decided which country to sell A-1 gas to." The official added that they were considering three options: selling the gas *via* pipeline, building an LNG plant, and construction of gas-based industries in the country.[46]

Several press reports have seen the Myanmar-PetroChina MOU as part of the expanding bilateral Sino-Myanmar political and economic relationship over the last ten years.[47] The oil and gas pipelines from Sittwe to Kunming in southeast China have obvious positive implications for China's energy security interests: they provide an alternative route for oil and gas from the Gulf to China bypassing the Malacca Straits. They also enable China to diversify its hydrocarbon supplies from the Gulf by obtaining access to Myanmar's resources through the most economical route. It is understood that an oil pipeline linking Myanmar's deep-water port of Sittwe with Kunming in China's Yunnan Province was approved by the National Development and Reform Commission (a department of the Chinese State Council) in early April 2006, with construction expected to begin this year.[48] There are reports that other Myanmar-China connectivities are being pursued vigorously with development of road, railway and inland waterway projects.[49]

Taking into account India's gas requirements and the impasse pertaining to taking the pipeline through Bangladesh, GAIL, the Indian lead-company in the pipeline project, commissioned a study to route the pipeline directly from Myanmar to India, bypassing Bangladesh. The project would include:

(i) a pipeline in Myanmar, 50-kilometre offshore and 200-kilometre onshore, up to the Indian border; and
(ii) a pipeline of 1,500 kilometres from the Indian border to Gaya, where it would join the Jagdishpur-Haldia pipeline.

The total cost of this project would be about $2.75 billion, and would provide India with 18 mmscmd of gas. The project envisages capacity augmentation to 28 mmscmd with additional compressors.[50]

Towards the end of 2006, there was continued uncertainty about the pipeline project, with reports from Myanmar indicating that the government had not been satisfied with the prices for the gas offered by the various bidders and that it would examine the LNG option for its gas. However, in January 2007, a senior Myanmar official said in New Delhi that there were no plans to shelve the pipeline project and that discussions on the price of gas were still on.[51] The official said that no decision had been taken whether to sell the gas as such or in the form of LNG. The main issue, he said, is the price and "we are ready to sell in any form given we are offered the right price." The news report noted that India was competing for the Myanmar gas with China, Thailand and Republic of Korea.

In the latter part of 2007, there were reports that Myanmar had decided to sell gas in the A1 and A3 blocks to PetroChina rather than to GAIL. This followed an earlier Myanmar Government statement in March 2007 when stakeholders of the A1 and A3 blocks had been informed that the Myanmar Government were considering export of gas in these blocks to China through a land pipeline.[52]

The difficulties that emerged with regard to the Myanmar-Bangladesh-India gas pipeline project have important lessons for those who are pursuing promotion of energy cooperation in Asia. Transnational pipeline projects are difficult and complex ventures since:

(i) they involve different countries with differing interests;
(ii) being transnational in character, and involving neighbouring countries, they frequently carry a substantial and complex political baggage of disharmony and discord; and,
(iii) the projects are beset with serious technical and financial difficulties, requiring the mobilization of huge resources from domestic and international sources in an environment of mutual trust and confidence.

These problems are particularly daunting in Asia which has been the theatre of considerable intra-continental discord and conflict, and has relatively few success stories in regard to regional and continental cooperation. It is also true that some of the issues that divide Asian countries, particularly neighbours, are fairly complex and are unlikely to be resolved in the near future.

The principal lesson that can be drawn from the thirty-five-year history of gas pipelines is that those projects are successful only if they are founded on a strong commercial base and at the same time, are effectively immunized from the vagaries of day-to-day political issues through arrangements based on government-to-government and commercial agreements. Bangladesh, by insisting on references to bilateral India-Bangladesh issues in the agreement pertaining to the Myanmar-Bangladesh-India pipeline project, ensured that the project would be a non-starter. On the other hand, the principal reason why we have been able to make so much progress in regard to the India-Iran-Pakistan pipeline project is due to a consensual agreement between the governments of the three countries concerned to see the project purely on a commercial basis and not to permit any whiff of day-to-day politics to influence the negotiations.[53]

The international community, over the last thirty-five years, during which thousands of kilometres of gas pipelines have been laid across all continents, has developed laws, rules, norms and practices that ensure that pipelines can be insulated to a considerable extent from day-to-day politics and made "safe and secure" on the basis of international best practice. Not surprisingly, today 130 transnational pipeline projects, valued at US$200 billion, are at various stages of implementation in Europe, Africa, North and Latin America and, above all, Asia.

While the challenges involved in the implementation of transnational pipeline projects are serious, what gives them impetus is the common interest of oil and gas producers to have stable markets for their products and for consumers to have assured supplies to maintain their economic development programmes. Though Asia has relatively little experience of transnational oil and gas pipelines, the availability of abundant hydrocarbons within the continent, as also the overwhelming demand for this resource, ensures that concerns of national security and energy security can and should coalesce.

Indian Perceptions of Energy Security

In the post-Cold War era, Western (primarily American) strategic thinkers and policy-makers frequently perceive their energy security interests as an area for competition, conflict and even hegemonic domination. Their fears pertain to the security of the sources of supply amid concerns relating to depleting global supplies; the possibly hostile role of major hydrocarbon producers in global politics, and the burgeoning demand for energy, particularly from Asia, that could, at some stage, jeopardize Western interests. An American commentator recently set out the U.S. position in the following terms:[54] "any serious threat to the stability of the energy marketplace is a threat to the United States. The grand strategy of the United States requires that it never lose the ability to respond effectively to any such threat."

While many American commentators do recognize the importance of a global and regional cooperative effort in regard to energy security, this is not often reflected in U.S. political and military policies on the ground, which actually contribute to the energy insecurity of both Western and Asian consumers. Thus, the United States' "dual containment" policy against Iraq and Iran in the 1990s; its war on Iraq as part of the global war on terror on the most specious grounds; its sustained and non-rational confrontation against Iran, with continued hydrocarbon-related sanctions under ILSA and its exclusion from hydrocarbon-related projects in Central Asia; and, finally, the emerging strategic confrontation against Russia, and even China, in Central Asia, all of these policies have left the gulf, with 65 per cent of global oil reserves and 40–50 per cent of global gas reserves, mired in uncertainty, insecurity and violence, while Central Asia too is increasingly emerging as a possible theatre of big power confrontation. Indeed, it could be said that the United States' own political and energy interests have been adversely affected by the burgeoning anti-U.S. sentiment in West Asia and much of the Muslim world, and the credibility that has been imparted to Islamic extremism in the region.

India does not see the pursuit of its own, Asian and global energy security interests in competitive and conflictual terms. Given the central role that energy security plays in the national development of a country, it has to be seen as an integral part of the national security of the country concerned. At the same time, India's view is that energy security has attributes that distinguish it from other aspects of national security: first, while various aspects of national security are generally *status quoits* in that they protect and sustain the existing order, be it national borders, national political structures or national values, energy security is a dynamic concept in that it enhances a nation's economic and, therefore, political status by providing it with the resources to pull its people out of poverty and pursue national growth and development.

Secondly, while national security has at its core the maintenance of a country's national interest, energy security cannot be attained on a purely national basis; it is inherently cooperative in character and is founded on engagements with other countries: given that hydrocarbon resources will continue to dominate the global energy mix (and, hence, the energy mix of most countries) for at least the next twenty-five years, if not longer, for the world's energy resources to be harnessed efficiently, a cooperative approach at bilateral, regional and international levels is both inevitable and urgent.

India's commitment to a cooperative approach in the pursuit of energy security interests is strengthened by the realization that the next few years will see a steady decline in hydrocarbon supplies, with consequent implications for prices, economic programmes and increased political contentions. Though advances in technology will provide the hydrocarbon resources required to meet global demand, at least over the next thirty to fifty years, new resources will be available in physically challenging areas such as the deep sea or frozen terrain or environmentally sensitive locations. Again, it will require huge investments for its extraction, amounting cumulatively to about US$5 trillion up to 2030, at the rate of US$20 billion per annum. Meeting the global demand for oil and obtaining the financial resources to ensure supplies requires the rejection of political contentions based on narrow national considerations and, in its place, calls for an integrated regional and global effort to pool together the world's human, financial and technological resources in a spirit of cooperation for mutual benefit.

In response to this challenge, the international oil industry is already integrating in significant ways: major companies are merging to pool together their financial resources and technological capabilities. Again, there is a clear trend in favour of national oil companies integrating across the hydrocarbon value-chain, from exploration to production, to transportation, to refining and petrochemicals. Finally, E&P contracts in developing producer countries are increasingly being linked to refinery proposals and, on occasion, even to other infrastructure development proposals such as roads, railways, power, mining and port development projects.

The surge in oil prices over the last one year, even as it has adversely affected economies in different parts of the world, has called for greater scrutiny of the organization and functioning of the world's oil markets — their non-transparent and non-rational foundations and procedures, with attendant calls for reform, particularly from developing countries that are seeing their hard-earned resources wither away and their development programmes in jeopardy.

India took the first significant step in setting up a platform for dialogue between the principal Asian oil and gas producers and consumers when it convened a Round Table of Asian Oil Ministers in New Delhi, in January 2005. Present at the Round Table were representatives of four principal Asian oil-consuming countries — China, Japan, Republic of Korea and India — in dialogue with the principal oil-producing countries of West Asia and Southeast Asia.

In his inaugural address, Indian Minister of Petroleum and Natural Gas Mani Shankar Aiyar, noted that the Round Table was "historic" and affirmed the commitment of the countries present to "our shared destiny". Minister Aiyar asserted that the interests of producer and consumer countries are best served in an order which is:

> a more fair, more just and more remunerative oil order for all of us in Asia- in which the Asia producer is ensured a stable, secure and sustainable return for a most precious but depleting natural resource, and the Asian consumer is assured a stable, secure and sustainable regime within which to promote progress and prosperity for that deprived one-half of humankind that inhabits our shared continent of Asia.[55]

The Indian minister noted that Asian producers and consumers would obtain stability, security and sustainability in the Asian oil and gas economy through mutual inter-dependence, which called for "mutual investments in each other's countries by producer and consumer nations of the Asian oil community". The minister envisaged a future "in which Asian countries can become major participants in the massive investments which need to be made in the Asian countries represented at this table, running to an estimated

US$1,580 billion over the next twenty-five years in upstream, midstream and downstream oil and gas development in all our countries put together."[56]

This Round Table of Asian Oil Ministers approved a consensual "Chairman's Statement" which stated:[57]

(a) Asian cooperation in the oil and gas economy must include "moderation, dialogue, mutual understanding and respect, security of international supplies, demand-supply equilibrium, and strategic partnerships based on a reciprocity of interests."
(b) There is a scope for improving Asian markets for petroleum and petroleum products.
(c) Prices should be sustained at levels which encourage Asian consumers to increase their purchases of Asian produce; at the same time, prices should be such as to encourage Asian producers to promote investment in oil and gas for Asian consumer destinations as an economic priority.
(d) Criss-cross investments all along the entire oil and gas products chain through reciprocal investment interlocking of producers and consumers will guarantee security of both supply and demand, thus contributing to stability of prices and thereby security of both supply and demand.
(e) The Round Table endorsed the importance of energy conservation for the protection of the environment and issues of climate change, and the need for technological cooperation in the pursuit of cleaner and more environmentally-sound fossil fuel technologies.
(f) To this end, cooperation among Asian research and development centres and the promotion of conservation awareness among the general public were recognized as key instrumentalities.

This Round Table of Asian Oil Ministers was followed by a second Round Table in New Delhi, in November 2005, when the representatives of the same four principal Asian consumer countries met ministers from North Asia (Russia) and Central Asia. At this Round Table, the assembled dignitaries approved a consensual document committing themselves to promoting greater regional cooperation in the Asian oil and gas economy. Specifically, they agreed to study "the promotion of developing gas and oil interconnections through LNG and through transnational oil and gas pipelines within the Asian region for integration energy markets as well as improving the transportation infrastructure." The studies to be undertaken will focus on "the exploration of alternative linkages by land and sea throughout Asia". The assembled Asian Oil Ministers recognized that Asia's interests in providing gas from Central and West Asia to markets in Southeast and Northeast Asia would be best served through the development of an Asian Gas Grid.[58]

India has just commenced a constructive energy-related engagement at bilateral, regional and global levels. It is increasingly being seen as a significant player in the international energy economy and as a valued partner in the world's quest for energy security. The Bay of Bengal has emerged as a new area to pursue policies of regional cooperation for the common interests of the countries concerned. Thus, India has liberalized its upstream hydrocarbon sector which has given opportunities to foreign and Indian public and private sector companies to use state-of-the-art technology to tap this under-explored region.

At the same time, the logic of energy security has encouraged Indian companies to participate actively in the region's E&P proposals for mutual benefit, particularly in Myanmar and Sri Lanka, and to pursue transnational pipeline proposals. Beyond the upstream sector, the rest of the hydrocarbon value chain, from refineries to petrochemicals and the attendant infrastructure development, as also R&D, technology transfer and training are areas that hold considerable promise for bilateral and regional cooperation, so that common energy security interests bind the littoral states in a framework of partnership for mutual benefit.

NOTES

The views expressed in this chapter are the personal views of the author and do not reflect the views of the Government of India or the Indian Council of World Affairs.

1 "Report of the Group on India Hydrocarbon Vision-2025", in *Oil and Gas in India's Security*, edited by Jasjit Singh (New Delhi: Knowledge World in association with IDSA, 2001), pp. 131–230.
2 *BP Statistical Review of World Energy*, June 2005, p. 28.
3 "Integrated Energy Policy: Report of the Expert Committee", Planning Commission, New Delhi, p. 27, henceforth IEP.
4 Dagmar Graczyk, *Gas to Power — India* (Groningen: International Gas Vision/ Energy Delta Institute, 2006), p. 6.
5 IEP, p. xiii.
6 IEP, p. 28.
7 IEP, p. 22.
8 IEP, p. 29.
9 IEP, p. 22.
10 IEP, p. 45.
11 M.R. Srinivasan, R.B. Grover, S.A. Bhardwaj: "Nuclear Power in India — Winds of Change", *Economic and Political Weekly*, Mumbai, 3 December 2005, p. 5184.
12 IEP, p. 46.
13 Ibid.

14 Information provided to the author in an unofficial note dated 1 September 2006 by the Director General of Hydrocarbons, Ministry of Petroleum and Natural Gas, Government of India, New Delhi; henceforth DGH.
15 DGH.
16 DGH.
17 DGH.
18 DGH.
19 DGH.
20 "GSPC find to go in production by 2007", *Projects Today*, 29 June 2005, downloaded from <www.projectstoday.com>.
21 "India Finds Natural Gas and Oil in West Bengal Coast", 16 February 2005, downloaded from <www.indiadaily.com>; and *The Telegraph*, Calcutta, 15 February 2005.
22 "ONGC Discovers Huge Gas Reserves in Bay of Bengal", 17 December 2006, downloaded from <www.hindustantimes.com>.
23 "India Maps Huge Gas Reserves around Andaman Islands", remarks of Avinash Chandra, DGH, at launch of NELP-IV, downloaded from <www.projectsmonitor.com>.
24 A.K. Sethi, A.V. Sathe and M.V. Ramanna, "Potential Natural Gas Hydrates Resources in Indian Offshore Areas", paper presented at the AAPG Hedberg Conference, Vancouver, 12–16 September 2004, downloaded from <searchanddiscovery.net/documents/abstracts>.
25 Reshma Patil, "India Marks Turf in Undersea Treasure Hunt", *Hindustan Times*, New Delhi, 18 September 2006.
26 B.G. Verghese, "For an Ocean Outlook", *The Hindu*, Chennai, 25 November 2003, downloaded from <www.hinduonnet.com>.
27 Monzur Hossain, "Bangladesh: Natural Gas Export", *South Asian Journal*, July–September 2005, downloaded from <www.southasianmedia.net/magazine/journal>.
28 Ibid.
29 Ibid.
30 Ibid.
31 Ibid.
32 *People's Daily*, 17 April 2006, downloaded from <English.people.com.cn>.
33 Quoted in Anand Kumar, "Oil Poaching Controversy in Bay of Bengal", *South Asia Analysis Group*, 14 July 2006, downloaded from <www.saag.org>; also, *The New Nation*, Dhaka, 29 August 2006.
34 Sharier Khan, "Bad Timing for Third Round Bidding", *The Daily Star*, Dhaka, 29 August 2006.
35 Ibid.
36 Ibid., and "Survey Discovers Possible Oil Reservoir in Bay", 13 August 2006, downloaded from <darkcrunk.wordpress.com>.
37 Kumar, "Oil Poaching Controversy".

38 Ashild Kolas and Stein Tonnesson, "Burma and Its Neighbours: The Geopolitics of Gas", Nautilus Institute at RMIT University, 24 August 2006; p. 4, downloaded from <www.nautilus.org>.

39 Details of Myanmar Blocks from John Mueller: "Myanmar Places Offshore Prospects in the Spotlight", *Offshore Engineer*, 1 February 2004, p. 1, downloaded from <www.oilonline.com>.

40 Kolas and Tonnesson, "Burma and Its Neighbours", p. 6.

41 Mueller, "Myanmar Places Offshore Prospects in the Spotlight", p. 3.

42 Ibid.

43 Kolas and Tonnesson, "Burma and Its Neighbours", p. 12.

44 *The Economic Times*, New Delhi, 16 June 2006; and *Petrowatch, Mumbai* 10, no. 9, 24 August 2006, p. 3.

45 Kolas and Tonnesson, "Burma and Its Neighbours", p. 11.

46 "Thailand Eyes Myanmar's Natural Gas Reserves", AFP Report, 31 July 2006, downloaded from <www.hindustantimes.com>.

47 See: C.S. Kuppuswamy, "Myanmar-China Cooperation: Its Implications for India", *South Asia Analysis Group*, paper no. 596, 3 February 2003; Ramtanu Maitra, "The Energy Ties that Bind India, China", *Asia Times*, 12 April 2005; David Fullbrook, "Resource-hungry China to Devour More of Burma's Gas and Oil Industry", 1 February 2006, downloaded from <www.irrawaddy.org>.

48 Kolas and Tonnesson, "Burma and Its Neighbours", p. 14.

49 Fullbrook, "Resource-hungry China"; Maitra, "The Energy Ties"; Kolas and Tonnesson, "Burma and Its Neighbours", p. 14.

50 Powerpoint presentation by GAIL at the Ministry of Petroleum and Natural Gas, New Delhi, on 19 September 2006.

51 "Burma Gas Pipeline Project On", *The Asian Age*, 17 January 2007.

52 "Myanmar aims to sell gas to China" — Indian Minister, Reuters, 26 April 2007, downloaded from <http://asia.news.yahoo.com/070426/3/30xjo.html>; Gideon Lundholm, "China trumps India in Myanmar gas stakes", 11 September 2007, downloaded from <http://www.atimes.com/atimes/printN.html>.

53 See Talmiz Ahmad, "Advantages of Transnational Gas Pipelines", *The Hindu*, Chennai, 24 April 2006, for details of India's perceptions of pipeline projects.

54 Eckart Woertz, "Demand for Gulf Oil Set to Grow", *Trade Arabia*, 30 August 2006, downloaded from <www.tradearabia.com>.

55 Mani Shankar Aiyar, Minister of Petroleum and Natural Gas, India, Inaugural Address at First Round Table of Asian Oil Ministers.

56 Ibid., p. 11.

57 Chairman's Statement on the Conclusion of the First Round Table of Asian Oil Ministers, New Delhi, 6 January 2005.

58 Chairman's Statement at the Conclusion of Second Round Table of Asian Oil Ministers, New Delhi, 25 November 2005.

APPENDIX 3.1

Demand Scenario for Natural Gas — India
(By Various Agencies/Organizations)
(In million metric standard cubic metres per day)

Year	Projections by the Various Agencies									
	EIA (2004)			EIA (2004)	IHV-2025 (2000)	India Vision-2020 (2002)		Power & Energy Division's Projections (2003–04)	IRADe & PWC*	
	Reference Case	High Case	Low Case			BAU	BCS		BAU	HOG
Base Year	2001 (62 mmscmd)	2001 (62 mmscmd)	2001 (62 mmscmd)	2000 (67 mmscmd)	1999–2000 (110 mmscmd)	1997 (59 mmscmd)		2001–02 (81 mmscmd)	2003–04 (685 mmscmd)	
2004–05	74	77	74	91	195	89	87	98	93	95
2009–10	95	101	93	140	277	115	111	134	145	164
2014–15	124	132	109	189	329	149	142	183	226	285
2019–20	155	171	132	228	358	194	177	249	356	493
2024–25	195	225	155	259	391	258	226	326	488	738
2029–30				295				430	667	1,111

EIA – Energy Information Administration, USA
IEA – International Energy Agency
IHV – India Hydrocarbon Vision 2025
IRADe – Integrated Research and Action for Development
BAU – Business as Usual
BCS – Best Case Scenario
PWC – Price Waterhouse Coopers
HOG – High Output Growth
* includes Natural Gas & N G equivalent of Naphtha

Note: As the available projections by the various agencies are for different years, the same have been interpolated or extrapolated to bring them to common years and have been converted into MMscmd for the purpose of comparison.
Source: Integrated Energy Policy: Report of the Expert Committee, Planning Commission, New Delhi.

4

Macroeconomic Challenges for the Growth of the Energy Sector in Bangladesh in the Context of Regional Integration

Debapriya Bhattacharya and Tazeen Tahsina

Introduction

Global Outlook: Demand and Composition

Demand for energy in the developing regions, particularly in Asia has been following an upward trend. Predictions of the International Energy Agency (IEA) found that in 2030 world demand would increase by 66 per cent compared to demand in 2000. Figure 4.1 shows that Asia's contribution to the world's energy demand will increase from 20 per cent in 2000 to 27 per cent in 2030. On the other hand, demand from the Organization for Economic Cooperation and Development (OECD) countries is expected to decline from 59 per cent in 2000 to 47 per cent in 2030. It seems that over the next decades energy use will continue to grow inexorably, fossil fuels will continue to dominate the energy mix and developing countries will fast approach OECD countries as the largest consumer of commercial energy. Moreover,

Figure 4.1

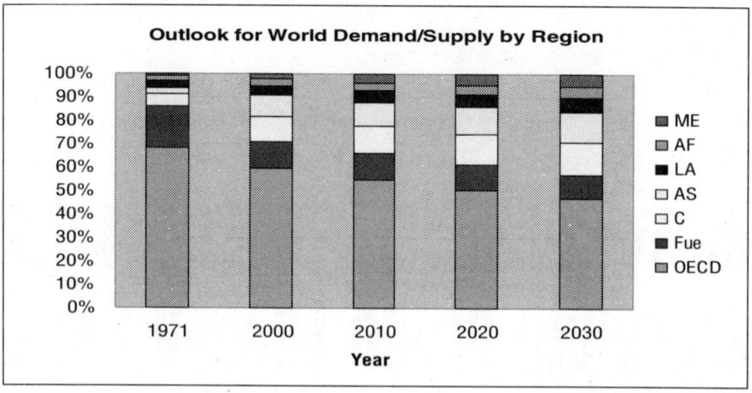

Source: IEA/World Energy Outlook (* ME = Middle East, AF = Africa, LA = Latin America, AS = Asia, C = China, FUe = Former Soviet Union etc.)

world energy use would see a constant rise till 2030. During this period, global primary energy demand would increase by 1.7 per cent per year from 2000 to 2030 reaching an annual level of 15.3 billion tonnes of oil equivalent. But in order to meet this demand, huge capital flow from the industrialized nations to the developing world is required. Forecasts have also been made by the IEA that the importance of natural gas as a source of energy would substantially increase by 2030 (from 23 per cent in 2000 to 28 per cent in 2030). However oil would remain as the world's major energy source that currently occupies 38 per cent of total energy supply.

Table 4.1 portrays that according to the World Development Indicator 2006, per capita consumption of energy in the developing countries is still much lower than the developed nations. However, energy consumption in Bangladesh is not only lower compared to the developed countries, it is also below the per capita consumption of energy in other developing countries in the South Asian region. The table also depicts that energy use in all these countries remained stable and there has not been any surprise. However, energy consumption in China and Vietnam shows faster growth compared to the other developing and least developed countries.

South Asian Scenario and Bangladesh

Despite having a population of over one-fifth of the world's population, South Asia accounts for only about 5 per cent of total world primary

Table 4.1
Energy Use (kg of oil equivalent per capita)

Country Name	2001	2002	2003
Bangladesh	153.23	154.80	159
India	507.70	513.34	520
Pakistan	457.08	454.14	467
Sri Lanka	422.97	430.32	421
Nepal	356.83	352.96	336
China	894.44	959.52	1,094
Vietnam	496.94	530.25	544
United States	7,899.61	7,942.64	7,843
United Kingdom	3,969.62	3,824.28	3,893
Japan	4,066.49	4,057.54	4,053

Source: World Development Indicators 2006.

commercial energy demand. One of the major concerns of the region at the moment is energy security because of lack of stability in price and the supply situation. A distinguishing factor of energy consumption in South Asia is the large dependence on the conventional sources of energy. Dependence of the transport sector on petroleum products is another matter of concern.

Figure 4.2 shows that within the region Bangladesh uses more conventional energy (56 per cent of total energy use) than India and Pakistan. Sri Lanka, Nepal and Bhutan on the other hand use a higher quantity of conventional energy compared to Bangladesh. Among the South Asian countries, India and Pakistan uses more than 50 per cent of their energy supply from commercial sources while in the rest of the countries major portion of energy supply comes from conventional sources.

Objectives and Scope of the Chapter

Energy shortages for much of the past decades have been the bottleneck for the economic development of Bangladesh. The per capita energy use is very low in the South Asian region compared to the world while the number for Bangladesh remains one of the lowest within the region. The scale of shortage has been increasing as demand continues to dominate supply. In such a situation, the economy is on the verge of becoming paralysed in the midst of declining productivity. Thus, the country is unable to make use of its full potential and the booming sectors may be affected soon. This study has attempted to identify the major macroeconomic challenges that are constraining the development of the energy sector. The chapter also focuses on the difficulties the economy might face if the present situation continues

Figure 4.2

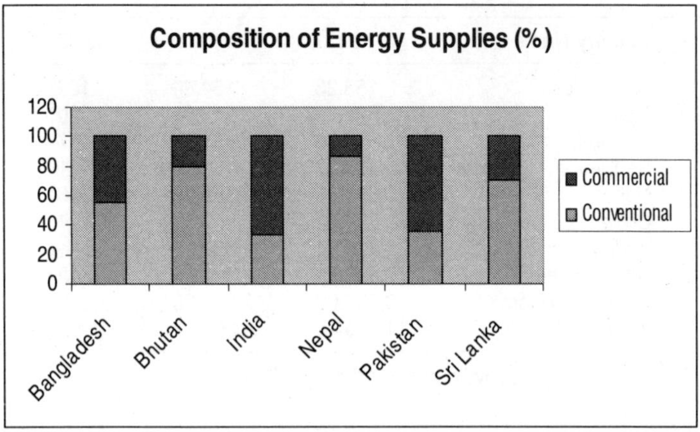

Source: Lama (2003).

and also tries to find immediate and long-term solutions to the problems arising from the shortages in energy and power supply.

The chapter is divided into four sections. It first compares the position of Bangladesh in terms of supply and usage of energy of the world and the South Asian region. It then moves on to discuss the current consumption scenario of the major sources of energy and looks at the growth in energy consumption over time. After analysing the situation, it discusses the existing policies related to energy and the reforms that have taken place so far, and identifies the major loopholes in the existing energy policy. In the next phase the chapter discusses the challenges posed by the shortage of energy in the growth and poverty situation of the country and identifies the features related to investment and pricing of energy resources. Finally the chapter looks into the need for regional cooperation and analyses the rationales behind such a policy, its scope and the policies that have to be adopted in order to be successful in power generation with support from countries in the region.

Overview of the Energy Sector of Bangladesh

Bangladesh is one of the least developed countries of the world with per capita gross domestic product (GDP) of about US$400. Being a signatory of the Millennium Development Goals (MDGs) of the United Nations, the country strives to halve its poverty level by 2015. The GDP in the previous fiscal grew by 6.7 per cent despite the continuous price hike and the removal of Multi-Fibre Arrangement (MFA). Only a rapid growth in the economy can help to achieve the ambitions set at MDGs, and energy is no doubt one of the driving forces for further development. It has been mentioned earlier that economic development and energy consumption have a linear relationship whilst in Bangladesh per capita energy consumption is about 220 kilogram of oil equivalent (kgoe) and per capita electricity is about 150 kilowatt/hour (kWh). Only 40 per cent of the population have electricity access while 60 per cent of the area is covered under the national grid (Hossain 2007).

The Power Division of the Ministry of Energy and Mineral Resources (MEMR) oversees the power sector of Bangladesh while it plays both the roles of owner and regulator of this sector through a number of statutory government bodies.

While the above-mentioned organizations manage the whole energy sector under the MEMR, there also exists the Independent Power Plants (IPPs) and the International Oil Companies (IOCs). Some of the IPPs sell

Figure 4.3
Power Sector of Bangladesh

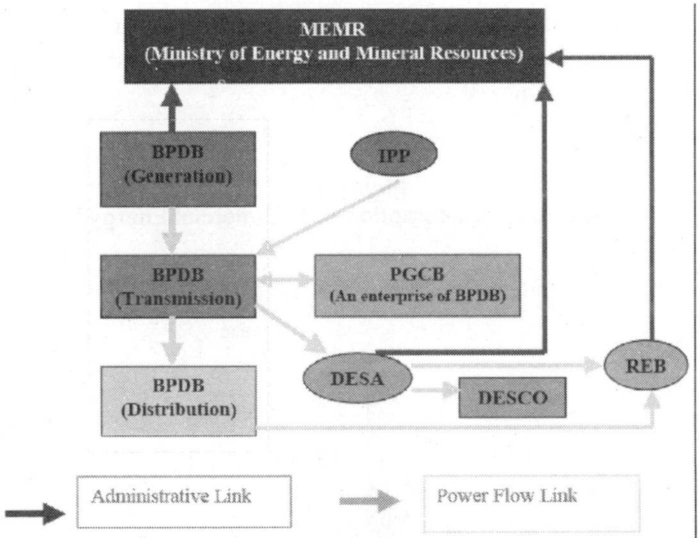

BPDB = Bangladesh Power Development Board; DESA = Dhaka Electricity Authority; DESCO = Dhaka Electric Supply Company Ltd. EA & CEI = Electrical Advisor and Chief Electric Inspector; MEMR = Ministry of Energy and Mineral Resource; PBS = Palli Biddyut Samity (Rural Electric Cooperative); PGCB = Power Grid Company of Bangladesh; REB = Rural Electrification Board.
Source: Malek (2001).

to Bangladesh Power Development Board (BPDB) as per their agreement while BPDB is responsible for the generation, transmission and distribution of power throughout the country. The IOCs perform their activities independently until production. After that, the gas is transmitted by the local transmission companies like Gas Transmission Company Limited (GTCL) and others. But no matter who gets their product, the payments are made through Petrobangla. Besides these organizations, there is the Energy Regulatory Commission. The commission is a statutory body to regulate the activities of the entire energy sector. Major functions of the ERC include regulating generation, purchase, transmission, distribution, supply and utilization of electricity and energy, quality of service and tariff and approving programme of licensees for generation, transmission, distribution and supply of electricity and energy. REB, PBS, DESA, DESCO, Power Cell, RPC, etc. have been formed as part of a reform initiative to improve the performance of the energy sector.

Energy Consumption by Sector

Figure 4.4 shows that non-energy (raw materials) is the major sector of energy consumption in Bangladesh while transport is the second. Only 1 per cent of energy is being used for commercial purposes and 10 per cent by the industrial sector while 17 per cent of the energy is consumed by the households.

Figure 4.4
Sectorwise Final Consumption of Commercial Energy (2004)

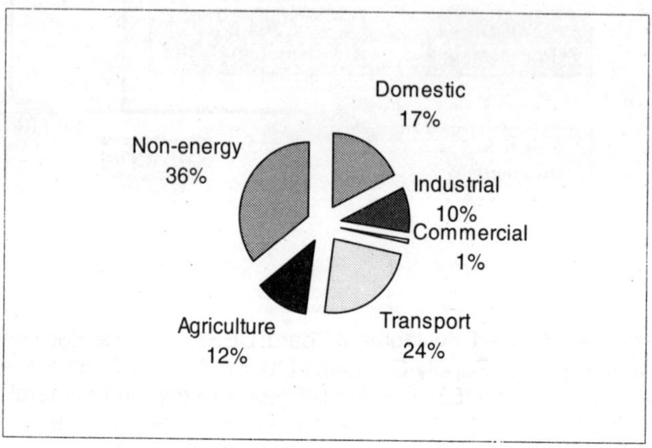

Source: Petrobangla (2006).

Gas Consumption

The dependence of the power sector on gas is reflected from the gas consumption pattern depicted in Figure 4.5. It shows that the power sector takes up about half (48 per cent) of the total consumption of natural gas. Fertilizer industries use up 19 per cent of the natural gas while the industrial sector and households consume 14 per cent and 12 per cent of total gas.

Figure 4.5
Gas Consumption by Category

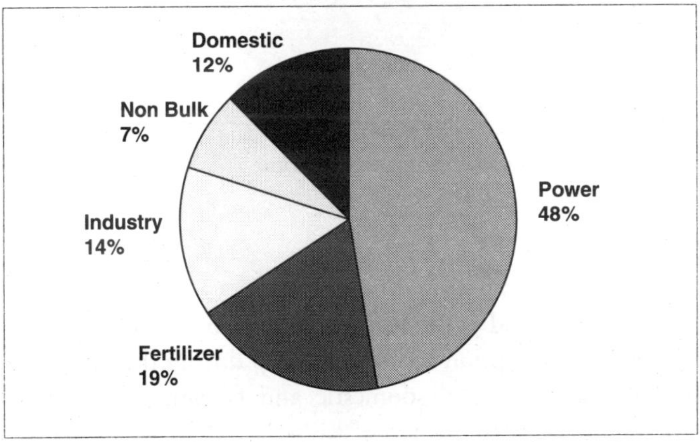

Source: Statistical Yearbook of Bangladesh 2004.

Consumption of Electricity

Figure 4.6 shows that the major usage of electricity takes place in industries and households. However, only around 18 per cent of the population (25 per cent in urban areas and 10 per cent in rural areas) have access to electricity (IEA 2006). During the past ten years, electricity consumption of the country rose by 3.5 per cent while the domestic and industrial sector registered 6.1 per cent and 4.7 per cent annual growth throughout the same period.

Natural gas has been the single largest source for electricity generation in Bangladesh. Estimates also show that total thermal electricity generation accounted for 96 per cent of the total. Dependence on the natural gas as a source of electricity generation has increased from 74 per cent in 1995 to 89 per cent in 2004 while the use of hydro sources has been declining for electricity generation.

Figure 4.6
Consumption of Electricity by Category (2004)

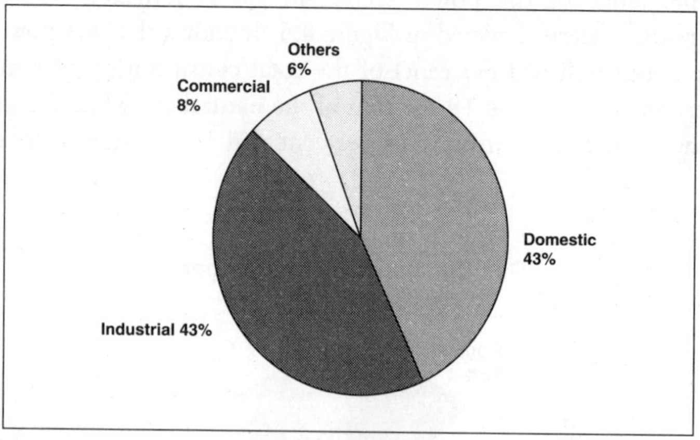

Source: Statistical Yearbook of Bangladesh 2004.

Growth of Consumption

Growth of electricity and gas consumption had been steady between 2000 and 2004. Coal consumption has seen a jump during the same period. The availability of coal from both domestic and foreign sources has made it popular mainly for brick burning.

Figure 4.7
Average Growth of Consumption by Item from 2000 to 2004

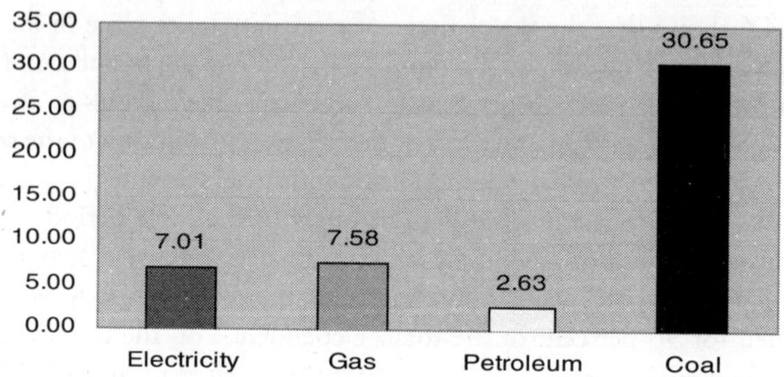

Source: Statistical Yearbook of Bangladesh 2004.

Recent Scenario

Bangladesh has been suffering from severe supply shortage of electricity. Recent information shows that according to the BPDB, the demand for electricity in Bangladesh is 4,300 MW while the unofficial report shows that the demand is as high as 5,400 MW. However the country's supply capacity is 3,300 MW leaving a shortage of about 2,000 MW. This large unfulfilled demand for energy is growing by 10 per cent every year (United States Agency for International Development).

One the main reasons behind the disruption in electricity supply production recently is the lack of maintenance. Moreover, during the last five years only one project has been undertaken with a capacity of 80 MW only, whereas the number of connections went up from 50 lakhs to 85 lakhs.

Recently the government has set a plan to increase power generation by 957 MW by completing the plants under construction and renovating the existing units as well as by adding supply from independent producers. The work plan also includes the installation of thirteen new power plants that is expected to add 3,435 MW of electricity to the existing capacity. Moreover, the government is trying to minimize the use of energy by encouraging efficiency energy use.

Energy Policy in Bangladesh

The National Energy Policy (NEP) for Bangladesh was released in May 2004. The two main features for the energy policy of Bangladesh are that it ensures the ownership of all natural resources to the Government of Bangladesh with the objective to ensure the right of energy to all the people in the country.

Major Objectives: Apart from the above-mentioned goals, the major objectives include the avoidance of operational, structural and other deficiencies, specifically system loss, system reliability, poor quality, load management, unscientific pricing management, unsatisfactory billing and bill collection. The policy also strives to improve the performance of the sector by bringing reliability and quality in electricity supply, and to promote competition among the constituents of the sector through private sector participation. While incorporating a regulatory framework, the policy also aims to restructure the utilities and facilitate transparency and accountability along with an improved managerial and financial performance. Rationalization of the tariff structure, transforming the public sector entities into public limited companies in phases, evolving a mix of fuel for power generation, bridging the gap in supply between the west zone and the east zone, and ensuring regional and international cooperation for importing electricity from neighbouring countries plus exchange of experience in power development and training of human resources are the other main objectives of the energy policy. This policy strives to ensure electricity for all by 2020. To summarize, the NEP aims to ensure energy security in the country. Apart from the NEP, there are a number of other policies related to the energy sector of Bangladesh.

Coal Policy: A coal policy in Bangladesh has been underway since the middle of 2005 but unfortunately could not be finalized for the past two years. The initial draft policy was formulated at the end of 2005 by IIFC as part of the contract with the MEMR. The second version was prepared in the beginning of 2006 and was made public. But the policy came under debate for seeking high royalty from the developers and several other issues. Since then, it has been going through modifications and is yet to be finalized.

PSCs in the Gas Sector: Petrobangla went for production sharing contracts (PSCs) back in 1974, limited to the offshore area of Bangladesh. The next

Figure 4.8
Framework of the National Energy Policy

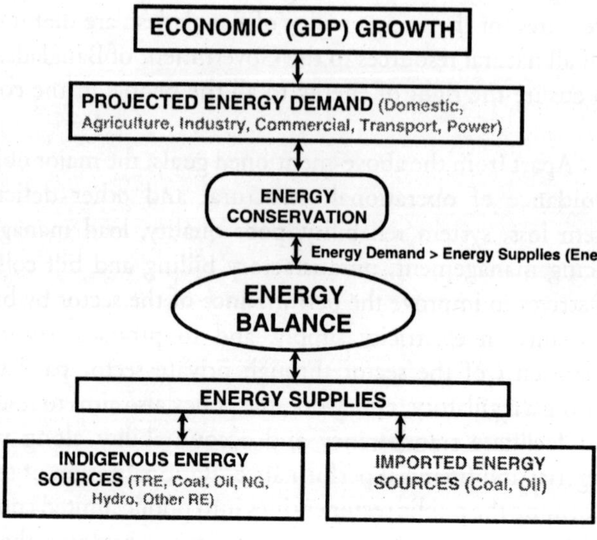

Source: Islam (2007).

major round occurred in 1993, after the promulgation of the NEP. This time the whole territory of the country was divided into 23 blocks and both offshore and onshore blocks were offered.

At present, among 22 blocks, 13 blocks have been allocated to the IOCs entirely or partially. Among 22 fields, 12 fields are producing, production is suspended in 3 fields and 7 fields are undeveloped. As of June 2003, recoverable reserve remains to be 15.4 trillion cubic feet (tcf), and the latest figure shows that among 68 producing wells, 50 wells are operated by the domestic companies and the remaining 18 by the IOCs. Of the total production, 67.5 per cent comes from domestic companies and 32.5 per cent from the IOCs. However, the IOCs are producing 98.1 per cent of their production capacity while the domestic companies are producing only 66.2 per cent. The exploring for natural gas in the offshore fields are still very limited in practice. The Bangladeshi government is now preparing for a third bidding for hydrocarbon explorations in the offshore areas.

PSC in the Gas Sector — The Debated Issues: Investment in the energy sector in Bangladesh dominated the FDI inflow throughout the 1990s. But investments during this period also came under question regarding the quality of the contracts. The criticism came up from various fields in terms of accountability of the PSCs, lack of domestic ownership, high cost of production presented by the IOCs and accountability of the IOCs. So far, most of the PSCs signed between IOCs and the Government of Bangladesh is not done through bidding. Initially, the blocks were allocated through negotiations. As of today, only one block has been allotted through the bidding procedure. A report by the Hydrocarbon Unit of the MEMR reveals that during the second round, discrepancies in terms of profit sharing among the contractors have been observed. The report suggested revising the provisions for the contracts. The need of foreign investment in the energy sector is well recognized but it is also noted that the sector also suffered investment cut-off from the domestic sector. Quite a few gas fields discovered by the domestic organizations (Petrobangla/BAPEX) have been handed to the IOCs. Moreover, the share to the IOCs are quite high and in fact, in some cases, the wells developed by Petrobangla or BAPEX were handed over to the IOCs. In addition to that, the obligation of payment through the foreign exchange is expected to have an adverse effect on the balance of payment of the country.

According to GUC, Petrobangla has significant advantage over the IOCs in cost of production. Petrobangla produces 1 million cubic feet (mcf) of gas at Tk 8 only at Rashidpur while an IOC produces the same quantity at Tk 35 at Jalalabad (a field Unocal acquired almost free of cost) and Tk 56 at Sangu (offshore) (CPD Task Force Report, 2003). The main difference lies in its personnel compensation between Petrobangla and the IOCs. However the picture is simply opposite to the IPP operation for the generation of electricity. Cost of generation under the IPP operation shows low tariff (US 2.73 cents/kWh for 360 MW Haripur and US 2.79 cents/kWh for 450 MW Meghnaghat plant) compared to over US 3 cents/kWh in the public sector plants (under BPDB).

In addition to the above, accountability of the IOCs have come under question several times. Bangladesh had suffered major accidents from the gas fields operated by the IOC. The incident in Magurchara and twin accidents at Tengratila caused millions of dollars to the country that the government could not compensate at any time. Recently, different scams against the IOCs have made their activities even more controversial. Despite all these, the fact that although at present Bangladesh is still producing gas below its capacity, the present reserve will be exhausted in the near future, should push the country towards the IOCs for exploring new sites and sources of energy.

Along with the above-mentioned drawbacks in the existing policies, there are a number of macroeconomic challenges that emanate from the energy sector. The problems lie in terms of economic growth and poverty alleviation, investment demand in the energy sector and pricing of the energy commodities. All of these challenges underpin the goal of energy security.

Macroeconomic Challenges and Reforms

Growth-Energy Linkage

The significance of energy as an input in the growth and development process has became more prominent following the oil price increases in 1973/74 and 1978/79. In this era of rapidly advancing technology, access to energy is the key to transform quality of lives and foster economic growth. Other than direct contribution to the economic activities, it improves health standards and assists in providing better education. In the rural areas, it helps to retard rural-urban migration, enhances opportunities for income and employment generation. In short, energy is an asset to a country that can bring revolutionary changes in the economy. Elias and Victor (2005) observed that there exists a correlation between per capita GDP and the evolving patterns of the use of energy. They found that the developed countries, particularly the United States during the industrial revolution, have seen rapid growth in per capita consumption of energy relative to growth in GDP, while the developing countries today follow a slower growth rate in per capita energy consumption compared to their growth in GDP.

Supporting this idea Toman and Jemelkova (2002) stated,

> Energy intensity in today's developing countries probably peaks sooner and at a lower level along the development path than was the case during the industrialization of the developed world. But even with trends toward greater energy efficiency and other dampening factors, total energy use and energy use per capita continue to grow in the advanced industrialized countries, and even more rapid growth can be expected in the developing countries as their incomes advance.

Demand and Supply

The demand forecast made by Petrobangla in April 2001 was based on information/data collected mainly from bulk consumers such as BPDB, BCIC, and other end-use consumers such as industries, domestic and commercial sectors. The projection suggests that power sector will be the dominant sector even in the near future. The result obtained by the Petrobangla shows that the reserve of gas will be exhausted by 2020.

Table 4.2 summarizes the projections of the National Reserve Committee, Petrobangla and Gas Utilization Committee (GUC). The National Gas Reserve Committee conducted a domestic demand for gas for 2010–50 taking each ten-year period cumulatively and considering different economic growth scenarios. With Bangladesh having accelerated its growth rate to 6 to 7 per cent, the reserve scenario looks more vulnerable.

Table 4.3 shows 4,121 billion cubic feet (bcf) recoverable reserve (RR) at the end of 2020 out of the total RR of 15,197 bcf available when 5 per cent

Table 4.2
Gas Demand Projection (2002) (in tcf)

Higher intensity/year			Up to 2010	2020	2030	2040	2050
Annual growth	4.5%		4.7	13.5	27.7	46.6	69.0
	6%		5.1	16.1	36.3	66.9	110.0
	7%		5.4	18.1	43.8	86.6	152.0
Lower intensity/year							
Annual growth	4.5%		4.7	12.6	24.7	41.8	64.0
	6%		5.0	14.9	32.2	60.0	101.0
	7%		5.3	16.8	38.8	77.7	141.0
PETROBANGLA			4.8	13.7	26.8	43.7	63.9
GUC at	5%	Gas growth		11.1			
	6%	rate		11.6			
	7%			12.0			

Source: CPD Task Force Report (2003).

Table 4.3
Mid-term Demand/Supply Scenario

Cases[1] (demand growth	Start of Bibiyana Gas Supply (yrs from 2002)	Supply of gas per day at 2010 (MMcfd)			Reserve at 2020 (tcf)	Unmet demand		Actual Reserve at 2020 (tcf)
		PB	IOC	Total		Year	Total up to 2020 (tcf)	
M1 (5%)	2011 (9 yrs)	1,277	280	1,557	5.284	2017	0.673	4.611
M2 (6%)	2007 (5 yrs)	1,272	408	1,680	4.770	2016	1.398	3.372
M3 (7%)	2007 (5 yrs)	1,282	529	1,811	4.334	2014	2.354	1.980

Source: Hydrocarbon Unit. Ministry of Energy, Power & Mineral Resources.

growth in demand is assumed. Considering the RR of 757 bcf of non-producing fields (Begumgonj, Kutubdia, Semutang) and 406 bcf of the fields in Chattak, Kamta, Feni at present under suspension, the total gas reserve is calculated at 5,284 bcf. Estimates also show that a demand growth forecast of 6 per cent, gas reserve will be 4,770 bcf and the reserve will fall to 4,334 bcf if the demand growth forecast goes up to 7 per cent. With the daily demand in excess of 3,000 mmcfd towards the end under both 6 per cent and 7 per cent growth forecasts, the RR is a little over four years. Under a more modest demand forecast of 5 per cent growth, the total RR of 5,284 bcf is five years' reserve. Despite these estimates of the reserves, the table discloses that part of the demand will not be met from 2017 due to limitations in production. (Hydrocarbon Unit).

The Power Policy Statement (2000) indicated a forecast of 15,000 MW (72,000 GWH) by 2020. The forecast is in fact conservative as the demand has gone beyond 5,000 MW in 2005 (see Table 4.4). "The maximum

Table 4.4
PSMP Forecast of Electricity Demand (1995)

Year	Max. Demand	Gross Energy Generation (GWH)
2000	3,149	16,500
2005	4,597	24,000
2010	6,779	35,000
2015	9,906	52,000

Source: CPD Task Force Report (2003).

demand and gross energy generation forecast under PSMP remained short by 9 per cent, consequently, resulting in higher load shedding during the summer of 2002." (CPD Task Force Report 2003). With the dependence on natural gas, meeting the demand of electricity is a major challenge for Bangladesh. Bangladesh has small coal reserves and has consumed little coal in the past.

Bangladesh began commercial coal production in April 2003 with the opening of the Barapukuria Coal Mine, which is expected to produce 1 million short tonnes of coal per year, principally for electricity generation. This mine is being used to fuel the 250 MW Barapukuria Coal-Fired Power Plant in Parbotipur, which began commercial operation in January 2006.

South Asia contains coal reserves of 105.3 billion short tonnes or approximately 11 per cent of the world total. Nearly all of the coal in this region is produced and consumed by India, the only South Asian country with significant coal reserves (102 billion short tonnes) and the world's third largest coal producer after the United States and China.

Total hydropower potential of the country is estimated to be 753 MW of which 230 MW has been harnessed at Kaptai. Potential hydropower sources are the rivers Sangu, Muhuri, and Brahamaputra. There are also some potential sources of renewable energy such as solar, wind, tidal and wave, and mini-hydro. Out of these, only a few solar photovoltaic units are in use now with significant subsidy. But within the existing framework it is very hard to ensure energy security for a country that is largely dependent on natural gas.

Leakage

Apart from production limitations, a large quantity of the produced output is lost due to the lack of quality supply. In the power sector, the lost output is as high as 1 per cent of GDP (The Policy Statement of the Government of Bangladesh, January 2000). According to a study conducted by CPD, Bangladesh had suffered a total loss of Tk 6,850 crore in 2004 due to power supply shortage. This figure was equivalent to about 2 per cent of the GDP. The estimate also shows that the commercial sector accounted for maximum share of the loss (58 per cent) followed by industry (34 per cent) and agriculture (8 per cent). Of course, the origin of all these troubles is weak governance.

Investment Needs in the Energy Sector

The Government of Bangladesh's Policy Statement (2000) on power sector emphasizes access to affordable and reliable electricity to the majority of the people by 2020 as a key development goal while Bangladesh's Power System

Master Plan (PSMP) foresees a cost of US$4.4 billion for achieving required generating capacity of electricity. Moreover, the demand for gas (as the only source of primary energy) is increasing day by day. These indicate a higher production of gas from the existing sources, the need for more sources of gas exploration as the present recoverable reserve seems insufficient to meet the future demand, and the need to search for new sources of energy. However, lack of expertise has made the problem even more acute. As suggested by Hossain (2007), much of the requirement for natural gas can be met by using liquefied natural gas (LNG) as liquefied petroleum gas (LPG) in cylinders and the diesel and petrol produced from it. The LPG can serve a larger share of the population than the small section (6 per cent) receiving gas for cooking through small pipelines.

Private Investment: The private initiatives in the energy sector in Bangladesh started mainly from the 1990s when IOC came in the exploration and production of gas fields. Realizing the need for more investment in the gas sector of Bangladesh, the Government of Bangladesh had called for foreign investment in the sector, popularly known as PSC (production sharing contract). The need for foreign sources arose from the need for a huge amount of capital and the prevailing gap in technology and knowledge level in the country. Obviously the increasing demand plays the most crucial role for the need of private investment in the energy sector.

Diversity

Natural gas has been the single source of commercial energy in Bangladesh. Official statistics shows that back on 30 June 2001, the net recoverable reserve of natural gas was 14.96 tcf. The National Gas Utilization Committee in 2002 showed that the reserve at 16.1 tcf will be exhausted by 2014–15. EIA's recent (January 2006) estimate shows that Bangladesh has approximately 5.0 tcf of gas while South Asia's proven natural gas reserves were estimated at 62.1 tcf, approximately 1 per cent of the world total. India's and Pakistan's reserves are 38.9 tcf and 28.2 tcf, respectively.

Pricing

After the oil price increases in 1973/74, policy choices of Asia's developing countries were heavily determined by the effects of oil price changes on a country's balance of payments, economic growth, and inflation. In both groups, the relationship of energy and economic development and the effects of prices on real incomes and income distribution were recognized. The basic objectives of energy pricing policy include the achievement of economic efficiency and social equity while maintaining financial viability. These objectives may be translated into criteria of fixing administered price. "Lifeline rates" for electricity, subsidized kerosene for meeting basic needs, control of inflation, encouragement to utilize domestic resources, incentives for conservation, subsidies for investment in renewable energy technologies and profitability and efficient management of public sector units.

The Government of Bangladesh has taken initiatives to readjust the tariff rate for all the commodities in the energy sector. The price of natural gas had been rescheduled four times in three years between 2002 to 2005. In Bangladesh, gas is distributed at a lower price than the production cost. The objective of the rescheduling of price was to reduce the loss incurred by the public sector to maintain the fiscal balance. The adjustment of energy price is also influenced largely by the donor agencies. But the increase in energy price adversely affects the economy by increasing the price of almost all the commodities.

Pricing of Natural Gas

Commercial and industrial consumers are paying US$3.37 and US$2.14 per mcf respectively which are the highest tariffs for gas consumption. During three years period the brick industry and domestic consumers experienced the highest price hike for gas. Although tariff for the industry sector was amongst the lowest, the power and fertilizer industries along with the commercial sector also experienced the heat of the price hike. The present

Table 4.5
Natural Gas Tariff in Bangladesh (US$/mcf)

Sector	Tariff (2005)
Power	1.07
Fertilizer	0.92
Industry	2.14
Commercial	3.37
Tea Estate	2.14
CNGV	1.01
CAP. Power	1.53
Brick	3.37
Metered (Domestic)	1.88
Single Burner*	5.06
Duble Burner*	5.78

Source: Petrobangla.

caretaker government, however, has suggested another revision of the tariff structure for the IOCs, stating that the tariff rate should be US$1.50 per tcf instead of the prevailing rate of US$1.34 per tcf as the share of the IOCs has gone up in the PSCs.

The price adjustment also took place for petroleum commodities. The price of all the petroleum products doubled during last five years .The price of kerosene in particular fluctuates very frequently, going beyond the government price. This affects the poor people directly as they are more dependent on kerosene for their energy supply. In the latest review of the prices of oil products, the government once again increased the price of diesel, kerosene, octane and petrol with a view to bring down Bangladesh Petroleum Company's loss from about US$289 million per month to about US$130 million per month.

Table 4.6
Pricing of Oil Products (In US$)

Year/Oil price	Diesel	Kerosene	Octane	Petrol
Current price	0.58	0.89	0.96	0.94

Source: Financial Express.

Bangladesh needs 37 lakh tonnes of refined oil per year and Bangladesh Petroleum Company (BPC) meets the demand by importing it from Middle East sources. The country needed about US$2 billion to import the petroleum fuel during the last fiscal 2005–06. BPC is under tremendous pressure with huge due subsidy. In 2003 the subsidy was US$1,445.28 million, in 2004 it was US$3,902.27 million, and in 2006 it became US$2,456.98 million. This would have been much higher if the price had been adjusted. Unfortunately, BPC is still running short of funds and looking for bank loans to resolve the situation. This has adversely affected availability of loans for the private sector.

Poverty Alleviation

Energy is needed for economic and social development and in essence aimed at poverty alleviation. An underlying objective of energy sector projects is to give low-income households and communities in rural and semi-urban areas better access to modern fuels to allow them to shift from biomass fuels to kerosene or gas for cooking, to put electric lighting in a school or power a refrigerator in a community health clinic or to access electricity for lighting, etc. These kinds of interventions are expected to have important and direct effects on the welfare of the poor. The benefit of the better access to energy for the poor can be found in a number of areas. There are various direct effects on the well-being of poor by the means of improved access to lighting, etc.; saving time by not gathering biomass and other fuels; and improved access to information (through radio, TV, and telecommunications). Access to energy will also lead to improved quality of air in the houses; reduce fire hazard; improved quality of health service through better lighting; use of equipment and refrigeration; speed up establishments of the health centres; improved facilities and access to education; and opening up new windows of opportunities for the poor. Moreover, better access to energy through easier establishment and greater productivity of business as well as positive impact on the environment is expected to give rise to a trickle-down effect and reduce poverty.

A range of existing constraints in the energy sector is holding back the economic development and poverty alleviation processes of the country. As mentioned before, a large gap between the demand and supply of energy already prevails and it is spiralling with time as no appropriate step has been taken to meet the required demand. Adding to that, the outreach of energy facilities is very limited and there is a growing disparity between the rural and urban areas. The PRSP provides two strategic goals for the energy sector that includes assessing non-renewable indigenous resources and ensuring conservation measures for economic and efficient use of energy.

Energy Price and Inflation

Food price inflation is one of the major concerns for the economy at present. Increased energy prices also add to the food inflation and are expected to be prominent in the coming months as a result of the recent price hike. The higher price of fuel oil, especially diesel, has raised the cost of production as it is used for irrigation purposes.

Energy Security

Energy security is now a global concern. A stable and cost-effective supply of energy is desired in any economy. Energy security issues emerged in the early 1970s with the imposition of the Arab oil embargo in 1973, along with rise in crude prices from US$2/bbl to more than US$10/bbl. This 1973 oil price hike did hurt the developing countries more than the developed countries as they had offset the price hike by increasing costs of services, materials and capital goods to the developing world.

Energy security, today, encompasses both internal and international dimensions. Dependence on imported oil and geographic locations of oil supplies have made energy security a complex issue and it is to be dealt by accessing all feasible options. Different countries view energy security differently considering spatial, temporal and economic dimensions. Resources, supply and demand factors plus stable access to supply sources are considered basic ingredients of energy security by many countries, both developed and developing. A shared view of the meaning of energy security in a national context is stable and cost-effective supply of energy. For Bangladesh (and also for other countries in the South Asia region), a third dimension is availability of energy to the vast poor population at an affordable price. The impact of the price hike in South Asia during 1990–91 went to the extent of effecting 1.2 per cent of India's and 4.5 per cent of Sri Lanka's GDP (Quader 2004).

The dimensions of energy security shown in Figure 4.9 for Bangladesh has been discussed in the Task Force report prepared by CPD in 2003. The dimensions to be highlighted to ensure a sustainable path for energy security are temporal and spatial. Islam (2007) in a presentation on sustainability and energy security of Bangladesh discussed the temporal dimensions in terms of short, medium and long-term energy security while the spatial dimensions

Figure 4.9
Different Dimensions of Energy Security

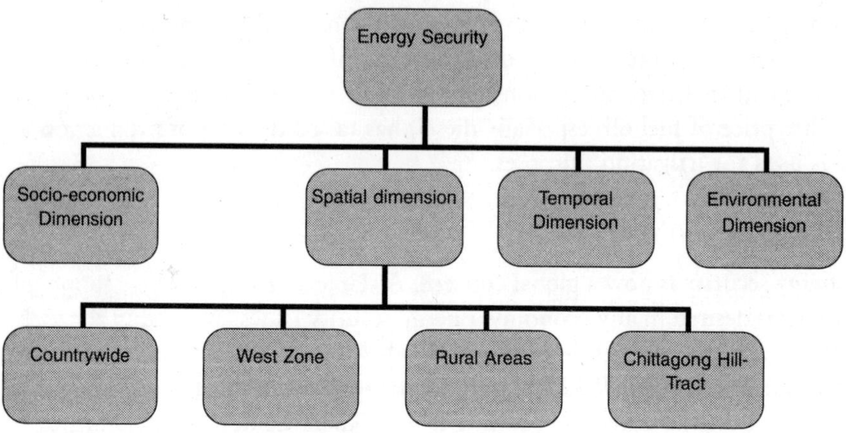

Source: CPD Task Force Report (2003).

were divided into the areas of the Chittagong Hill Tracts (CHT), west zone, coal zone and rural areas. He also pointed out the need to take care of local environmental issues in areas like Kaptai where the Karnaphuli Hydropower Project has been established as well as the areas where open-cut coal mining projects are taking place.

Energy is needed for economic and social development and in essence aimed at poverty alleviation. Other than natural gas and hydroelectricity (a small scale of production), no other commercial energy source has been exploited on a commercial scale. Recent attempts to produce coal has yet to make an impact on the energy security of the country. The increasing rate of growth in energy demand has brought about the challenge of determining the level of energy security. Energy insecurity in the western zone of the country has been a burning issue for a long time but hardly has there been any effort to resolve the relevant issues. In sum, the present energy insecurity clearly speaks of low energy development in the country.

Reforms

The government has taken up several reform initiatives in order to meet the necessary requirements to develop the energy sector. Among the major reforms are: the creation/establishment of REB, PBS, DESA, DESCO, Power Cell, RPC, etc.; adoption of the petroleum policy in 1993; the Power System Master Plan (PSMP) in 1995; the National Energy Policy in 1995 and the revised NEP in 2004; Private Sector Power Generation Policy in 1996; PGCB taking over the transmission business of BPDB since 1996; Small Power Generation Policy in 1998; drafting of the Bangladesh Electricity Reform Act in 1999, and the Energy Regulatory Bill approved by parliament in early 2003. Among others, corporatization and creation of strategic business units (SBUs) are some of the measures to be highlighted.

The Private Sector Power Generation Policy outlines the procedure for the participation of the private sector for Independent Power Producers' (IPP) projects on a build-own-operate (BOO) basis. For establishing mini power plants with capacity of up to 10 MW, the government also approved the "Policy Guideline for Small Power Plant in Private Sector" in the private sector (Quader and Gomes 2003). Hossain (2007) mentioned another reform initiative approved recently under the RAPSS model that supplements the REB. The model strives to extend electricity in some of the remote areas of Bangladesh through private sector investment. Under the programme, some distribution lines have also been built to power from a small CNG-run power plant.

The Energy Regulatory Commission Act 2003

Among the major reform initiatives, the Energy Regulatory Commission Act 2003 provides for an Independent Energy Regulatory Commission (ERC). Apart from these duties, the commission is also responsible for applying uniform accounting procedures for all the licences, settling disputes and differences between the licences and between consumers and licencees and referring to arbitration if necessary, enforcing codes and standards including safety, quality and reliability of services for the sector and coordinating with the Department of Environment on environmental matters.

However, this long-awaited act contained a number of major shortcomings. The bill made no serious effort to highlight the energy security issues of the poor people to support sustainable development. It contains a number of contradictions regarding the independence of the regulator, with no clear mention of a balance between independence and accountability.

Nevertheless, the present government has already taken some steps to be implemented immediately. These include rationing the use of electricity in the urban areas, staggering of load distribution and steps to reduce non-technical system loss. The hydrocarbon cell of the Energy Division has also been working to improve the performance of the energy sector. But unless successfully implemented, these initiatives will remain fruitless.

Policy for Bangladesh

Based on the above discussion, there are a number of measures that need to be carried out immediately. First of all, supply energy should come from diversified sources. There should be a mixture of energy sources, not only in terms of sources of energy within the national territory, but also the sources of import should not be concentrated within a small number of suppliers. Moreover, in order to build on the existing gas reserves, newer explorations have to be done by the local companies and gas explored by the international companies should not be exported. In the process, a reserve should be built for petroleum/crude. The challenges in the energy sector may also be addressed through international cooperation. But most importantly, and the issue that this study has emphasized in particular, is the generation, transmission and distribution of energy through regional cooperation.

Energy Cooperation

Why the Need for Energy Cooperation

With energy crises occurring at regular intervals since the 1970s either due to disruption of oil supplies or volatile oil price (from US$2 per bbl in 1971 to

US$60 or more per bbl in 2005), energy cooperation among countries, developed or developing, is recognized as a strategy for sustainable development.

Developing countries, tied to import energy especially crude oil and oil products, have suffered by paying a high price for oil and paying excessively for the import of capital goods and services from the developed countries. Energy cooperation among these countries in a region empowers them to bargain in forums where global strategies are formulated.

Energy cooperation can also achieve development of harmonized and standardized policies, regulations and procedures for cooperation among its members to be a recognizable stakeholder in the global trading of crude oil. It also can bring about inter-dependency and thereby change mindsets by removing mistrust. Economic efficiency and energy security improve while integration strengthens the bargaining capability with IOCs and FDIs for IPPs. As elaborated by Quader and Gomes (2004),

> Cooperation like EEC eventually enables its citizens to be the citizen of the community by removing the geographical boundaries among constituents with opportunities for job and investment in the region as a whole. This leads to uniform regulatory frameworks, fiscal policy, etc. without undermining political sovereignty; rather it enhances political stability nationally as well as regionally as a result of economic stability, growth of trade and efficient use of natural resources and technological advantages.

Cooperation for Bangladesh can be in various forms. For example, trading can take place in the form of finished commodity like electrically, piped natural gas, LNG, petroleum products, coal, etc. The region can develop common infrastructure such as a power transmission system and pipelines for gas and petroleum products/crude oil. Moreover, integration can also take place in the form of common resource development projects like hydro or thermal power plants, gas and oil exploration and development, etc.

Potential Barriers in Power Projects: Barriers in power projects include: past history of such projects both at national and bilateral levels; sharing of water of the common rivers; size of investment; assessment of existing perspective rights of each side; sharing costs and benefits of projects; implementation mechanism; funding arrangements including credit and guarantee mechanisms; legislative framework; technology and management; environmental issues; cross-border institutional linkage; political necessity and compulsion; economic rationale for trading; cost of transmission line and its sharing mechanism; inter-connection issues; determination of power tariff; payment mechanism including the currency to be used; power supply reliability and sustainability;

regulatory framework including institutional arrangements; immunization from geo-political contingencies; environmental issues, and cross-border institutional linkages.

Potential Barriers in Power Trade: Unfortunately there are a number of challenges that exists as barriers to building strategic partnerships among the countries within the region. One of the major challenges for trade would be to bring all the SAARC countries together for an agreement. The governments of these nations have to reach a consensus for energy sharing. However, before going into such inter-connection, the viability of such a measure has to be reviewed with scrutiny. Even if it appears feasible, such a project would require huge financing. Thus there remains the question of finding a suitable financer to fund the project. In addition, there exists no laws and regulations for exchange as the mechanism would require fully transparent policies and procedures (Malek 2001).

In addition, there are large differences between the size of the economies which sometimes can become a psychological barrier for the smaller economies. Reluctance of India as well as other states in opening up their economies to other neighbours is another barrier towards developing a common platform for power sharing. Finally, lack of appreciation for each other regarding the steps and policies initiated by member countries in the block leads to information failure between the countries.

Strategies to Overcome the Barriers: In order to overcome these barriers, people have to get across the borders at all levels to discover that their common enemy is poverty and denial of social equity, and not political divide based on religion or ethnic identity or geographical boundary. Governments have to make bilateral trade easier by abolishing procedural wrangling. By adopting unified tariff structures, procedures for trading and FDIs, fiscal policies, etc., governments need to overcome the non-trade barriers. Bilateral trade in petroleum products on a long-term basis at private and state levels need to be promoted. Also, uncalled-for bashing of the neighbours in the media has to stop. Promoting exchange programmes at technical and institutional levels for harmonizing norms and standards in energy technology as well as matters in regulatory and policy regimes, etc. can also be an option. Investment potentials of all South Asian countries could be developed in a coordinated manner under a common investment framework. But for that, harmonization of the rules and procedures and mutual recognition of the rules and standards are essential. The South Asian countries have yet to build on their infrastructural facilities in order to operationalize intra-regional cooperation initiatives.

Scope for Regional Cooperation

Advantages of Inter-connections: Inter-connection of power systems of contiguously located countries provides immense technical and economic benefits. It also contributes to the quality of electricity supplied to customers as well as reduces environmental damages. The economic criterion of inter-connection and the power transfer are invariably determined on the basis of configuration of transmission system and the regional demand. Inter-connection can significantly decrease the cost of electric energy particularly when power generation is highly capital-intensive in nature.

Power Trading Mechanisms: The two generally accepted trading mechanisms are pool-based and bilateral power trade.

Pool-Based: In the case of pool-based mechanism, if the power market is available, the daily pay System Marginal Price (SMP) is used to establish competitiveness in the power trade. This can possibly provide support to develop competitive long-run market equilibrium in the regional power trade.

Establishing a South Asian Association for Regional Cooperation-Regional Power Trading Corporation (SAARC-RPTC) would also be highly beneficial to the South Asia region. This in essence would be the pooling of surplus power generated by individual plants in the participating countries and transporting into deficit ones by a coordinated exchange mechanism depending on demand and consumer categories (estimating consumer surplus). The success of such power trading depends on the efficiency of the dispatch centres and speeds up the payment mechanism.

Bilateral Power Trade: Cross-border power trading already takes place widely between India and Bhutan and to a certain extent between India and Nepal.

Bangladesh-India Gas Pipeline: There are strong possibilities and scope for exporting gas to India from Bangladesh through pipeline. According to Unocal, the Government of Bangladesh could expect to begin receiving estimated revenues and tax receipts of at least US$3.7 billion over the twenty-year life-time of the project. At present, the proposed plan has been dissolved in consideration of Bangladesh's energy security. The export possibility must be considered only if new exploration is possible. This possibility, however, needs to be examined from both economic and socio-political perspectives.

The swapping of Indian gas with Bangladesh is another proposal whereby ONGC would sell the gas found in northeast India to Bangladesh, which would in turn sell an equivalent quantity of gas to India in return. This proposal is quite similar to what had been stated before for an alternative "Bangladesh-India Gas Pipeline" option.

Another proposal would be to allow the right-of-way to lay a gas pipeline across Bangladesh to bring Indian gas, stranded in the northeast, to mainland India. This will bring transit fees to Bangladesh without any gas sales from the country.

Other Options: Bangladesh and Thailand could jointly conduct a study to determine probable areas of collaboration prior to offshore hydrocarbon exploration in Bangladesh. Recently Petrobangla and PTTEP signed an MOU on behalf of their countries. Bangladesh is fully prepared on its side to be involved with Bhutan by involving India. Trading with Nepal is also a possibility. There can be a partnership among Bangladesh, Bhutan, Nepal and northeastern and Eastern regions of India.

TATA's Investment Proposal: The proposal by TATA offered to make the largest ever FDI in Bangladesh worth US$3 billion with a view to pacing up industrialization all over Bangladesh. Such a venture would lead to a rapid rise in Petrobangla's cash inflow as well as give a boost to the country's overall balance of payment situation. The project is expected to provide employment for 24,000 people and upgrade the overall infrastructural situation of the country. Moreover, the project offered substantial level of activities like developing a fertilizer technical training institute, farmers' training centre, technical training institutes and the establishment of two hospitals separately for the steel and coal mine projects under the company's corporate social responsibility programme. They offered a formula for setting the gas price depending on the price of urea and HR coil. Gas price was expected to stay within the range of US$2–US$4/MMBTU. The agreement was supposed to be completed by June 2006 and negotiation on the contract was expected to begin during August. But due to continuous delaying and reluctance in decision-making by the Bangladeshi government, this proposal had been suspended by TATA in September 2006.

Asia Energy: Asia energy had an investment plan of US$2.5 billion for thirty years along with the installation of a 500 MW coals fired power plant. The company waited for about eight years before a deal could be finalized due to continuous criticism from political parties and environmentalists. Asia Energy signed the contract with the Bangladeshi government in February 1998 although many energy experts also considered the proposal harmful for the country. Delay in the finalization of the coal policy was also a reason for the process to become lengthy. The company would export two-thirds of extracted coal and Bangladesh would receive a royalty of only 6 per cent. Based on an average price as US$50/tonne of coal, the government was expected to earn an estimated US$7 billion in terms of taxes, royalties, duties, etc. Although the company began its operation at the Phulbari Coal Mine, it could not last because of protest from the local community. At present, the government has a plan to re-negotiate the contract to look for new options regarding coal exploration.

Energy Cooperation: Policy Options

Bangladesh, as mentioned, is running a deficit on its supply of energy. Demand for power and energy for both commercial and domestic use is much higher than the supply. About 50 per cent of the population still uses conventional energy sources. In order to manage the national energy scenario, the government needs to revise and harmonize the policies related to the energy sector. The tariff structure should also be thoroughly reviewed to ensure that subsidies that have not been planned are not being provided quietly. A presentation on "Visions of a National Energy Policy" held in April this year has recommended to charge on-peak prices for all consumers during a mandatory period of the day to reduce demand. The presentation also highlighted the efficient use of energy by means of co-financing and reducing theft by establishing pre-paid meters. However, in order to ensure sustainability in the energy sector, the major emphasis should be put on regional cooperation.

The creation of a South Asian energy market and cooperative development of the available diverse energy sources in the region would help increase the level of energy security in the region, and thus, can subsequently contribute to achieving a sustained higher economic growth. A suitable power trading model for this region should be taken into consideration on a long-term basis. This also implies establishing proper institutional, legal and payment mechanisms.

Nonetheless, both power projects and power trading are vital as they complement each other. Besides political risks, commercial risks involved in the exchange of power should also be avoided. Building capacities of the policy-makers in the energy sector across the region to the advantages of cross-border energy exchanges are also very important. Cooperation always implies that certain resources are shared, and thus, the national control over them has to be transparent. Therefore the issues of benefit sharing, unless determined on a scientific and mutually convincing manner, would continue to crop up as a key hurdle.

For this, a regional consortium of the SAARC members could be set up in order to attract regional and sub-regional investment partners in the energy sector. Power trading would be based on bulk supply and would have to have a more detailed framework of contracts and operating procedures. One of the prerequisites for a scientifically drawn-up power purchase agreement would be the fixing of power tariff both at the generation and distribution levels.

Policy harmonization in terms of national level energy sector policies and regulations is essential. An information network for SAARC needs to be designed to facilitate regular exchange of data on demand-supply gaps for various forms of energy; policy changes; price and market conditions; technological innovations and inputs, investors and investment opportunities, energy expertise; seismic and other geological and environmental data. As mentioned in Bangladesh Vision for 2021, the ever-growing need for electricity can be met by developing a regional power grid along with Nepal, Bhutan and India, using the region's enormous capacity to produce hydroelectricity. (Nagorik Committee 2007)

The member states should promote technical cooperation for joint research, information exchange and technology transfer programmes in energy systems. The countries should look for new technology acquisitions and adaptation for energy conservation, use of waste products and the monitoring of environmental impact of energy systems in a joint project.

There are a number of organizations and institutions both in the public and private sectors working on the energy sector cooperation issues in South Asia. All these initiatives and studies carried out by the institutions across South Asia need to be pulled together to create regional synergy on energy cooperation.

REFERENCES

"South Asia Overview Energy Data, Statistics and Analysis — Oil, Gas, Electricity, Coal", 14 September 2006 <http://www.eia.doe.gov/emeu/cabs/South_Asia/Full.html>

"Visions of a National Energy Policy", A Symposium on Bangladesh Energy Sector: The Way Forward, Ministry of Energy, Power & Mineral Resources and GTZ-German Technical Cooperation, Dhaka, 12 April 2007.

Ahmed, Ahsan Uddin. *Energy and Sustainable Development in Bangladesh*. Helio International, 2002.

Bangladesh Bureau of Statistics. *2004 Statistical Yearbook of Bangladesh*, Government of Bangladesh, 2004.

Centre for Energy Economics. *Gas Monetization in Bangladesh*. Austin.

CPD Task Force Report. "Policy Brief on "Development and Governance of the Energy Sector". Centre for Policy Dialogue (CPD), 2003.

Dey, Dipanker. *Energy and Sustainable Development in India*. Helio International, 2006.

Elias, Rebecca J. and David G. Victor. *Energy Transition in Developing Countries: A Review of Concepts and Literature*. Stanford, 2005.

Hossain, Anwar. "Present Energy Scenario of Bangladesh". A Symposium on Bangladesh Energy Sector: The Way Forward, Ministry of Energy, Power & Mineral Resources and GTZ-German Technical Cooperation, Dhaka, 12 April 2007.

Huq, A. S. M. Bashirul. "Energy Security for Bangladesh". *Energy and Power*, 1–15 February.

Islam, M. Nurul. "Sustainability and Energy Security for Bangladesh". A Symposium on Bangladesh Energy Sector: The Way Forward, Ministry of Energy, Power & Mineral Resources and GTZ-German Technical Cooperation, Dhaka, 12 April 2007.

Jaswal, Pragya and Mitali Das Gupta. "Energy Demands and Sustaining Growth in South and East Asia". Asia 2015 Conference, 2006.

Lama, Mahendra P. "Energy Cooperation in South Asia: Opportunities, Strategies and Modalities". Centre for Policy Dialogue (CPD), 2003.

Malek, M. A. *Major Issues and Benefits of Regional Power Trade*. Bangladesh, 2001.

Ministry of Power, Energy and Mineral Resources. National Energy Policy, Bangladesh, 2004.

Nagorik Committee 2006. *Bangladesh: Vision 2021*. Centre for Policy Dialogue. 2007.

Petrobangla E. R. Natural Gas Tariff in Bangladesh (Table No.) at www.petrobangla.org/bd/ <http://www.petrobangla.org.bd/data/natural%20gas%tariff.html>, Bangladesh petrobangla, 2006.

Quader, A.K.M.A. "Regional Cooperation in the Energy Sector in South Asia: Bangladesh Perspective". Centre for Policy Dialogue (CPD), 2003.

Rahman, Mustafizur. "Bangladesh Gas and Coal Policy: Energy Security or Questionable FDI?". *The Daily Star*, 18 February 2006.

Raza, Hilal A. "Pakistan Country Study on Regional Cooperation in the Energy Sector in South Asia". Centre for Policy Dialogue (CPD), 2003.

The Energy and Resources Institute (TERI). "Energy Sector Co-operation in South Asia India Perspective". Centre for Policy Dialogue (CPD), 2003.

U.S. Department of Energy. *International Energy Outlook 2006*. Washington D.C., 2006.

Usman Aminuddin. "World Energy Outlook and Regional Co-operation in Energy".

5

Energy in the Bay of Bengal Region: Myanmar's Perspective

U Than Tun

The regional group in the Bay of Bengal known as BIMSTEC initially selected nine major areas, for example, trade, investment and industry, technology, transport and communication, energy, tourism, agriculture, fisheries and human resources development for sub-regional cooperation. However at the Second Ministerial Meeting of BIMSTEC in Dhaka in 1998, six priority areas were identified. The energy sector was among the six areas, and as a result of the developments that took place, Myanmar was designated the lead country and the chair country for the energy sector. Two projects are identified for cooperation.

The projects are:

1. The Energy Infrastructure Development (natural gas) Project, and
2. The Development of New and Renewable Sources of Energy Project

Following this identification, Thailand and India were designated coordinating countries respectively for the two projects.

Overview of the Energy Situation in the Sub-region/Bay of Bengal

The BIMSTEC region has a very large population; over 21 per cent of the total world population live in this region. The region has a very low per capita energy consumption with the main energy source provided for by traditional sources such as wood fuel and agriculture wastes. The sub-region — Bay of Bengal — has good prospects for economic growth and industrial expansion. However, it is currently experiencing high population growth and urbanization, increasing substitution of traditional fuels by commercial fuels and is under heavy stress from high commercial energy demand growth.

Although some of the member countries of the sub-regional group in the Bay of Bengal are endowed with primary energy resources such as coal, oil and natural gas and sharing of resources has already been in progress, the region as a whole is currently a net importer of commercial energy. Supply of electricity for population in most member countries still leaves much to be desired. Moreover, a large part of the population in the member countries live in remote areas where the availability of commercial energy is quite limited even for social purpose, let alone income generation.

Against this energy scenario, there is a dire need for the region to increase its efforts to develop the energy sector to the extent possible. The BIMSTEC Energy Sector Cooperation Programme is one such arrangement to achieve this objective and would concentrate its effort on developing untapped energy resources and cross-border sharing. It would also support the development of the power sector to enhance productivity and raise the social and economic standard in the region. The programme will most importantly develop the renewable sources of energy in the region to promote energy services in supporting the livelihood of the population through promotion of income generation activities.

The identified projects for implementation under the BIMSTEC Energy Sector Cooperation Programme are designed to cover the full aspect of this strategy, and implementation would involve:

1. the establishment of a resource inventory to provide a guideline to formulate further development strategies;
2. development and strengthening of energy infrastructure;
3. development and promotion of rural energy programmes; and
4. promoting of private sector participation in energy development programmes.

Guidelines for Implementation

There are three main guidelines for implementing the energy sector cooperation programme. They are:

- the role and functions of lead countries in identified sectors of cooperation;

- the role and functions of chair countries in sub-sectors; and
- the modalities of implementing projects and functions of project coordinating countries.

Status of Implementation

Myanmar, since its designation as the lead country, has as its first agenda established the Committee of Experts/Officials as per guidelines mentioned in the role and functions of the lead country. The committee is comprised of five members, from each member country, and the first meeting was organized to finalize the implementation of the two identified projects, Development of Energy Infrastructure (Natural Gas), and Development of New and Renewable Sources of Energy. The meeting also agreed to establish an Energy Information Centre in Myanmar and to establish two task forces to implement the two identified projects.

To speed up the pace of implementation, Myanmar organized the Third Meeting of the BIMSTEC Energy Sector Experts/Officials convened in Yangon in early 2002. It also made a presentation on the status of the Establishment of the Energy Information Centre. From the discussions after the presentation, the following transpired:

- Member countries agreed to furnish information necessary for the coordinating country Thailand to conduct a feasibility study for the Energy Infrastructure Development Project.
- With regard to the status of implementation of the Development of New and Renewable Sources of Energy project in the BIMSTEC region:
  (a) Member countries held a training programme on new and renewable energy technologies in New Delhi on 21–27 March 2002. The programme focused on application and barriers to penetration, policy and other required interventions;
  (b) On the subject of a demonstration project using biomass gasifier to be implemented in Myanmar, the meeting recorded that Myanmar would submit and amend proposal for utilizing the gasifier for the tobacco drying industry;

Potential for Cooperation

The seven member countries of BIMSTEC vary widely in their levels of development, this variance being most likely due, among others, to large population, the level of industrialization and economic growth. Energy, on the other hand, is an important ingredient for the development of the economy and the supply of adequate and reliable energy is a critical input to the development process. As such BIMSTEC member countries need to increase the input of this critical commodity through the development and management including resource sharing and development of new and renewable energy resources. One way of achieving this is through regional cooperation which can bring about economic and social prosperity to the individual member countries and to the region itself.

Based on the country reports and discussions at the meetings of experts/officials, it may be argued that potential for cooperation exists among member countries of this sub-regional group, especially in the field of developing and managing both commercial and non-commercial energy resources. In the field of commercial energy, member countries have the opportunity of trade and sharing of electricity and natural gas. Some of the countries, for example Myanmar and Thailand, are already in practice of cross border power trade in some sectors of the border.

The sharing of the large natural gas resource on the Myanmar side with users across the border on the Thai side is a significant achievement in this direction. It is expected that the BIMSTEC energy sector cooperation programme will enhance similar widespread sharing of resources in the sub-regional context throughout the region as well as in the Bay of Bengal.

Further Development of the Energy Sector Cooperation Programme

The BIMSTEC Sector Cooperation Programme has so far identified two significant and major projects. During the course of discussions for implementing the two projects, a third project, the Establishment of an Energy Information Centre was agreed for implementation to support the implementation of the two projects as well as the ongoing cooperation programme.

On the whole, the energy sector cooperation programme has made substantial achievements in initiating the implementation of the identified projects and is expected to make continued progress in the field.

The BIMSTEC Energy Sector Cooperation Programme in the Bay of Bengal is in its initial stage. Myanmar as the first country to take the position of the lead country in this sector has devoted much time and resources for the success of the programme. Much thought was given to solicit concurrence from member countries to engage with potential dialogue partners for the sustained development of the energy sector in the sub-region but the initiative has to come from higher levels. No outside agency or donor country is known to have expressed their interest on the activities of the regional group so far. Although member countries have kept to the self-reliant path and are proceeding towards the aims and objectives of cooperation programme with full trust, it is realized that BIMSTEC should eventually embark on a campaign to create awareness in the international community of its existence, programmes and activities.

As the lead country, Myanmar welcomes the support of development partners. It is fully committed towards the realization of the objectives set for the projects and will seek ways to further expand, intensify and accelerate the process of cooperation. Myanmar is also very honoured by the endorsement of the Fourth Ministerial Meeting of BIMSTEC to continue as the lead country. It pledges to take this opportunity to add momentum to its present activities and to further cooperation towards achieving its perceived objectives.

Existing Energy Cooperation between India and Its Neighbouring Countries

Hydroelectricity

A preliminary feasibility study is underway on the inter-connection of the transmission systems of Nepal, Bhutan, Bangladesh and India in the "chicken neck" region of northeastern India. This inter-connection will be able to match projected hydroelectric power surpluses in Bhutan and Nepal with projected deficits in India and Bangladesh.

So far, South Asia Regional Energy Coalition (SAREC) has identified several cross-border electricity transmission inter-connection projects such as double circuit 400 KV lines between Bhutan and India; three radial 132 KV lines from Nepal to India; two 220 KV direct current transmission between Bangladesh and India; and privatized 500 KV inter-connected between Pakistan and India.

Oil and Gas

Lanka IOC, a subsidiary of India Oil Corporation Limited, India, has launched downstream petroleum business in Sri Lanka.

Myanmar-Bangladesh-India Pipeline

The gas reserves in Myanmar, where Oil and Natural Gas Commission of India (ONGC) and Gas Authority of India Ltd (GAIL) have 20 and 10 per cent stake respectively, and India's own gas reserves in Tripura cannot be exploited optimally because of the absence of local market and gas transporting infrastructure. The proposal of transportation gas from Myanmar to India through pipeline via Bangladesh is one from which all the parties stand to gain. Bangladesh could think of supplying its gas to India on the same lines, adding to revenue earnings for allowing passage of Myanmar gas to India through its territory.

The proposed 290-kilometre pipeline would run through Arakan (Rakhine) state in Myanmar, then via the Indian states of Mizoram and Tripura before crossing Bangladesh to Kolkata (India). If this proposal does not materialize due to opposition from Bangladesh, then India could opt to ferry gas via a 1,450-kilometre route from Myanmar's A-1 gas field through the mountains of northeast India. However, that proposal is the least economical.

The former proposal would serve the primary aspects of regional cooperation as well as economic development since both the gas-rich countries (Bangladesh and Myanmar) would have a regional market (India).

Role of Bangladesh in Myanmar-Bangladesh-India Pipeline

The proposed gas pipeline is yet to see the light of day mainly because of ambivalent behaviour of Bangladesh. Due to strong domestic opposition, getting Bangladesh gas is almost impossible in the near future. Initially Bangladesh was not even willing to allow its land for transit but after the twelfth SAARC Summit, it has agreed in principle to allow the construction of the pipeline under certain conditions. It wants the pipeline to be laid along its existing roads and highways and the project jointly managed by India and Bangladesh. It will allow the use of land for laying the pipeline from Myanmar to India provided India allows Bangladesh a free trade corridor to Nepal and accompanying trade benefits. It also asked India to remove the existing trade barriers between two countries.

Bangladesh will benefit in a number of ways by the construction of this pipeline. These include revenue earnings from granting a right of way to the pipeline, an estimated US$100 million per annum.

Recently, Korea plans to extend a helping hand to India by mediating with Bangladesh to secure the rights for an overland pipeline to ferry gas from Myanmar's A-1 and A-3 blocks in which Korean companies — Daewoo and Kogas — are in partnership with OVL and GAIL.

Daewoo Set for Myanmar Gas Boom

DAEWOO International Corporation, one of South Korea's leading trading companies, announced in August 2006 that it has secured large gas reserves in Myanmar, which were officially certified by a U.K.-based evaluator and could bring the company additional profits of up to US$155 million.

The company said that oil industry consultant Gaffney, Cline & Associates Ltd evaluated three gas fields in the A-1 and A-3 blocks, with reserves ranging from 5.7 to 10 trillion cubic feet, equivalent to two billion barrels of crude oil.

"In three gas fields in the sea off northern Myanmar, 'Shwe' in Block A-1 and 'Shwe Phyu', 'Mya' in 'Block A-3' hold recoverable reserves of up to 4.8 to 8.6 trillion cubic feet", Daewoo International's president Lee Tae-young said at a press conference on 10 August 2006. Currently India, Thailand and China are keen on purchasing the gas through pipelines. "Korean, Japanese and Taiwanese companies are also interested in buying the gas. The company is now expecting to open a deal with these countries within the second half of 2007.

If the production of gas starts, the company is likely to see additional net profits of more than 100 to 150 billion won [US$$100–155 millions]", he added.

Daewoo International holds a 60 per cent stake in the A-1 and A-3 fields and has been spearheading the project jointly with Korea Gas Corporation (KOGAS), which holds 10 per cent, and two Indian oil companies, ONGC and GAIL, which had shares of 20 per cent and 10 per cent each respectively.

The company is planning to explore and test-drill in two places in the A-3 block in 2007, which are also thought to contain large amounts of gas.

GAIL Starts Talks with Myanmar for Gas Share

Energy development company GAIL (India) has started negotiation with the Myanmar government to buy its share of natural gas from A-1 block in that country. Myanmar had earlier agreed to consider GAIL as the preferential buyer of gas from the block.

It is estimated that the A-1 block has reserves of 4 trillion cubic feet (tcf) of gas. Production is anticipated to be about 16 million standard cubic metres a day during the plateau period of about fifteen years.

GAIL and ONGC Videsh Limited together hold a 30 per cent share in the A-1 block. The other partners in the consortium are Daewoo, which is the operator with a 60 per cent share, and KOGAS with a 10 per cent share.

MOGE's share of gas in the A-1 block would be approximately 11 million standard cubic metres a day including royalties and share in profit gas by virtue of participation in the development project, said officials, adding that third-party reserve certification of the gas reserves was expected by May 2006 and commercial production was expected to commence by 2009.

Block A-1 entered the third extension period in August 2006, which was likely to be over by 31 October 2006, with a work programme of drilling six appraisal or exploratory wells. The drilling campaign has already been underway.

MOGE, Russia, India, Sign Production Sharing Contract on Oil and Gas Exploration

On 16 September 2006, a production sharing contract of Mottama offshore Block M-8 was signed by Myanmar Oil and Gas Enterprise, JSC Zarubezhneft, Itera Oil and Gas Company of the Russian Federation and Sun Group of the Republic of India at Nay Pyi Taw, Myanmar.

The production sharing contract agreed on oil and gas exploration, drilling and production at Mottama offshore at M-8 in the Bay of Bengal.

Energy

Myanmar has significant potential for energy sector development. Energy production to date has largely been dominated by state-owned enterprises with consumption restricted to within Myanmar. However, recent developments and plans for regional power projects demonstrate that Myanmar has investment potential in the establishment of future power facilities. Within the energy sector, oil and gas explorations and production have proven to be the most viable industry for attracting foreign investment. Investment to date has come from Europe, the United States and regional countries such as Thailand.

Sector Management

The main activities of Myanmar's energy sector are administered under the Ministry of Energy, which are divided among two SOEs, the Myanmar Oil and Gas Enterprise (MOGE) and the Myanmar Electric Power Enterprise (MEPE). MOGE is concerned with the exploration and production of crude oil and natural gas from both onshore and offshore oil fields. MEPE is the main vehicle for energy production in Myanmar and is responsible for energy production and transmission through hydroelectric, thermal, natural gas and diesel power plants. However, it should be noted that power production is not the monopoly of MEPE since many SOEs under different ministries utilize their own sources.

In terms of foreign investment and joint venture agreements in the energy sector, Myanmar has primarily set up guidelines for projects in the oil and gas sector with the involvement of MOGE. There is a good potential existing in the energy production sector, with particular emphasis on hydroelectric projects and energy sharing agreements between Myanmar and neighbouring countries. While numerous projects are at the feasibility and planning stage, no actual power plants have been established under any agreements. It is expected that potential power generating projects with foreign investment will be established with guidelines relating to build-operate-transfer or other related structures.

With specific reference to onshore and offshore petroleum exploration and production, the guidelines set up by the Ministry of Energy stipulate that the national oil company, MOGE, has the exclusive right to explore, develop and produce petroleum. Petroleum licensing negotiations are carried out by the Ministry of Energy, while petroleum sharing contracts are handled by the contractor and MOGE.

Oil and Gas

The nationalization of the oil industry in 1965 gave the Myanmar Oil Corporation (MOC), later renamed as MOGE in 1985, exclusive rights to explore, develop and produce petroleum both onshore and offshore. Since the first mechanized well was spaded in 1987, exploration activity has yielded proven, probable and possible reserves estimated at some 801 million barrels of oil and 5,648 billion cubic feet of gas. Cumulative production to the beginning of 1993 was estimated at 509 million barrels of oil and 343 billion cubic feet of gas.

Of significant interest in the oil and gas sector is the investment and involvement of foreign partners with MOGE through petroleum sharing contracts. Table 5.1 lists those foreign contractors that have explored potential areas and either relinquished their designated block or commenced operations.

Table 5.1
Ya Khine Offshore Project, Block A-1 Natural Gas Production

• Videsh	20%
• Daewoo	60%
• GAIL	10%
• Korea Corporation	10%
• Reserve Gas	13–47 (tcf)

Source: Maung Maung Aye, "The Increasing Situation of Global Oil Commodity Prices and the Fuel Problems", paper presented to the National Defence College, Yangon, 24 January 2006.

Further regional investment in the oil and gas industry has been initiated by the Petroleum Authority of Thailand (PTT) which has acquired 25 per cent of the Yadana oil field from the French operator company Total, which enabled PTT to transport natural gas via pipeline.

Hydropower

Myanmar has an abundance of potential hydropower resources in its main river system, the Ayeyarwaddy, Chindwin, Thanlwin and Sittoung. Existing hydroelectric facilities include:

- Lawpita with a capacity of 196 megawatts;
- Kinda with a capacity of 56 megawatts;
- Sendawgyi with a capacity of 25 megawatts;
- Zaungt with a capacity of 18 megawatts.

The exploitable hydropower capability of the country is assumed to be around 366 terawatt hours annually.

Coal

Some fifteen coal deposits have been identified so far representing a total of about 256 million tonnes. Approximately one-third of these resources might be recoverable. The main use of coal are small-scale power generation, mineral processing industries and sponge iron production.

Key Investment Opportunities

The annual capital requirement to meet projected power demand in Myanmar was estimated to be around US$115 million in 1995, increasing to about US$180 million by the year 2000. This is not including any potential hydropower projects for export to neighbouring countries which would require substantially higher investment.

Hydroelectric Projects

Current hydroelectric power projects are tailored to cover the domestic energy demand which is greatly depressed. However, opportunity for export-related investment and development exists in the region of the Thanlwin River basin, particularly for Thailand. The Thanlwin upper (4,540 megawatts) and Thanlwin lower (792 megawatts) projects are both located where the Thanlwin River forms the border with Thailand. Joint involvement between

Myanmar and Thailand can also be extended to the transmission systems concerning the above-mentioned projects. Furthermore, the proposed Tamanthi (1,200 megawatts) site on Chindwin River and located north of the country is a possible source of energy supply to Bangladesh or India. Key potential hydroelectric projects are summarized in Table 5.2.

Other opportunities related to hydroelectric projects and power generation include the establishment of new transmission lines from new hydropower projects to the existing grid.

Strategies for Increasing Investment

In order to attract investment in Myanmar's energy sector, there is a need to analyse the existing energy prices in Myanmar which neither reflect the economic cost of supply nor the scarcity of energy resources and capital. There is consequently a need for continued reforms related to pricing structures, exchange rates and an adjustment to domestic energy prices to reflect real economic supply costs and international prices.

There is currently no private capital market in Myanmar which could provide capital for energy investments. However, irrespective of what happens

Table 5.2
Hydroelectric Power Plants from 2001 to 2006

No	Project	Location	Megawatts
1	Paung Laung hydroelectric power	Mandalay T/ship	280
2	Mone hydroelectric power	Magwe T/ship	75
3	Tha Pan Seik hydroelectric power	Sagaing T/ship	30
4	Phyu hydroelectric power	Bago T/ship	65
5	Kha Paung hydroelectric power	Bago T/ship	30
6	Kyung Chaung hydroelectric power	Bago T/ship	60
7	Ye' Nwe hydroelectric power	Bago T/ship	25
8	Baw Ga Hta hydroelectric power	Bago T/ship	160
9	Thut Yay Khut hydroelectric power	Bago T/ship	150
10	Shwe Kyin hydroelectric power	Bago T/ship	75
11	Ye' Ywar hydroelectric power	Mandalay T/ship	780
12	Shwe Li hydroelectric power	Shan State (North)	200
13	Kyaing Daung hydroelectric power	Shan State (South)	20
14	Taung Na Win hydroelectric power	Bago T/ship	2
15	Pa Thi hydroelectric power	Karen State	2
	Total		1945

Source: Maung Maung Aye, "The Increasing Situation of Global Oil Commodity Prices and the Fuel Problems", paper presented to the National Defence College, Yangon, 24 January 2006.

so far as domestic production is concerned, the domestic demand is going to ensure that Myanmar's import dependence will be of the order of 85 per cent.

Gas: The Situation in the Bay of Bengal

> "On gas, the situation is in some ways more encouraging and in some ways a little more alarming. It is encouraging as our (India's) production of gas in the 1980s was about 9 million metric standard cubic metres per day (mmscmd) and now it is 90 million. So to increase output by a factor of ten within two decades is a fairly impressive achievement reinforced by the kind of finds we've been having particularly in the Bay of Bengal, where gas has been found in the Palk Straits further north offshore the Cauvery basin; further north still, in very substantial quantities offshore the Krishna-Godavari basin, the 2002 find of Reliance having been the single largest gas discovery ever made anywhere in the world; and almost adjacent to that ONGC has in September 2006 made a very, very significant gas discovery.
>
> Bangladesh, as all of us know is floating on a lake of gas; and along the eastern littoral we ourselves are involved in the discovery of gas in the A1 and A3 blocks off the Arakan coast, which is now called the Rakhine coast. And if you fall off the shelf of Myanmar into the sea then the two large offshore gas fields from where Thailand is being supplied are in the Andaman Sea. The potential is so considerable that before we quite wake up to it, it might turn out that the Bay of Bengal is the North Sea of South Asia. ("Energy Cooperation: India and Its Neighbours" by Mani Shankar Aiyar, former Indian Minister for Petroleum and Natural Gas).

Thailand Closes in on Myanmar Energy Deals

On 7 August 2006, the Thailand and Myanmar governments verbally agreed to increase natural gas production at the Yetagun gas field by a quarter to supply Myanmar's energy-thirsty neighbour.

PTT Exploration and Production, a unit of Thailand's largest energy Firm PTT Plc, holds a 14.17 per cent share of the Yetagun project and is negotiating with its partners to buy an additional 100 million cubic feet of gas a day (mcfd) on top of the 400 mcfd it pipes from the project in the Gulf of Mottama.

Thailand buys all the gas from the Yetagun project, which is operated by Malaysia's Petronas which has 56.67 per cent stake, MOGE with a 15 per cent stake, and Nippon Oil and PTTEP with about 14.17 per cent each.

The contract to buy gas from the field would be over twenty years and this period would be increased if further gas reserves were found in the areas.

Myanmar started selling Thailand 200 mcfd of gas from Yetagun gas field in 2000 and increased the amount to 400 mcfd in 2005. Reserves at the existing Yetagun project have been placed at 3,946 billion cubic feet (bcf) with a sale reserve of 2,437 bcf.

PTTEP already has five projects under development in Myanmar, mainly in the Gulf of Mottama and pipes about 1 bcf of gas a day from Myanmar. On 4 August 2006, PTTEP revealed it had submitted bids to the Myanmar government for more petroleum concessions.

On 31 July 2006, PTT confirmed it had joined the race against China and India for exclusive rights to gas in the A-1 block off the Rakhine State coast. Thailand's former Prime Minister Thaksin Shinawatra, in a weekly radio address on 5 August 2006 reaffirmed his country's reliance on Myanmar energy production and said "Myanmar will continue to be Thailand's biggest sources of energy."

His comments came after an announcement on 2 August by PTTEP that an affiliate of the company had discovered a new petroleum source at the offshore "Zatilal-1" well, in the M-9 area about 250–300 kilometres south of Yangon.

Energy Planning Department and Petronas Sign MOI

A ceremony to ink a Memorandum of Intent (MOI) between the Energy Planning Department of the Ministry of Energy of the Union of Myanmar and Petroliam Nasional Berhad (Petronas) of Malaysia was held at the meeting hall of the ministry at Nay Pyi Taw, Myanmar on 9 August 2006.

According to the MOI, technicians of the Ministry of Energy and Petronas will cooperate in conducting feasibility survey on commercial and technological matters to sell natural gas through pipelines to neighbouring countries and manufacture liquefied natural gas (LNG) based on existing natural gas deposits and potential natural gas resources in Myanmar.

Measures Taken by Myanmar for Fuel Management

In Myanmar, most widely and commercially used non-renewable energy are crude oil and natural gas. Oil and natural gas industries are almost exclusively government-owned with the exception of a limited of joint ventures. Most oil is produced onshore on seventeen geological valleys and offshore production in Rakhine. Gulf of Martaban and Tanin Tha Yi regions. Production has been carried out in Central Myanmar, Chindwin, Pyi, Ayeyar Wadi delta region and Rakhine coastal region. Unexplored oil fields in some regions have not been widely surveyed or searched yet. Onshore reserve crude oil is estimated to be 3,109.77 million barrels and 4,072,418 million cubic feet of natural gas, and offshore reserve crude oil is estimated to be 98.662 million barrels and natural gas is about 83.013 trillion cubic feet as at 1 April 2003. The consumption of crude oil and natural gas was 14.90 per cent in 1988–89 but significantly rose up to 28.3 per cent in 2002–03. Domestic oil production began to fall behind its growing oil consumption after 1990–91 as Myanmar has adopted market-oriented economy.

At present, onshore output is 12,000 barrels of crude oil and over 140 million cubic feet of natural gas. Offshore is 950 million cubic feet of natural gas and 8,500 million cubic feet of lightweight gas. MOGE has sought foreign investments for oil exploration and production. Already 34 onshore and 19 offshore joint venture agreements have been signed and so far drilling is now going on 11 onshore and 12 offshore blocks. Massive reserves of natural gas is found on land in Apyauk and Nyung Don. Ya Danar offshore project can produce 5.7 trillion cubic feet of natural gas and a total of 6.5 trillion cubic feet can be extracted with the additional new-found sites in the Diamond and Ruby projects. As agreed, 525 million cubic feet of natural gas is to be sent daily for thirty years to Thailand. Domestic consumption is 1,285 million cubic feet per day. Ye' Dagon natural gas was found in November 1992 and can produce 4.1 trillion cubic feet of natural gas and 84.63 million barrels of lightweight gas. Beginning from April 2000, MOGE is selling 200 million cubic feet of natural gas to Thailand and increased to 260 million cubic feet in October 2002. Sales of natural gas to Thailand has risen to 400 million cubic feet since April 2004. From 2000, Myanmar has become a major exporter of natural gas by pipeline in the Asia-Pacific region.

Myanmar is an active participant in the energy sector in the region and acts as a focal point in collaboration with the ASEAN countries. The offshore project is part of the Trans-ASEAN gas pipeline scheme. In addition, Myanmar is responsible in the energy sector of BIMSTEC, the members of which are India, Bangladesh, Myanmar, Sri Lanka, Thailand, Bhutan and Nepal. Moreover, countries in the Mekong region made an agreement to implement the plans to use natural gas in the region.

Suggestions on the Management of Fuel in Myanmar

Natural gas has been called the environmentally friendly fossil fuel since it releases fewer harmful contaminants. World production of dry natural gas was 73.7 trillion cubic feet and accounted for over 20 per cent of world energy production. In 1990 Russia account for about one-third of world natural gas. The second largest producer was the United States having about one quarter of world 1990 natural gas production. Natural gas may be increasingly used in place of oil for applications such as power generation and transportation. One reason is that the world reserve of natural gas has doubled since 1976, in part because of the discovery of major deposits of natural gas in Russia and in the Middle East. New facilities and pipelines are being constructed to help process and transport this natural gas from production wells to consumers. The United States consumes more natural gas than other country in the world.

Environmental issues have urged countries towards examining and supporting legislation to subsidize the development of cleaner vehicles that use compressed natural gas (CNG). Even with a push towards the use of CNG-burning vehicles, the numbers are quite small when compared with gasoline vehicles. Italy has used CNG since 1935 and has the largest usage with 30,000 vehicles in 1994. Argentina, which ranked sixth, had 15,000 vehicles. In Myanmar, CNG-burning vehicles have been in use since 1986 and was about 587 in number. With effect from 1 August 2005, 1,697 buses have been converted in Yangon division and 12 CNG stations are being opened and more will be extended in the near future. Some 200 buses in Paleik township and 122 vehicles have already converted to CNG. By using more CNG vehicles, demand on gasoline and diesel is likely to slow down. According to the Ministry of Energy second quarter reports, an average of 13,640 gallons of gasoline and 17,066 gallons of diesels were reduced by the use of CNG as substitute. Therefore, it is advisable to use alternative fuel instead of relying on conventional gasoline and diesel.

Suggestions on fuel management in Myanmar include the following:

(a) As a nation's GDP is linked to energy consumption and its GDP will slow down if consumption of energy is cut short, it is essential to explore new sources both onshore and offshore.
(b) It is also necessary to produce more energy from hydropower. Measures must be taken to explore hydropower reserves to obtain cheap, renewable and clean energy. It is estimated that there are about 39,720 megawatts of hydroelectric opportunities to be expanded for hydropower energy.
(c) By using more natural gas Myanmar can reduce its reliance on crude oil. Daily production of natural gas is over a 150 million cubic feet from onshore and 950 million cubic feet from offshore. Natural gas should be used more to power electric power stations, factories, transportation, productions, etc.
(d) The government should lay down policies to make industries adopt energy-conserving technologies and develop high-tech guidelines on saving

energy. National strategic oil reserve must be established in order to avoid an emergency energy crisis.

(e) Measures must be taken to research and produce energy from hydro, solar, wind and bio-fuel and use the renewable energy in both agricultural and production sectors through careful planning and constructive management.

(f) As adequate energy is an incentive for domestic and foreign counterpart to promote the economic growth of Myanmar, the energy issue is crucial and should be given priority over other matters.

As the domestic consumption of gasoline and diesel has significantly risen in recent years, the daily production of crude oil from the various oil fields cannot meet the demand, and import has to be made for enterprises like fisheries, timber corporation, gem exploration, etc. (see Table 5.3). Oil reserves have already been stored in Than Lyin oil refineries tanks with 8.3 million gallons of gasoline, 38.3 million gallons diesel and 2.8 million gallons jet fuel in August 2005. Another 1.5 million gallons gasoline, 6.65 million gallons diesel and 0.87 million gallons jet fuel are being stored as national strategic oil reserves.

Table 5.3
Total Import of Gasoline and Diesel (million/barrels)

No	Financial Year	Gasoline	Diesel
1	1988–89	–	–
2	1989–90	–	0.145
3	1990–91	–	0.197
4	1991–92	–	0.249
5	1992–93	–	0.819
6	1993–94	–	1.106
7	1994–95	0.043	1.390
8	1995–96	0.026	1.778
9	1996–97	0.275	2.674
10	1997–98	0.037	2.597
11	1998–99	0.341	3.742
12	1999–2000	0.374	5.404
13	2000–2001	0.758	6.295
14	2001–2002	0.761	6.871
15	2002–2003	0.451	6.105

Source: Maung Maung Aye, "The Increasing Situation of Global Oil Commodity Prices and the Fuel Problems", paper presented to the National Defence College, Yangon, 24 January 2006.

Synthetic Fuel

Synthetic fuels do not occur in nature but are made from natural materials. Gasohol, for example, is a mixture of gasoline and alcohol made from sugars produced by living plants. Although making various types of fuel from coal is possible, the large-scale production of fuel from coal will likely be limited by high costs and population problems, some of which are not yet known. The manufacture of alcohol fuels in large quantities will likely be restricted to regions, such as part of Brazil, where a combination of low-cost labour and land, plus a long growing season, make it economical. Gasohol is now being used as a fuel in Brazil, American, Korea and Japan. Research and mass production should be carried out in Myanmar where abundant land and skilful labour are available.

Bio-fuel

A bio-fuel which consists of 5 per cent of palm oil was experimented in Malaysia last June. There is no specific date when this green fuel could be used commercially but there is now talk of producing it in large scale. In Myanmar, experiments are now underway to produce bio-fuels by mixing palm oil and castor oil with diesel. There should be more research on the widespread use of bio-fuels.

Nuclear Plants

In 2001 a total of 435 nuclear plants operated worldwide. Another 35 reactors were under construction. Eighteen countries generate at least 20 per cent of their electricity from nuclear power. The largest nuclear power industries are located in the United States (104 sectors), France (59), Japan (52), Britain (35), Russia (29) and Germany (19). In the United States, no new reactors have been ordered for more than twenty years. Public opposition, high construction costs, strict building and operating regulations and high cost of waste disposal make nuclear power plants more expensive to build and operate than plants that burn fossil fuels.

Table 5.4
Income from Offsore and Natural Gas Projects in Myanmar
(In US$ million)

No	Financial year	Ye'Dagon Project	Yadana Project	Total
1	1998–1999	–	21.68	21.68
2	1999–2000	–	104.16	104.16
3	2000–2001	58.09	190.31	248.40
4	2001–2002	105.34	186.70	292.04
5	2002–2003	65.37	139.73	205.30
	Total	228.05	642.58	871.08

Source: Maung Maung Aye, "The Increasing Situation of Global Oil Commodity Prices and the Fuel Problems", paper presented to the National Defence College, Yangon, 24 January 2006.

Table 5.5
Crude Oil Sources in Myanmar

- Chindwin Valley
- Central Myanmar valley
- Pyi region
- Aye yar wa di region
- Ra khine region
- Sittaung region
- Thibaw, Lashio region
- Maplay region
- Mawlamyaing region
- Nan Myaw region
- Kalaw region
- Bago Yoma region
- Hukaung region
- Shwe bo, Mon Ywar region

Source: Maung Maung Aye, "The Increasing Situation of Global Oil Commodity Prices and the Fuel Problems", paper presented to the National Defence College, Yangon, 24 January 2006.

Table 5.6
Crude Oil and Natural Gas

- In Myanmar, commercially used non-renewable energy are mostly crude oil and natural gas. There are 17 regions in Myanmar according to the geological situation. They are:

Onshore

- Hukaung region
- Chindwin Valley
- Shwe bo-Mon Ywar region
- Central Myanmar Valley
- Pyi region
- Aye Ya Wa Di delta region
- Bago Yoma region
- Sittaung region
- Thi baw-Lashio region
- Maplay region
- Mawlamyaing region
- Nan Myaw region
- Kalaw region
- Rakhine region

Offshore

- Rakhine offshore region
- Martabban offshore region
- Taninthayi offshore region

Source: Maung Maung Aye, "The Increasing Situation of Global Oil Commodity Prices and the Fuel Problems", paper presented to the National Defence College, Yangon, 24 January 2006.

Table 5.7
Outlook of Fuel in Myanmar

Location	Natural gas (million cubic feet)	Crude oil (million barrels)
Onshore	4,072,418	3,109,776
Offshore	83,013	98,662

- Coal reserves — 710,771 million tonnes
- Hydropower reserves — 39,720.00 megawatts
- Solar energy — 51,973.80 terawatts/per year
- Wind energy — 365.10 terawatts/per year
- Geo-thermal — 93 locations

Source: Maung Maung Aye, "The Increasing Situation of Global Oil Commodity Prices and the Fuel Problems", paper presented to the National Defence College, Yangon, 24 January 2006.

Table 5.8
Onshore Crude Oil Reserves in Myanmar
(In million barrels)

No	Region	Approved	Prospect	Probable	Total
1	Chindwin	8.880	–	1,590.000	1,598.800
2	Central Myanmar	108.786	353.760	810.854	1,272.781
3	Pyi	4.660	38.847	143.729	180.236
4	Aye Ya Wa Di	1.923	0.314	0.132	2.896
5	Rakhine	0.890	6.700	48.00	55.590
	Total	125.041	202.620	2,592.115	3,109.776

Source: Maung Maung Aye, "The Increasing Situation of Global Oil Commodity Prices and the Fuel Problems", paper presented to the National Defence College, Yangon, 24 January 2006.

Table 5.9
Domestic Production and Importation of Crude Oil
(In million barrels)

No	Financial year	Domestic crude production	Imported crude oil	Total
1	1974–75	6,772	1,840	8,612
2	1984–85	11,199	–	11,199
3	1994–95	5,040	2,437	7,477
4	1995–96	4,277	3,552	7,829
5	1996–97	3,787	2,703	6,490
6	1997–98	3,632	4,794	8,426
7	1998–99	3,378	5,077	8,455
8	1999–2000	3,480	5,003	8,383
9	2000–2001	4,138	4,724	8,862
10	2001–2002	4,836	3,929	8,765
11	2002–2003	6,387	3,433	9,820

Source: Maung Maung Aye, "The Increasing Situation of Global Oil Commodity Prices and the Fuel Problems", paper presented to the National Defence College, Yangon, 24 January 2006.

Table 5.10
Imported Gasoline and Diesel
(In million barrels)

No	Year	Gasoline	Diesel
1	1988–89	–	–
2	1992–93	–	0.145
3	1997–98	0.037	2.579
4	1998–99	0.341	3.742
5	1999–2000	0.374	5.404
6	2000–2001	0.758	6.295
7	2001–2002	0.761	6.871
8	2002–2003	0.451	6.105

Source: Maung Maung Aye, "The Increasing Situation of Global Oil Commodity Prices and the Fuel Problems", paper presented to the National Defence College, Yangon, 24 January 2006.

Table 5.11
Increased Oil Production by Location (up to August 2005)

No	Location	Average daily production	
		Crude oil (barrels)	Natural gas (m/cfeet)
AA	Nyung Done	74	8.3840
BB	Myaung Aung/Shwe Pyi Tha	80	0.1510
CC	Htauk Sha Pin/Kun Ni	·303	2.5
DD	Mann	106	0.5689
EE	Ye nan Chaung	3	–
FF	Chauk/Lan Ywar	55	–
GG	Tha Gyi Daung/Sa Bai'	8	3.8670
HH	Let Pan Do/Ah Yar Daw	65	0.9750
	Total	694	16.4937

Source: Maung Maung Aye, "The Increasing Situation of Global Oil Commodity Prices and the Fuel Problems", paper presented to the National Defence College, Yangon, 24 January 2006.

REFERENCES

Energy Cooperation among the BIMST-EC countries, *BIISS journal* 24, no. 4 (2003).

Khosla, I. P. *Energy and Diplomacy*, Konark Publishers Pvt Ltd, New Delhi, 2005, p. 24.

Maung Maung Aye. "The Increasing Situation of Global Oil Commodity Prices and the Fuel Problems". Paper presented to the National Defence College, Yangon, 24 January 2006.

Myanmar Times, August and September 2006.

"Myanmar: Trade and Investment Potential in Myanmar". United Nations, New York, 1996, ST/ESCAP/1671.

New Light of Myanmar, August 2006.

Union of Myanmar report of the BIMST-EC Energy Sector, Third Meeting of the Committee of Experts/Officials, Yangon, 2002.

6

Marine-related Energy Resources in the Eastern Indian Ocean: Indonesian Perspective

Sugiarta Wirasantosa

INTRODUCTION

The Indian Ocean with average depths of 3,900 metres is the third largest ocean in the world, covering an area of more than 69 million square kilometres, or about 20 per cent of the Earth's water surface. It is bounded on the north by southern Asia; on the west by the Arabian Peninsula and Africa; on the east by the Malay Peninsula, the Sunda Islands, and Australia. The ocean is nearly 10,000-kilometre wide at the southern tips of Africa and Australia, but it spans 5,500 kilometres between Africa and Indonesia at the equator. Indonesia borders it on the east, but in the south, it opens wide facing Antarctica. The largest depths of the Indian Ocean floor are found in Java Trench and in Wharton Basin that exceeds 7,250 metres and 6,000 metres, respectively.

The ocean floor of the Indian Ocean is dominated by the Mid-Indian Ocean Ridge consisting of the Southeast Indian Ocean Ridge, Southwest Indian Ocean Ridge, and Ninety East Ridge. It reflects a long and complex history of plate dynamic since the Mesozoic. Plate interaction in the eastern boundary, namely Indo-Australian plate, Eurasian plate and Pacific plate, has produced numerous sedimentary basins in the area presently known as Indonesia. Some of these basins are proven to contain coal and hydrocarbon. In addition, tectonic plate interactions in the eastern boundaries have produced chain of volcanoes along the active margin involving magmatic and hydrothermal processes that potentially can be tapped as non-conventional energy resources.

At present and probably in the years to come, hydrocarbon and coal still are prime sources for energy in the world since the contribution of other energy types to the energy mix is still low. Large reserves of hydrocarbons are being tapped in the offshore areas of Saudi Arabia, Iran, India, Indonesia and Western Australia. An estimated 40 per cent of the world's offshore oil production comes from the Indian Ocean. However, the price of oil keeps increasing, and it seems that the era of low oil price is over. As energy demand increases due to better economic conditions, an unstable supply of energy resources due to security and political reasons in producing economies has to be considered as potential problems in the near future. Therefore, alternative sources of energy have to be explored and developed, and energy efficiency improved, particularly in some economies of the eastern Indian Ocean region.

Alternative sources of energy are even more critical to an archipelagic country such as Indonesia. Statistics show that even though Indonesia produces oil, its high energy demand has put the country as a net oil importer. On the other hand, contribution of non-oil energy sources to the country's energy mix is low and has to be improved. Development of non-conventional energy resources such as bio-diesel, bio-fuel, geo-thermal, and hydroelectric power is considered as temporary solution to balance the increasing energy demand. Another way to improve the share of non-conventional energy resources is to develop wind energy and ocean current-generated electricity suitable to the geographical condition of the country. Therefore, in the context of alternative energy development, research in oceanography is critical in terms of determining the characteristics of ocean current in potential areas.

The intention of the chapter is to discuss energy resources in the eastern Indian Ocean, particularly in Indonesia, as a perspective towards energy potential, demands and alternative resources. Attempt is made to a certain extent to discuss alternative energy resources such as marine-related energy resources.

Sedimentary Basins

The eastern boundaries of the Indian Ocean are geologically active areas because they are affected by tectonic interaction between the Indian Ocean and Eurasian plates. The crust of Sundaland, which dominates Southeast

Asia, was first assembled during the Triassic and is not a monolithic block (Clift et al. 2002). Instead it is surrounded on three sides by subduction zones and has continued to deform. Deep sedimentary basins have developed in a region of high heatflow and lower crustal flow. Different basins within Sundaland have experienced variable amounts of Neogene tectonic inversion that controls the flow and the accumulation of sediment. Inversion has thus had a major influence on the stratigraphy and development of hydrocarbons in Southeast Asia (Clift et al. 2002). The collision of subcontinent India to Asia during the Cenozoic has been estimated to occur around 30 million years ago, affected lithosphere deformation in the surrounding marginal seas.

Tectonic and geologic history of the region in the eastern Indian Ocean has produced numerous sedimentary basins, some of which are proven to contain hydrocarbons. It is estimated that 60 tertiary sedimentary basins are formed in the Indonesian area (Figure 6.1). However, only 38 basins have been drilled so far. The drilled basins show that 23 basins indicated hydrocarbons accumulation, 15 of which are productive, and 8 are not in production yet. Until 2007, there have been 227 petroleum working areas consisting of 121 onshore areas, 61 offshore and 45 areas onshore and their continuing offshore (Figure 6.2). Offshore work areas are located in the Java Sea, East Kalimantan, Macassar Strait, Natuna Sea, the sea around the Bird Head area of Papua, Cenderawasih Bay and Arafura Sea (Figure 6.3). It appears that onshore explorations are still attractive to investors.

The remaining 22 of the known tertiary basins are considered frontier basins, and most of them are located offshore in eastern Indonesia. The frontier basins need to be studied and further explored to determine their potential resources.

Energy Types and Its Potential

Major types of energy used in the eastern Indian Ocean are mostly fossil energy in the form of oil, gas and coal. Indonesia as oil producer is considered to produce barely sufficient energy for its own use. Indonesia oil reserve is only accounted for 0.6 per cent of the world's reserve, the gas reserve is 1.4 per cent, and the coal reserve is 3.1 per cent (Sectoral Agenda 21, Energy). Oil and gas have been the primary fuel source for domestic needs and a major foreign exchange for the country. In the year 2002, oil and gas contributed 25 per cent of the country's income. However, two-thirds of domestic energy needs is dependent on oil, and the domestic demand of energy for household, industry and transportation increases at an average of 7 per cent annually. Energy supply in the year 2002 was

Figure 6.1
Tertiary Sedimentary Basins in Indonesia

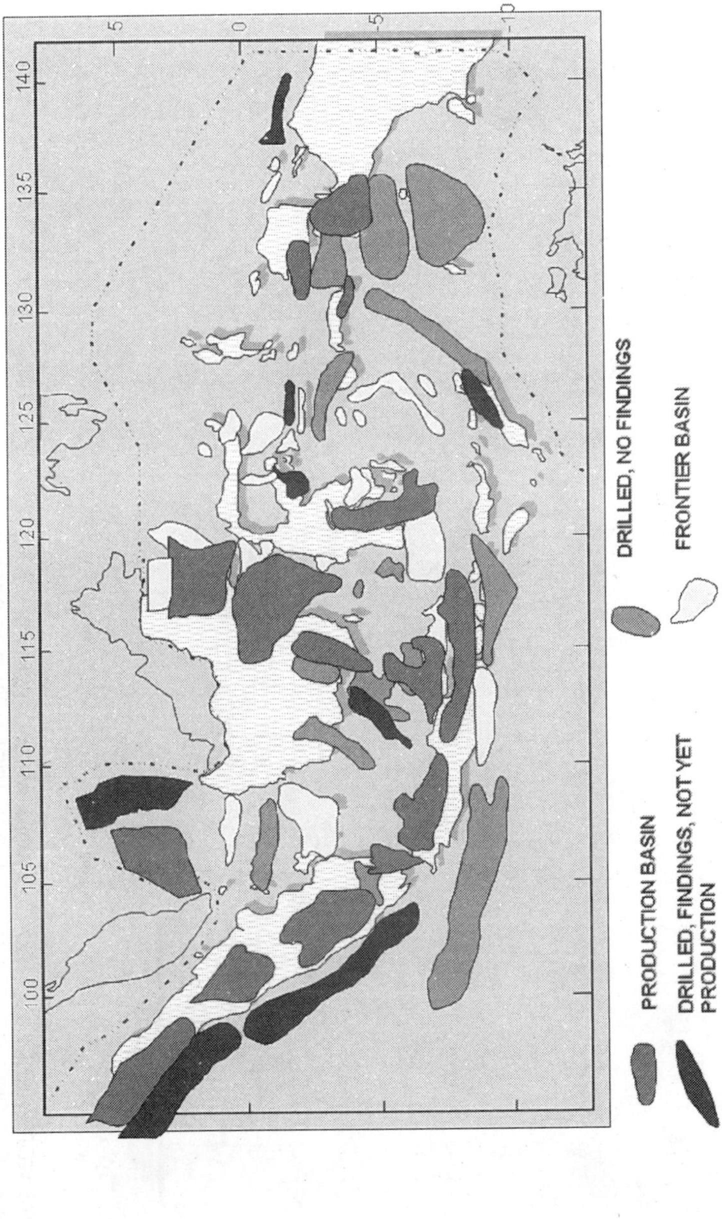

Source: Figure reproduced courtesy of D.G. Oil and Gas, 2007.

Figure 6.2
Exploration Work Area in Indonesia (July 2007)

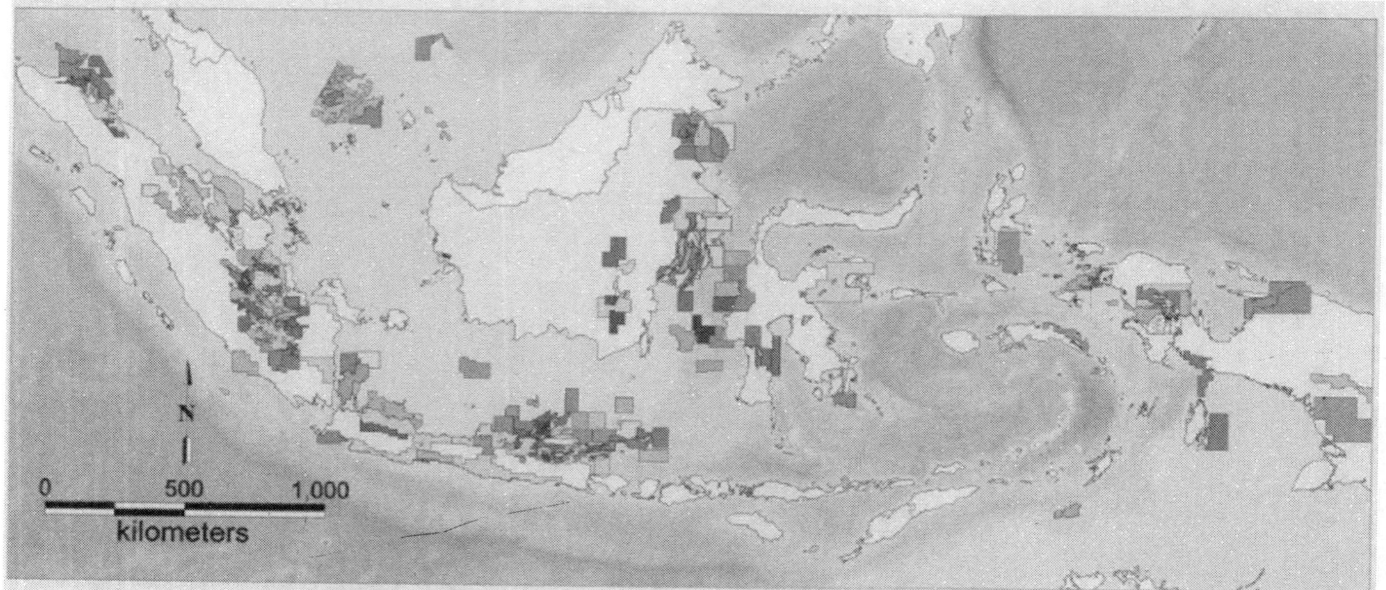

TOTAL WORK AREA	: 227	WORK AREA OFFSHORE	: 61
WORK AREA ONSHORE	: 121	WORK AREA ONSHORE-OFFSHORE	: 45

Source: Figure reproduced courtesy of D.G. Oil and Gas, 2007.

Figure 6.3
Offshore Oil Activities

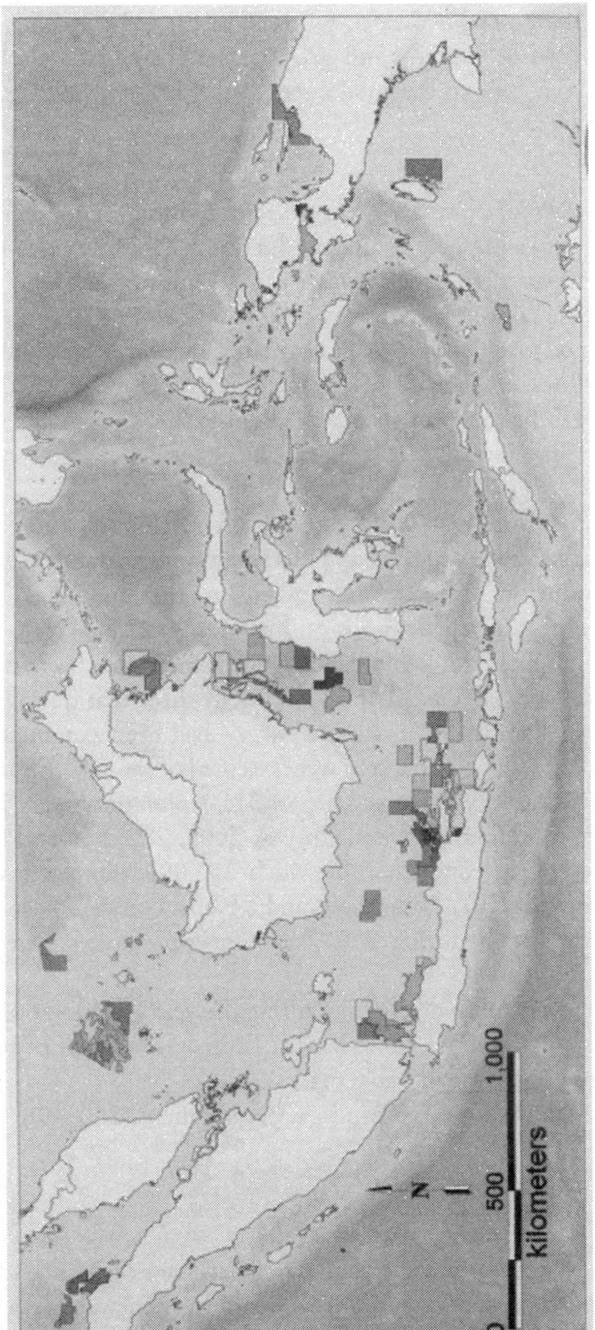

Source: Figure reproduced courtesy of D.G. Oil and Gas, 2007.

dominated by oil (54 per cent), followed by gas (23 per cent), and coal (17 per cent). Hydroelectricity and geo-thermal energy contribute only 4 per cent and 2 per cent to the total energy mix (Prasetyo 2005).

Fossil Energy

Table 6.1 shows total primary energy reserves and annual production. Assuming current reserves and stable annual production, oil is expected to last within 12 years, gas 30 years, and coal 50 year of consumption.

In spite of continuing effort to maintain primary energy production, the Indonesian oil production is declining naturally from 1.55 million barrels per day in 1998 to an estimated 1.1 million barrels per day in 2007 (Table 6.2).

Total gas production increases slightly to 8.2 mmscfd even though onshore production decreases, as shown in the following Table 6.3 (D.G. Oil and Gas, 2004).

In the past three years the average gas production was around 8 billion scf per day. Gas has been exported and used in power generating plants, fertilizer, chemical industries, refinery fuels, and city gas for households. In contrast to oil production, gas production is estimated to be stable.

Effort to maintain hydrocarbon production has been done through exploration. Data (D.G. Oil and Gas, 2004) show that during 1995–2000, 1.27 million kilometres of seismic survey has been conducted, of which 966,000 kilometres or 76 per cent were executed offshore. Offshore exploration drilling in the same period was done for 311 exploration wells (57 per cent of a total of 526 exploration wells). In year 2001, 282 thousand kilometres of seismic survey was conducted, of which 252,000 kilometres was offshore. During the year 2001, 77 onshore and 84 offshore wells were drilled. This data confirmed that during 2001, offshore explorations were higher than onshore activities.

Offshore exploration activities during the year 1995 to 2003 have shown oil and gas discoveries in some basins. Estimated reserves of oil and gas in those basins are shown in Table 6.4.

Onshore and offshore oil and gas development (2004–08) are shown in Table 6.5.

Renewable Energy

Renewable energy is generally referred to renewable non-fossil energy resources which can be used in a sustainable manner. Renewable energy includes biomass, geo-thermal, solar energy, hydropower, wind energy and ocean current. Although renewable energy is considered as clean energy, the share of

Table 6.1
Total Energy Reserves

Energy Type	Total Reserves	Proven Reserves	Production	Ratio (Reserves/Prod.)
Oil	86.9 billion bbl	6 billion bbl	500 million bbl	12 years
Gas	385 tscf	90 tscf	2.9 tscf	30 years
Coal	50 billion tonnes	5 billion tonnes	100 million tonnes	50 years

Source: Prasetyo, H. "Indonesian Energy Policy Development, Challenges and Opportunities" (Ministry of Energy and Mineral Resources Republic of Indonesia, 2005, unpublished).

Table 6.2
Oil Production up and Forecast (in thousand barrels per day)

	1998	1999	2000	2001	2002	2003	2004	2005	2006	2007
Onshore	1,049	1,036	1,007	955	902	830	803	808	826	803
Offshore	508	464	409	387	351	317	312	314	321	312
Daily	1,557	1,500	1,416	1,342	1,253	1,147	1,115	1,122	1,147	1,115

Source: "Oil and Gas Offshore Exploration Prospect in Indonesia" (D.G. Oil and Gas, Ministry of Energy and Mineral Resources Republic of Indonesia, 2004, unpublished).

Table 6.3
Gas Production and Forecast (In mmscfd)

	1998	1999	2000	2001	2002	2003	2004	2005	2006	2007
Onshore	4.21	4.46	3.45	3.00	3.64	4.39	3.69	3.59	3.67	3.60
Offshore	2.38	2.68	3.10	3.33	3.38	3.74	4.17	4.38	4.48	4.60
Daily	6.59	7.14	6.55	6.33	7.02	8.13	7.86	7.97	8.15	8.20

Source: "Oil and Gas Offshore Exploration Prospect in Indonesia" (D.G. Oil and Gas, Ministry of Energy and Mineral Resources Republic of Indonesia, 2004, unpublished).

renewable energy in the national energy mix is still low. Some reasons are commonly considered to be related to the slow development of renewable energy. These reasons include high investment cost, lack of supporting policies, lack of knowledge and awareness, lack of incentive and funding mechanism, and domestic oil price that is still below its economic value.

Different types of renewable energy have been developed and used by the general public for different purposes. Relating to their development stage,

Table 6.4
Offshore Oil and Gas Discoveries, 1995–2003

No.	Basin	Oil	Gas	Discovery
1.	West Natuna	248 mmbo	1 tscf	10
2.	East Natuna	–	5 tscf	1
3.	Kutei	1.4 bbo	6 tscf	36
4.	Bintuni (pre 1995)	87 mmbo	14 tscf	1
5.	South Makasar	195 mmbo	1.4 tscf	1
6.	Sunda	19 mmbo	–	6
7.	NE Java	23 mmbo	0.3 tscf	6
8.	NE Java and NE Java Sea	1.5 bbo	3 tscf	24
9.	Aru	–	10 tscf	1

Source: "Oil and Gas Offshore Exploration Prospect in Indonesia" (D.G. Oil and Gas, Ministry of Energy and Mineral Resources Republic of Indonesia, 2004, unpublished).

renewable energy can be put into three categories. First are renewable energy types in commercial development such as biomass, geo-thermal and hydropower. Second are those not fully developed, but are in limited use such as solar energy and wind energy. Third are renewable energy types still in research stage such as ocean energy.

Biomass energy is used widely in rural areas. It is used for cooking, home industry, agriculture, small-scale power generators, and other uses. It is estimated that the total potency of biomass energy is 50,000 megawatts (MW). Data show that biomass supports 36 per cent of total national energy consumption. Geo-thermal energy, however, is used directly for drying agricultural products, hot water for households and public use, and indirectly for power generators. Considered as a volcanic rich area, along the volcanic belt from Sumatra, Java, Bali, Lombok, to Timor and Sulawesi, it is estimated that geo-thermal potency can be developed in 51 locations. Geo-thermal resources in 17 locations are calculated as being capable of generating electricity of 20,000 MW of electricity for thirty years. Nevertheless, the present utilization of geo-thermal is relatively low, that is, 804 MW or 4 per cent of the total energy mix. This is due to several factors, such as, the economic price for water vapour is high in comparison to conventional energy, and the locations of geo-thermal resources are generally remote and at large depths of more than 1,000 metres. The potency of hydropower, on the other hand, is quite high. Present estimates of hydropower potency is 75,000 MW from 1,315 locations, including 34,000 MW that can be developed as a large capacity power station of more than 100 MW. National utilization of

Table 6.5
Onshore and Offshore Oil and Gas Development, 2004–2008

No.	Company (Field)	Start up	Oil Prod. (bopd)	Condensate (bopd)	Gas (mmscfd)	LPG/LNG Prod.
1.	PREMIER OIL (Gajah Baru)	2006			100	
2.	CONOCOPHILIPS (S. Natuna Sea)	2004	100,000		420	28,000 LPG(bpd)
3.	UNOCAL (Merah Besar)	2005	20,000		38	
4.	UNOCAL (West Seno)	2004	27,000		150	
5.	UNOCAL (Seturian)	2007		300	28	
6.	SANTOS (Maleo, Seram)	2005	20,000			
7.	BP Indonesia (Tangguh LNG)	2007		4,384	962	7,000 LNG (mton/yr)
8.	JOB EXSPAN (Tiaka/Senoro)	2004	6,593			
9.	SANTOS (Maleo, Madura)	2005			100	
10.	KODECO (Ke-30 Madura)	2005		4,000	90	
11.	KODECO (Ke-40, Madura)	2004	3,500		30	
12.	LAPINDO BRANTAS (Wunut)	2004			80	
13.	SANTOS (Oyong Sampang, Madura)	2004	3,500	80	40	
14.	AMERADA HESS (Ujung Pangkah)	2004	798		100	
15.	BP MURIAH (Kepodang)	2006			140	
16.	CNOOC (SES Gas)	2005		60	100	
17.	CONOCOPHILIPS (Mengoepeh)	2006	4,500			
19.	JOB YPF (Jambi Merang)	2005		4,800	70	5,427 LPG(bpd)
20.	PETROCHINA (Betara Complex Ph.3)	2007		10,948		11,208 LPG(bpd)
21.	CONOCOPHILIPS (Suban 2)	2005			700	
22.	CONOCOPHILIPS (South Jambi B)	2004	636	600		

Source: "Oil and Gas Offshore Exploration Prospect in Indonesia" (D.G. Oil and Gas, Ministry of Energy and Mineral Resources Republic of Indonesia, 2004, unpublished).

hydropower is 4,208 MW, or 5.6 per cent of the total. In Java, however, hydropower has been utilized 2,389 MW or 53 per cent of the total potency in the island, in addition to 64 MW of micro-hydropower in rural areas. Estimated total potency of micro-hydropower in Java is 460 MW.

Solar energy and wind energy are still in development. Solar energy is abundant in a tropical country like Indonesia with average daily radiation of 4.8 kWh per square metre. Solar thermal energy is used directly in agriculture and household and solar photovoltaic energy is used to generate small-scale electric power for rural areas. Installed capacity of solar photovoltaic energy in 2002 was 5 MW.

Table 6.6 summarizes the potential of renewable energy and their installed capacity (Prasetyo 2005)

Table 6.7 shows cost of producing renewable energy from various types of generator. The most expensive energy cost per kWh is the energy generated through wind, and the cheapest energy cost is the energy from ocean (current exchange rate of Rp9,000/US$; it costs only Rp36–Rp65 per kWh). However, the investment cost for generating energy from the ocean is the highest.

Marine-related Energy Resources

A study on the assessment of fuel consumption in Indonesia (2002) predicted that energy demand in 2010 would be, respectively, for industry 39.6 per cent, transportation 37.2 per cent, household 17.4 per cent, commercial 3.0 per cent and others 5.8 per cent. Electricity demand in 2010 is estimated to be 12 per cent of the total energy mix, and 81 per cent of it is for supplying Java and Bali. In terms of final energy mix, Prasetyo (2005) reported that in 2002 contribution of oil was 54 per cent, gas 23 per cent, coal 17 per cent, hydro-electricity 4 per cent, and geothermal 2 per cent. The data show that contribution of electricity is still low, although the demand is predicted to increase. Therefore, ocean energy and other marine-related energy resources are worth considering for the reason that it is suitable for geographic conditions of Indonesia. Moreover, the production of fossil energy as the main component of energy resources is declining and exploration of deep-sea sedimentary basins is more difficult

Ocean energy and other marine-related energy are also worth considering as alternative energy resources that can be developed in the long-term because ocean and other marine-related energy are abundant in an archipelagic country such as Indonesia. Although the investment cost is high, the cost to generate electricity from ocean energy is low in comparison to other means of electricity

Table 6.6
Renewable Energy, Their Potential and Capacity

Energy Type	Potential	Installed Capacity
Hydro	75.67 GW	4,200 MW
Geothermal	27.67 GW	802 MW
Mini/Micro hydro	712 MW	206 MW
Biomass	49.81 GW	302.4 MW
Solar	4.8 kWh/m2/day	5 MW
Wind	3-6 m/sec	0.5 MW

Source: Prasetyo, H. "Indonesian Energy Policy Development, Challenges and Opportunities" (Ministry of Energy and Mineral Resources Republic of Indonesia, 2005, unpublished).

Table 6.7
Renewable Energy Cost

Generator	Investment Cost (US$)	Energy Cost (Rp/kWh)	Assumption on Energy Cost
Micro Hydro	<200kW: 1,200/kW 200–500kW: 2,000/kW	194	Generator: 20 kW age: 10 years BOP: 4% Investment Interest: 10%
Wind	3,000 /kW	2,000–2,500	Depends on installed capacity and energy production
Solar - photovoltaic	Module: 3.5–5/Wp System: 7–10/Wp Wp – Watt peak	1,000–1,500	Module life age: 10–15 years. Battery life age: 3–4 years. Other component life age: 5–10 years
Biomass	900–1,400/kW depends on capacity and technology	10 MW: 100 50MW : 250	
Ocean	2,000–7,000/kW	0.004–0.007 US$/kWh	

Source: Sectoral Agenda 21, *Energy Agenda for Developing Sustainable Quality of Life* (Sectoral Agenda 21 Project, 2001. Cooperation between The State Ministry of Environment and UNDP).

production. Therefore, in the long-term, it is cost efficient. Potential energy resources such as wave energy, tidal energy, ocean thermal energy and ocean current energy have been researched for quite a long time. However, utilization of ocean energy and other marine-related energy is still low. It is known that the energy of a wave front is estimated to be an average of 20–70 kW/metre of coastline, or 1 kilometre of coastline is impacted by 20–70 MW. With the assumption of 50 per cent efficiency, wave energy along 1 kilometre of coastline potentially can be converted into electric power of 10–35 MW. Research on wave-generated electric power with a capacity of 1.1 MW is conducted at Baron Beach, on the southern coast of Yogyakarta.

Tidal energy can be used to run an electricity generator when the difference between high and low tide is reasonable. Tidal energy in Indonesia, however, is considered low because the tidal difference is low. Nevertheless, some bays have indicated reasonably high tidal difference sufficient for turning an electricity generator.

Ocean thermal energy works through a thermodynamics principle when a temperature difference between the ocean surface and at depth is available. The working temperature of ocean thermal conversion is when temperature at the ocean surface is around 25° C and 5° C at depth. The potential used of ocean thermal conversion in Indonesia is quite high, but it needs to be supported by research and actual measurement. When used to generate electricity, the overall efficiency is between 2 and 2.5 per cent (Sectoral Agenda 21).

Oceanographic data show relatively strong ocean currents in several locations and depths during a normal year. Strong ocean currents might therefore be used to generate electricity in the future. However, research on this matter has to be conducted. The locations of relatively strong ocean currents are shown in Table 6.8.

Table 6.8
Strong Ocean Current during Normal Year

No.	Location/depth	Month												Current Vel. (m/s)
		Jan	Feb	M	A	M	J	Jul	A	S	O	N	D	
1.	Karimata strait/50 cm	√	√	√									√	1 – 1.5
2.	South of Lombok/50 cm					√	√	√						1 – 1.5
3.	West of Mentawai/50 cm					√	√	√		√	√			1 – 1.5
4.	Central part of Makasar strait/50 cm								√	√				1 – 1.5
5.	North of Papua/50 cm	√											√	1 – 1.5
6.	Sulawesi sea and East Kalimantan/300 m	√	√	√	√	√	√	√	√	√	√	√	√	0.5 – 1
7.	Sulawesi sea and northern coast/1,250 m	√	√	√	√	√	√	√	√	√	√	√	√	0.25 – 0.50

Source: Supangat, A. "Marine Current Characteristics in Indonesian Waters and Its Relation to Climate Variability" (Regional Meeting on Marine Current Energy, Cooperation between The State Ministry of Research and Technology Republic of Indonesia and UNIDO, 2005).

Another possibility for alternative energy in the future is to tap gas hydrate found in sediments in accretionary complex and forearc basins. Accretionary complex is deformed sediments of complex structures generally found on the landward side of subduction areas. Djajadihardja et al. (1999), reported that distribution of pockets of gas hydrate appears as strong reflector on seismic sections recorded along the Sunda arc, particularly from south Bengkulu waters, south of the Sunda Strait and south of the Cilacap waters. Natural gas hydrate is an ice-like mixture of gas and water in which methane gas molecules are trapped within a framework of cages within clathrates of water molecules. Methane in nature is formed either through biogenic processes that expel gas from micro-organisms during the digestion of organic compounds, or through decomposition of organic matter by heat and pressure known as thermogenic processes. Alternatively, methane can be accumulated from reaction of deep crust gases with minerals or seepage of hydrogen and carbon from the Earth's interior. Further research on this matter has to be conducted to determine whether gas hydrate can be utilized as alternative source of energy in the future.

Energy Policy

The government policy on renewable energy development and energy conservation (green energy), 2003, stated that its mission is to:

1. assure national security of sustainable energy supply;
2. optimize the utilization of renewable energy resources;
3. promote the utilization of clean and efficient technology;
4. promote social culture of energy efficient;
5. improve implementation of reliable, safe, environmentally friendly and efficient green technology;
6. promote equal opportunity in public welfare.

The national policy on energy is focusing on the development of supporting aspects such as:

- policy on the utilization of renewable energy;
- policy on investment of energy resources development;
- policy on investment incentive;
- policy on energy pricing;
- policy on human resources development related to energy;
- policy on public awareness;
- policy on standardization and certification;

- policy on research and development;
- policy on institutional development.

Policy on the utilization of renewable energy in electricity generation aims to promote the utilization of renewable energy resources to at least 5 per cent from the installed capacity for a newly-built generator, or at least 5 per cent from the total energy production for a generator that has been in operation.

Policy on investment should promote the opportunity for investment on green energy by local and national stakeholders, cooperatives, private businesses, and government enterprises. It should include policies on fiscal, financial, monetary and energy pricing to support investments on green energy. Furthermore, appropriate energy pricing will increase efficiency, and discourage the misuse of energy and smuggling. As is known, energy efficiency in Indonesia is quite low, as reflected by the high intensity of energy, in comparison to average ASEAN economies. In 1998, energy intensity in Indonesia was 392 tonnes of oil equivalent (toe)/million U.S.$, while it was 364 toe/million U.S. dollar for the average ASEAN economy and 202 toe/million U.S. dollar for the average developed countries.

Summary

Major types of energy used in the eastern Indian Ocean are mostly fossil energy in the form of oil, gas and coal. Oil, gas and coal have been the primary fuel sources for Indonesia, while hydroelectricity and geo-thermal contribute only 4 per cent and 2 per cent to the national energy mix. While production of oil is declining, domestic demand of energy for household, industry and transportation is increasing 7 per cent annually.

Data show that contribution of electricity is still low, although the demand is predicted to increase. Therefore, ocean energy and other marine-related energy resources are worth considering for the reason that they are suitable given the geographic conditions of Indonesia. Moreover, the production of fossil energy as the main component of energy resources is declining and the exploration of sedimentary basins located at deepsea is more difficult.

REFERENCES

Anonymous. *Sectoral Agenda 21, Energy Agenda for Developing Sustainable Quality of Life* (Sectoral Agenda 21 Project, Cooperation between the State Ministry of Environment Republic of Indonesia and UNDP, 2001).

———. *Study on the Assessment of Fuel Consumption in Indonesia on 2002* (Cooperation between Advanced Engineering Associates International, Washington, U.S.A. and Center for Research on Material and Energy, Institut Teknologi Bandung, Indonesia, 2001, unpublished).

———. *Indonesian Energy Prediction for 2010* (Cooperation between Center of Energy Information, Ministry of Energy and Mineral Resources Republic of Indonesia and Energy Analysis and Policy Office, 2002, unpublished).

———. *Policy on Renewable Energy Development and Energy Conservation (Green Energy)* (Ministry of Energy and Mineral Resources Republic of Indonesia, 2003, unpublished).

———. *Oil and Gas Offshore Exploration Prospect in Indonesia* (D.G. Oil and Gas, Ministry of Energy and Mineral Resources Republic of Indonesia, 2004, unpublished).

———. *Policy on National Energy 2003–2020* (Ministry of Energy and Mineral Resources Republic of Indonesia, 2004, unpublished).

Clift, P. et al., ed. *Continent-Ocean Interactions within East Asian Marginal Seas.* AGU Chapman Conference, San Diego, November 2002.

Djayadihardja, Y.S. et al. *Investigation of Methane Venting and Hydrothermal Activity in the Sunda Trench, Southern Offshore of West Java Island.* Proceedings of Indonesian Association of Geologists, Vol. II, The 20th Annual Convention, Jakarta, Indonesia, 1999.

Prasetyo, H. *Indonesian Energy Policy Development, Challenges and Opportunities* (Ministry of Energy and Mineral Resources Republic of Indonesia, 2005, unpublished).

Sudibyo, R. *Offshore Oil & Gas Exploration and Exploitation Activities and Status* (BP. Migas, 2004, unpublished).

Supangat, A. *Marine Current Characteristics in Indonesian Waters and Its Relation to Climate Variability* (Regional Meeting on Marine Current Energy, Cooperation between The State Ministry of Research and Technology Republic of Indonesia and UNIDO, 2005).

<http://www.cia.gov/cia/publications/factbook/print/xo.htm/>.

<http://geography.laurentia.ca/cb/geopol/region.htm/>.

7

Energy Trading and Singapore's Role as a Hub

Ong Eng Tong

INTRODUCTION

This chapter examines energy trading and Singapore's role as a hub. Singapore is the third largest refining centre in the world after Houston and Rotterdam.

The refineries serve as a swing refinery whereby it will supplement those countries with insufficient refining capacity as well as serve countries whose product shortfalls arise out of refinery outage or extremity of weather.

Due to its strategic location, Singapore has served well as a hub where large cargoes of oil are received from Europe and the Middle East and the products are stored and reshipped in smaller lots to suit the requirements and port facilities of the surrounding countries.

In view of the above, Singapore also emerged as a major oil trading centre together with New York and London. All the major oil companies are present here and so are most of the Middle East oil producers and refiners, the Chinese, Japanese and the South Korean refiners and oil trading companies.

Besides refining 1,300,000 barrels per day of oil, Singapore imports 939,000 barrels per day and exports 1,145,000 barrels per day of finished product.

Refining Capacity (Appendix 7.1)

The Singapore refining capacity remains at 1.3 million bbl per steam day. Except for some debottlenecking at ExxonMobil, the latest addition to the refining unit, a condensate splitter, was added by Shell in 2003.

All the refineries in Singapore are sophisticated, that is, on the downstream side there are many upgrading units such as reformers, hydrocrackers, visbreakers, fluid catalytic crackers, residue catalytic crackers, etc.

There are many hydrodesulphurizers which can reduce the sulphur content of all the products to meet the current environmental friendly specifications.

The range of products produced are liquefied petroleum gas, used for cooking and transportation, naphtha for upgrading to gasoline as well as feedstock for the petrochemical industries, jet fuel for aviation use, kerosene for heating, cooking and lighting, diesel for industries and transportation, fuel oil for ship's use and for power generation, bitumen for making roads, sulphur for industrial use, propylene for petrochemical use, and last but not least, lube oil base stock for making lubricating oil for automotive, ship and industrial use.

During 1996–99, there was a surplus in refining capacity around the region and Singapore's refineries were running at 60 per cent operating capacity. The situation changed dramatically in 2003 due to the surge in demand of petroleum products by China and currently, there is a shortage in refining capacity, thus most refineries are running practically at full capacity.

Recently, Concorde Energy announced that they will put up a condensate splitter, of 75,000 bbl per day, which will probably be operational by 2009. This will bring up Singapore's refining capacity to 1.4 million barrels per stream day.

Due to Singapore's strategic position, straddled between East and West Asia, its refineries have always been in position of a swing refinery, that is, catering both to scheduled and unscheduled shutdowns of refineries in the region and to abnormal swing in demand due to weather or other calamities.

Crude Import (Appendix 7.2)

Since Singapore's refineries were mostly designed and built in the early seventies, before the first energy crisis, it is not surprising that all of them were designed to run Middle-Eastern crude. Thus, in most years the composition of the crude imported from the Middle-Eastern countries exceed 80 per cent of the total crude import.

Today, the Middle East seems to be a vulnerable area. Thus, any major mishap in that region would be a serious blow to Singapore's oil industry. Of course it can run other crude, but this cannot be done without sacrificing efficiency, although in a true emergency situation, Singapore's needs are only a minute of what its refineries have to produce (see Appendix 7.3).

Although Singapore has crude oil practically at its doorstep, that is, Malaysia, Brunei, Vietnam and Indonesia, most of these crude are sweet, that is, low sulphur and which fetch higher prices in Japan where the environmental needs are greater. Besides, some of the crude are too waxy, such as, Minas from Indonesia and Bach Ho from Vietnam, as our refineries are not geared to store waxy crude.

If an emergency arises, Singapore will have to rely on its ASEAN neighbours to supply the necessary crude under the ASEAN Petroleum Security Agreement. However, its track record shows that due to the economics of refining ASEAN crude, it is not a regular off-taker of ASEAN crude. This may not augur well when an emergency arises.

Product Import

Singapore's strategic position between East and West Asia augurs well in the distribution of oil products. As most of the surplus oil is in the Middle East and most consuming countries are in the Far East and the Pacific Islands, it is convenient for Singapore to import the products, store, blend, and break them into smaller parcels before shipping to the consuming countries.

It would be worthwhile to note that, in view of Singapore's deep harbour facilities, it is capable of taking big cargo lots of 80,000 metric tonnes to Very Large Crude Carrier (VLCC) size of 250,000 metric tonnes, whereas the other receiving countries can only take cargoes in the range of 20,000–50,000 metric tonnes. Due to the high cost of oil nowadays, Singapore is probably in a better position to finance the large cargoes than the consuming countries, for example, with the high cost of oil, an 80,000 metric tonne will cost US$21 million, and not many companies, beside the majors, can afford to open a letter of credit of that size.

Lately, a new role for Singapore has emerged, whereby it takes gasoline from China, Taiwan and Thailand, stores and upgrades them for redistribution to Vietnam, Indonesia and Australia. To a certain extent, it also takes diesel from Kuwait, South Korea, Thailand and Taiwan for redistribution and blending to meet the specifications of Australia and the other ASEAN countries.

However, Singapore's main import has been fuel oil. As it is the biggest bunkering port in the world, it needs up to 25 million tonnes of fuel oil to supply the bunker needs. All its refineries are very sophisticated, as most of the fuel oil is upgraded to lighter and higher value products. Thus, it is always short of fuel oil, and has to import a large amount to satisfy the bunker demand. Nevertheless, it is still exporting large amounts of fuel oil to Australia, China, Indonesia, Malaysia and Vietnam.

In order to cater to the massive amount of bunker to be delivered to ships, that is, an average of 70,000 metric tonnes a day, Singapore has a huge fleet of over 100 bunkering barges ranging from 1,000–6,000 metric tonnes. To load these barges, Singapore has at least forty jetties that can load the barges up to 1,000 metric tonnes per hour.

Thus it will not be easy to displace Singapore as one of the world's top bunkering ports as the infrastructures needed will take years to build up. Besides, there are first rate back-up facilities like the financial services and laboratory testing services.

Product Export

Singapore's oil export data show that ASEAN countries are its main off-takers, in particular Malaysia and Vietnam. The Indian sub-continent used to be a big outlet, but this role has been taken over by the massive Indian refinery expansion. Singapore is a big exporter to China especially in jet fuel and fuel oil.

One of its export areas often overlooked is the Pacific Islands. These islands have great potential to expand especially since they have the raw materials which China requires. Currently Singapore's advantage is due to its logistics position whereby it has a constant fleet of tankers on call at any time.

Product Storage (Appendix 7.4)

Singapore currently has 3.6 million cubic metres of oil storage outside of the refineries. By 2008, there will be an addition of 4.1 million cubic metres, which are under construction or in the final stage of planning.

The question remains whether, by 2008, with the doubling of oil storage capacity, there will be a surplus of oil storage capacity. Of course, if you require storage today, you will face a "No Vacancy" sign. This was the result of the past few years where oil prices were in contango all the time, that is, the prices increase in future months as reflected in the paper futures.

Thus, unless the contango can be maintained in 2008, then the "No Vacancy" is still relevant. However, the fear is that between now and the year 2008, oil price may shoot into the $100/bbl range. By then, if the contango persists, it may ruin the economies of many developing countries.

Sometime ago, the government announced the commencement of the construction of Phase One of the underground caverns for the storage of oil.

The total project is understood to be 25 million barrels or 4 million cubic metres. Each phase will probably be around 1 million cubic metres.

The cavern will most likely be used for crude oil storage rather than for oil product storage for the following reasons:

1. Measurement of quantity may not be the most ideal.
2. Quality control will be a problem unless there is an efficient way to drain out water. Furthermore, the more volatile products may dissolve the minerals in the rock.
3. The storage capacity may be too large. Ideally, most oil products are stored in tanks between 20,000 to 40,000 cubic metres due to grade and product differentiation which require segregation. Each cavern may be as large as 100,000 cubic metres, which is definitely not ideal for product storage.

Thus the cavern is likely to be used to store Middle East crude, in case of any mishap in the Arabian Gulf.

Currently the Middle East is also supplying the bulk of crude to Japan, China, South Korea and Taiwan. In fact the Saudis are a shareholder of refineries in South Korea and the Philippines, and are therefore totally committed to supply crude to these two refineries come what may.

Should there be a mishap in the Middle East, Singapore would be the most ideal location for crude to be stored and used in the emergency until the situation eases.

Strategic Storage

The point to note here is whether there will be a partial or a total disruption of oil supply. The probability of a total disruption is very low; the most probable case will be partial disruptions which may not affect Singapore greatly as all major oil companies, with worldwide resources, have their presence here.

The other scenario is whether Singapore's port will remain fully open, partially open or totally shut off from the rest of the world. In the first two scenarios, Singapore will have no problem. In the third scenario, its domestic requirement is very small, that is, 70,000 barrels per day, and it can easily last one whole year, from the total oil stored in Singapore.

In fact Singapore's natural gas supply via submarine pipelines is its safest source of energy supply. Barring other problems, the gas should be flowing smoothly in any form of emergency, barring any dispute with its neighbours.

Outlook for Singapore

1. It may not be easy, but an attempt should be made to reduce the Middle East portion of Singapore's crude import. Since all its refineries are owned by commercial companies, economics is the final determining factor.
2. Vietnam has indicated that it would like to build one, if not two, new refineries. So far site preparation has been done, and it is understood that construction will start soon to complete the refinery by 2009. By then Singapore's 3.5 million tonnes of crude which Vietnam sends here will be consumed domestically; so will 4.9 million tonnes of product exports that Singapore exports to Vietnam will be wiped off our slate.
3. The easing of China cross-straits flow. If this happens, then the excess Taiwan refinery products can proceed directly to China without going through a third country. This may have a tremendous effect on Singapore's export of diesel, jet fuel and fuel oil to China.
4. Currently, India has a refining capacity of 3 million barrels per day. It has plans to double this capacity, which may happen as early as 2008. When that happens, India will probably take away most of Singapore's oil exports to Indonesia. It can access most Indonesian ports without having to transgress through the crowded Straits of Malacca.
5. The most unheralded news from China is their refinery expansion. What the media laments most is that China's economy is growing by 9 per cent each year and that they need plenty of oil to keep pace with the economical growth. What the outside world is unaware of is that the Chinese oil companies are building and upgrading their refineries. Why this news is not reaching the media is that no foreign company is involved in these projects. What will happen is that in a couple of years' time, China may be self-sufficient in oil product and leave the world with surplus refining capacity like what happened in 1996 to 1999. The moral of the story is that China needs crude oil and not finished oil product.

Singapore's Strategy

1. Currently Singapore still has a logistics advantage, that is, it has an efficient port and many tankers of suitable capacity and is strategically placed to ship cargoes both east and west of Singapore, at short notice.
2. It also has the financial structure so that break bulk activities can be carried out here, that is, it can finance the large cargoes which some of the off-takers may have problem financing. Its financial strength can go

a long way also to finance any infrastructure construction in relation to the petroleum industry.

3. However, it has to be aware of its costs. Singapore's neighbours, though not as efficient, may have a cost advantage over it.
4. Singapore is also a centre for anti-pollution activity. Should there be sea pollution whether by a tanker, a refinery or a production platform, the team here can be on-site in a matter of hours as they have planes, helicopters and all the cleaning equipment and materials in stock.
5. Singapore is also an engineering hub, whereby most of the world's offshore platforms are built here. Its engineering companies which specializes in petroleum and chemical industries have many years of experience and are well equipped to deal with problems within the Asian countries. In fact it should tap on both the resources from India, especially its IT industry, and from China, the manpower in order to establish the country as a centre for research for petroleum technology and engineering.
6. Singapore can be a hub for natural gas, whereby those countries who are rich in natural gas, for example, Malaysia and Indonesia, can pipe their gas to Singapore. It can in turn supply the gas to Thailand and the Philippines. To meet any shortfall or any disruption, Singapore can embark on a LNG Terminal which the government is seriously looking into now.
7. Singapore should form an Asian petroleum engineering and technology centre whereby it can marshal all the experts from India, South Korea, Japan and China to come together. In terms of some of the technology, these four countries are far more advanced than Europe and/or the United States.

APPENDIX 7.1

Singapore Refineries

Company	Location	Capacity
Shell	Pulau Bukom	436,000
Shell	Condensate Splitter	70,000
ExxonMobil	Pulau Ayer Chawan	280,000
ExxonMobil	Jurong	300,000
SRC (SPC & Chevron)	Pulau Merlimau	285,000
Total		1,371,000
Concord (2009) Condensate Splitter		75,000

Figures are in bbl per stream day.

Source: From industry sources.

APPENDIX 7.2

Singapore Crude Import, 1999–2005

1999–2005 COUNTRIES	1999	2000	2001	2002	Crude 2003	Condensate 2003	Crude 2004	Condensate 2004	Crude 2005	Condensate 2005
Angola/Algeria		0	0	330	0	0	82	0	151	0
Australia	889	3,058	4,088	3,746	848	2,812	606	1,607	1,015	1,424
Brunei	389	563	119	168	0	35	0	0	40	0
China/Korea	0	515	144	220	120	0	0	289	105	131
Ecudor/USA	0	0	130	0	11	0	0	0	0	0
Egypt	801	534	0	0	150	0	567	0	0	0
Gabon/Cameron	0	0	353	136	0	151	0	0	89	
Indonesia	0	0	0	0	0	0	0	0	355	357
Iran	1,111	1,491	352	1,169	741	578	1,076	581	442	8,86
Kuwait	4,972	4,572	5,833	4,909	5,433	0	6,291	116	7,528	0
Malaysia	701	722	307	130	386	171	854	386	1,470	404
Oman	1,064	465	3,048	2,264	169	435	86	537	130	471
Philippines	0	0	0	439	69	431	49	76	36	329
Qatar	5,075	5,383	3,565	5,518	4,739	1,434	6,209	921	6,111	1,574
Saudi Arabia	17,921	13,086	14,544	12,067	6,944	3,593	8522	3,746	10,938	8,696
UAE	4,904	3,997	3,698	4,345	4,039	149	3,716	799	2,816	6
UK/USA	254	404	0	105	0	0	252	0	0	652
Venezuala	0	0	0	0	0	0	0	0	121	0
Vietnam	1,845	2,414	3,116	3,583	1,052	2,198	917	2506	940	2,592
Yemen	1,870	711	1,407	792	425	0	962	0	75	0
O.C Africa	788	124	130	122	0	0	261	0	0	0
O.C. Europe	364	132	0	51	126	0	0	0	0	0
O.C.Asia	1,203	2,703	320	346	170	33	759	1,262	3,154	1,751
Total	44,279	40,874	40,801	40,657	25,558	11,869	31,360	12,826	35,427	19,362
					Total	37,427		44,186		54,789
ME	85%	74%	80%	76%	84%	69%	84%	52%	79%	60%
Others	15%	26%	20%	24%	16%	31%	16%	48%	21%	40%

Figures are in '000 mt

Source: Department of Statistics, Singapore.

APPENDIX 7.3

Singapore Oil Product Balance
(Based on 1,230 mbcd refinery run)

2005	Mogas	Naphtha	Kero	Diesel	Fuel Oil
Production	192*	192*	233*	320*	240*
Import	168	92	54	81	544
Blending	0	0	0	0	20*
Sub-total	360	284	287	401	804
Export	330	57	174	291	293
Blending	0	0	0	20*	0
Aviation	0	0	80	0	0
Bunker	0	0	0	45	407
Power Plants	0	0	0	0	18
Inland/Gas Stn.	17*	0	0	31*	0
Feedstock	13†	227†	0	0	95†
Sub-total	360	284	254	387	804

Figures are in '000 bbl per calendar day.

*Estimates
†Balancing

Source: From industry sources.

APPENDIX 7.4

Singapore Oil Storage (Additional)

Company	Location	Capacity
Vopak	Banyan	340
OilTanking	Seraya	240
Horizon	Jurong Island	850
Hin Leong	Jurong Island	2,300
Chemoil	Jurong Island	400
Total (Additional)		4,130
Total (Current)		3,556
Grand Total (2008)		7,686

(Figures are in '000 cu. metre.)

Source: From industry sources.

8

Bay of Bengal: Awakening of a Potential Giant Area

P. K. Singh

INTRODUCTION

For the last few years the Bay of Bengal region has come under focus for reasons of energy, trading, security and regional cooperation in general among the countries around the rim of the Bay.

The conference on the subject of "Energy in Bay of Bengal Region" held at the Institute of Southeast Asian Studies on 28–29 September 2006 was therefore an important milestone in that direction which needs to be carried forward.

This issue is addressed in its global perspective since there are many issues that link and affect the various countries of the region in multiple ways. Therefore any discussion on energy must be viewed as part of the overall picture.

The Bay of Bengal region comprises an area of more than 2.2 million square kilometres and 3.0 million, if we add the Andaman Sea and the Malacca Straits. It borders Sri Lanka, India, Bangladesh, Myanmar, Thailand, Malaysia, Singapore and Indonesia. In addition, if we were to also include the land-locked Bhutan and Nepal for whom the nearest sea exit is the Bay of Bengal, then the area and the issues involved become even more important.

Common Heritage

The area has historically been bound together for thousands of years for various reasons given the physical proximity in the first instance. It is a little known fact that Pu Breush Island in Sumatra is only 90 nautical miles or 170 kilometres or Phuket, Thailand is only 275 nautical miles both from Indira Point in Andamans and Nicobars, India. India alone shares maritime boundaries with Sri Lanka, Bangladesh, Myanmar, Thailand and Indonesia.

Not so long ago, Sanskrit was the common and dominant language in the region and the Hindu thought and later Buddhist philosophy created a common cultural thread among all the countries. Indeed, even the spread of Islam in certain countries of the area was from India. Extensive and well established trade between the countries of the region is well documented. Travelling across all these countries, from India to Indonesia, a common heritage is clearly inbuilt even though today each country has its own interests and agenda.

Given these historical ties, the question therefore arises where the region is today.

The Bay of Bengal Countries Today

Taken together these eight countries have a combined population of 1,650 million, that is, nearly 27 per cent of the world's total, occupying a land area of more than 7 million square kilometres and a coast line stretching to 8,300 kilometres.

At economics level, these countries have a combined gross domestic product (GDP) of above US$1,500 billion, producing 3 million barrels of oil per day and consuming nearly 6 million per day.

However the per capita levels are highly diverse — with Singapore leading the pack at a developed country level and Bhutan being at the level of the least developed economy while Malaysia remains a middle level economy. Indonesia, a member of the Organization of Petroleum Exporting Countries (OPEC), exports oil but is a net oil importer, and also a totally oil dependent country like Nepal.

Yet, unlike the trade that existed between the countries once upon a time, the current status presents a dismal picture. Except for the intra-ASEAN cooperation and exports to Europe or other developed countries, trade and cooperation within these countries themselves remains far below the potential. The list below shows each country's trading partners ranked in order of decreasing trade volume:

- Sri Lanka: U.S., U.K., India, China, Singapore, Iran, Continental Europe (C.E.)
- India: U.S., China, Middle East, U.K., C.E.
- Bangladesh: U.S., India, U.K., China, Middle and Far East
- Myanmar: China, ASEAN, India, Japan
- Thailand: U.S., Japan, China, ASEAN
- Malaysia: U.S., China, ASEAN, South Korea
- Singapore: Malaysia, U.S., China, Japan, South Korea
- Indonesia: Japan, China, U.S., ASEAN

A detailed analysis of the nature of commodities and services traded above may reveal or justify the nature of the current trading volumes but in the historical context of extensive trade that flourished once upon a time between these countries, it can safely be concluded that there does remain a great potential for significant growth of the inter-regional trade. In other words, the BOB countries have been trading with the developed economies of either the West or the East but not so much with each other. The time has now come to change direction. Let us now look at what are the potential areas.

Trade and Cooperation Potential

There exists an entire gamut of areas where the BOB countries can interact with each other without compromising on their political leanings, system of governance or cultural affinities. Some of the most important fields of cooperation are:

1. Oil
2. Gas
3. Energy and CO_2 Emissions
4. Maritime Security and Terrorism
5. Infrastructure
6. Tourism
7. Higher Education
8. Research, particularly in cutting edge technological fields like biotech

Each of these shall be examined in some detail below.

Oil

As we have seen above, the whole region remains globally energy deficient. To compound the situation, the rapidly developing economies of India and

China are creating an ever increasing demand which the region cannot match based upon the currently known reserves.

Taking India as an example, its most productive Bombay High oil fields located offshore have already peaked while the domestic consumption, and consequently the imports from outside, continue to rise. At the current rate of production of about 84,000 barrels per day, that is, about 42 million tonnes per year, and the increasing consumption, the known reserves may last only for another twenty to thirty years. India's oil import dependency in 2005 was 75 per cent. Based on International Energy Agency (IEA) estimates, India will be required to import up to 86 per cent of its requirement.

Similar energy deficiency is pushing China (and India as well) to tie up long-term energy contracts with countries in Latin America, Africa and Middle East.

However, this very situation creates space for regional cooperation which has started happening though on a modest scale. The Sri Lankan government has permitted India and China to explore oil and gas off its coast. There is good news in the form of International Seabed Authority's studies which estimate that India's extended continental shelf alone may hold up to 2 billion barrels of oil and up to 4 billion bbl of gas hydrate. The eventual estimate for the extended continental shelf of all the Bay of Bengal countries therefore holds great promise towards more energy finds.

Yet, paradoxically the overlapping offshore territorial claims between India, Bangladesh and Myanmar are slowing down joint exploration efforts. It is clear that it will take time to develop a joint effort mentality but the oil industry remains a major field of cooperation among the Bay of Bengal countries.

Gas

While oil prospects and cooperation has started moving in the right direction, the gas energy situation has remained mired in inter-regional rivalry and distrust.

Myanmar has proven reserves of about 300 billion cubic metres (bcm) while Bangladesh, based on the latest Shell estimates, is sitting on 1,000 bcm. The annual consumption in Bangladesh is 12 mcm with no export at all. Major gas finds on the coasts of eastern India and Myanmar indicate the possibility of more gas finds in the region.

In contrast, Indian gas reserves are currently pegged at 700 bcm with annual production at 25 bcm and growing at 7.3 per cent annually. IEA expects Indian gas demand to reach 54 bcm by 2010, that is, practically tomorrow.

There have been some discussions about the possibility of liquified natural gas (LNG) imports from Indonesia to India but so far nothing concrete has been achieved.

It can thus be seen that between the surpluses available in Myanmar and Bangladesh and the huge demand in India, there should be a mutual "fit". Unfortunately for a basket of political and other reasons, the level of cooperation, and consequently the full exploitation of the resources, remains inadequate. The most recent example is that of the gas pipeline that was proposed between India and Myanmar about which discussions on the price of gas, etc., are still reportedly on.

Energy and CO_2 Emissions

The rapid industrialization dependent as it is on higher fossil fuel consumption has inevitably led to high CO_2 emissions and global warming. Based on published statistics, Indian CO_2 emissions in 1997 were 880 tonnes, equal to Germany's emissions and somewhat lower than that of Japan at 1,085 tonnes.

IEA estimates that by 2020, Indian CO_2 emissions will touch 2,170 tonnes which will be twice of Japan's emission in 1997. China is already much higher. It is clear that we have not yet seen the end of these CO_2 emissions which affect the entire region and will call for drastic measures that can be effective only if taken collectively. In other words:

- Asia, of which the Bay of Bengal countries are an important part, remains a very high net importer of energy with very low per capita energy consumption.
- The same region is already one of the highest CO_2 emission areas in the world.
- Taken at a per capita level and given the population density, the CO_2 emissions are the lowest in the world.

The conclusion is obvious. With the continued economic and industrial growth, the ever increasing energy demand will lead to a huge surge in CO_2 emissions that the region can ignore only at its peril. Thus a joint effort to reduce these emissions and work together for the development of the related policies and technologies is a big challenge for the region.

Maritime Security and Terrorism

The Bay of Bengal region is home to some of the busiest sea lanes with continuous movement of crude oil, petroleum products and minerals that are required to sustain the explosive economic growth in the region. The Middle

East crude bound for Japan and China, in particular, passes through Malacca Straits and any disruption in oil supplies can have a disastrous consequences for the economies not only of the above two countries but of the region as a whole, given the huge inter-linked business investments within various countries. Some of the terrorist websites unabashedly proclaim the disruption of oil supply chains as their premier goal.

While the Malacca Straits area has been always infected with piracy, the region has also seen some of the worst terrorist activities in the last few years.

Complicating the situation here are the long-standing political, border, insurgency and immigration issues between Sri Lanka, India, Bangladesh, Myanmar, Thailand, Malaysia, Singapore and Indonesia. It is not the intent of this chapter to go into the details or causes of these disputes but to highlight the delicate balance that currently prevails.

In this prevailing climate, maritime security assumes a major significance. Moreover, in view of the vast spread of the region, a sustained security mechanism mandates regional cooperation.

Here the tidings are positive. The various concerned governments are realizing the need to work together for mutual good. India with Sri Lanka and India with Singapore have already conducted joint naval exercises in the Bay of Bengal area. For border insurgency issues, India and Myanmar are coordinating their army actions. In addition, India, Thailand, Malaysia and Indonesia are going to regularly patrol the Malacca Straits area. It is conceivable that in near future, the navies of all the Bay of Bengal countries may pool their physical and intelligence resources together to safeguard the whole of the Bay of Bengal region.

The need for this inter-regional cooperation was dramatically highlighted during the post-tsunami relief work. When U.S. troops reached Indonesian waters, they found that the Indian Navy from nearby Andaman's base had already reached the affected area and prepared a "beach-head" for the relief operations by all the agencies. This single event demonstrated not only to the Bay of Bengal countries but to the international community at large that the Bay of Bengal region can indeed become a viable and cohesive area of cooperation.

Infrastructure

Infrastructure levels in the region vary greatly. Singapore, closely followed by Malaysia, can rightfully boast of world-class roads, seaports, power plants and telecommunication network.

On the other hand, there are vast areas of Myanmar or Bangladesh which are remote. In India, roads have been a nightmare, seaports congested, and power supply highly erratic.

For all the four issues though, there is a huge scope for mutual cooperation and development and some beginnings have been made.

For road networks, Malaysian engineering and construction companies are branching out to India and other countries. There are concrete plans to build roads connecting Assam in India to Bangkok running through Myanmar.

With the start of India-ASEAN car rally terminating in Indonesia, the region has seen that a wide road network is not only feasible but essential to promote cross-border trade and movement of people by surface transport. It is indeed strange that despite the whole region being connected through a contiguous land mass, it is only recently that the awareness of the need for a road network has arisen.

In seaport management, Singapore has long acquired significant expertise that can be shared with others. The same applies for airport management, where Singapore Airlines proposed cooperation to build a new airport at Bangalore, India remained on the table for a number of years.

For telecommunication as well, Malaysian and Singaporean companies are reaching out to other countries, particularly to Thailand and India where a virtual explosion seems to be taking place for mobile telephony, adding nearly five million subscribers every month.

This South-South cooperation will be vital for developing similar facilities in Bangladesh, Myanmar, Thailand, Nepal or Bhutan.

It is also a known fact that the potential for electricity generation has not yet been fully explored and technically, it is certainly feasible to dream of a regionwide electricity grid to ensure that no area remains in power deficit.

Yet all the infrastructural requirements remain closely inter-linked and will have to be taken up as an integrated campaign.

Tourism

There is another area of huge cooperation potential which is only now beginning to be recognized. The region boasts of nearly every facet of what a tourist could be looking for.

From the lush rainforests of Indonesia and Malaysia, Asian lion and tiger population in India, soaring temples of Angkor, Borobudur and South India, Buddhist centres in Thailand, Sri Lanka, Myanmar and India, fun cities of Bangkok and Phuket, snow-capped Himalayan peaks, golden sand dunes of Rajasthan, ancient and historical monuments, the likes of Taj Mahal, spread all over, medical tourism centres growing rapidly in Singapore, Bangkok, Kuala Lumpur, Delhi and Mumbai, it is clear that the region has everything going for it.

One single statistic proves the potential: While France gets 75 million tourists; India's domestic tourists are now nearing 275 million; many of them with enough spending power to entice Thailand and Malaysia to start issuing "visa upon arrival" scheme.

This once again brings us back to the need of developing road and rail routes and augmenting the air links to encourage movement of people within the region to boost the economies and release the huge "energy" that has remained dormant so far.

Higher Education

Historically the affluent and the powerful from the region have sent their children to the West for higher studies. Many of the region's elite have received their degrees from institutions like Oxford, Cambridge, Harvard, MIT and the likes.

Yet it is a little publicized fact in the Bay of Bengal countries that within their own region, there are many institutions of higher learning that are world class and can be taken advantage of.

Particularly in the field of engineering and Management, names like Indian Institutes of Technology (IITs) and Indian Institutes of Management (IIMs) have become happy recruiting grounds for U.S. industry. Similarly, Singapore now boasts of some world-class institutions that have academic tie-ups with leading European institutes and offer either twinning programmes or have joint campuses.

The same success story is repeated for information and telecommunication technology courses and biotech research facilities in India and Singapore.

Some student movement towards these regional institutions has indeed started but to overcome the mindset will still take some time. This effort needs further encouragement.

First Concrete Steps towards Fuller Integration

The need for closer economic and security cooperation has been becoming clearer for some time now and this has started taking institutional shape in the form of various multilateral forums coming into existence, the more notable ones being:

1. Multilateral cooperation agreements between Myanmar, Bangladesh and India for oil and gas.
2. ASEAN + India to create a Free Trade Area (FTA) progressively by 2016.

3. Gradual consolidation of BIMST (Bangladesh, India, Myanmar, Sri Lanka, Thailand) and now including Nepal and Bhutan which commits to the FTA by 2017.
4. MOU for marine and fisheries between India and Indonesia

The collective will and efforts to tap the enormous energy of the region may be expected to accelerate in the not too distant future. However, all these initiatives will need a strong political will and sustained political stability to turn them into reality.

9

Energy Transportation Security in the Bay of Bengal

Vijay Sakhuja

> "One of the main causes for our enemies' gaining hegemony over our country is their stealing our oil; therefore, you should make every effort in your power to stop the greatest theft in history of the natural resources of both present and future generations, which is being carried out through collaboration between foreigners and [native] agents .... Focus your operations on it [oil production], especially in Iraq and the Gulf area, since this [lack of oil] will cause them to die off [on their own]."
>
> Osama bin Laden
> Audiotape December 2004[1]

> "Our brothers in the battlefields to direct some of their great efforts towards the oil wells and the pipelines."
>
> On an Islamist website, translated by the IAGS[2]

Post 9/11, the traditional concept of safety of maritime transportation system has changed. The threats at sea arising from terrorism and piracy have assumed significance in view of the determined bids by *Jihadi* terrorists to engage both military and civil targets by using suicide terrorist tactics. In terms of maritime security, attacks on *U.S.S. Cole* and French tanker *M.V. Limburg* have exposed the vulnerability of both warships and merchant shipping. Importantly, the latter attack has highlighted the possibility of terrorists engaging in such attacks to create a long-term slowdown of maritime commerce leading to economic disasters.

There are fears that an LNG (liquefied natural gas) tanker exploding in a seaport could be as devastating as the 9/11 attack in the United States. A VLCC (Very Large Crude Carrier) or a LNG tanker could be rammed into a major port or a large bomb could be set off by a suicide bomber or via remote control on board a large cruise ship. Terrorism experts believe that terrorist groups are obtaining specific maritime skills, thereby increasing their capability of launching more complex operations. Such fears about the attacks have forced the states to initiate several initiatives to provide greater protection to maritime infrastructure and maritime supply chains.

Energy infrastructure is an attractive target that can be devastated or destroyed with relative ease. In recent years, terrorist groups, armed militants, insurgents and mafia have targeted oil and gas wells, pipelines, refineries and oil and gas tankers, thereby highlighting the fact that energy-related infrastructure remains poorly protected against potential attacks and is highly vulnerable. Also, production and transportation of oil and gas are being interrupted by accidents and weather-related events throughout the world. Unfortunately, disruption of energy supply chains is becoming more frequent, more severe and more complex.

Significantly, energy infrastructure is a "soft" target and therefore relatively easy to hit. Notwithstanding exhaustive counter-terror mechanisms having been introduced and operationalized, attacks on energy infrastructure appear to be becoming more frequent thus exposing chinks in the armour of energy transportation security systems. Given the international geo-political situation, current energy infrastructure weaknesses and the rise of non-state actors like the Al Qaeda, long-duration disruptions should be expected, together with extremely large increases in oil and gas prices.

This chapter attempts to highlight the vulnerability of energy-related infrastructure in the Bay of Bengal. It begins by examining the concept of energy supply chains and underlines the economic impact of disruptions and its immediate global consequences. It then superimposes these vulnerabilities in the context of sea spaces in the Bay of Bengal and identifies the likely nature of threat in the region.

Energy Supply Chains and Security Dynamics

An "energy supply chain" is a process under which oil, gas and petroleum products are transported from the point of origin, that is, oil wells through refineries, to final destination, that is, consumers, and includes the movement of the these goods on board carriers on road, on the rail, and over the seas including pipelines. The process also involves transfer of shipping data both written and electronic and the associated processes, thus creating a dynamic link between the different participants. These participants include several entities, such as oil wells and related exploration facilities, energy logistics management firms, consolidators, truckers, rail and road carriers, port terminal operators, ocean carriers, customs agents, financial and information services, and final recipient of goods. It is evident that energy supply chains are dynamic in nature.

There is clearly a strong relationship between an efficient energy supply chain and security which is based on safe and secure route of transport over land, through pipelines, waterways and seas. A significant downstream consequence of a terrorist attack on the energy transportation system along a sea lane or pipeline network would most definitely entail disruption of the supply chain resulting in a range of impacts on the global economy, business continuity and economic loss. It would also have a significant impact on the competitiveness in the region, with expected losses to local and regional economies. A safe energy supply chain system is therefore critical to domestic and international business.

A modern energy supply chain involves a complex network of systems. The interactive complexity of these systems is critical to supply chains in the sense that the potential for incidents or inefficiencies in these systems, individually or collectively, exists because of vulnerabilities inherent in the design and operation and in their interaction with supply chains. There are at least seven systems that merit attention:[3] (a) gas and oil wells; (b) pipelines and pumping stations; (c) refineries and tank farms; (d) loading terminals and ports; (e) transportation systems; (f) IT-related data exchange; and (g) carriers both on land and at sea.

Gas and Oil Wells and Offshore Platforms

Onshore oil and natural gas is produced at over a million sites across the world, and most of these are located in rural areas, accessible only through long and often vulnerable road systems. There are very few cities that have oil and gas production facilities within the city limits and can be considered relatively safe since these employ more security measures than typical exploration and production facilities. While most of these sites have a tank for storage of the oil, the volume of oil stored onsite is limited. Like the onshore platforms, offshore platforms are also vulnerable to sabotage and have relatively less security systems to maintain the flow of oil or gas in case of any unusual event of disruption.

Pipeline and Pumping Station

Oil pipelines, both crude oil and refined petroleum products, are the most significant mode of petroleum transportation the world over. Pipelines play a key role in moving oil from producing areas and seaports to refineries and from refineries and large redistribution centres to smaller regional supply centres. Logistics hubs provide for the inter-connections of major pipeline systems. Nearly 40 per cent of energy resources are transported through pipelines and concentrations of pipeline assets vary based on whether the regions of the country are net producing regions or net consuming regions. These are generally built above ground, making them common targets for terrorists and insurgents. There are several instances when insurgents, militants and terrorists particularly in Iraq, Chechnya, Turkey, Nigeria, Colombia, Pakistan, India, and elsewhere, have attacked pipelines, costing local governments billions of dollars. In Iraq, pipeline attacks have been pervasive. It is estimated that pipeline sabotage has cost Iraq more than US$10 billion in oil revenues, despite the high priority coalition forces have put on pipeline protection.[4] There is concern that the insurgents are attacking Iraqi pipelines on a regular basis and they have gained a measure of expertise, which can be emulated elsewhere.[5]

Refineries and Tank Farm

Most refineries are located on coasts, primarily because of access to major sea transportation and shipping routes. The refineries process crude oil into a variety of petroleum products such as gasoline, heating oil, jet fuel, etc. Being large and complex, these are spread over large areas and their security is a major challenge. For instance, suicide bombers tried to storm the world's biggest oil processing plant in Saudi Arabia. Using two cars carrying explosives, they rammed into the outer gates of the heavily fortified complex of the Abqaiq facility resulting in an international oil price jump by US$2 a barrel.

Loading Terminals and Ports

Seaports are perhaps the most difficult security challenge that exists within an energy supply chain. The security of a port is the sum total of individual site security assessments. Consequence at one site in the port premises may multiply overall leading to consequences throughout the port. It may even damage the centre of gravity with a cascading effect beyond the gates of the port along the supply chain. Variations between facilities in a port require that individual facilities are assessed with a holistic perspective considering their part in an overall supply chain system as also in the context of the types of threats that are likely to be encountered within the system. Port security involves the entire port and that is a challenge of coordination. The concept of entire port planning and coordination may seem immense, but the entire marine community has to be involved to achieve success.

Transportation Systems

Nearly 60 per cent of the world's crude oil, its products and derivatives, petroleum gases and liquefied natural gas oil are transported through the maritime transportation network. This includes marine operations at terminals at the ship-to-shore interface. Tankers and barges carry crude oil and pipelines transport petroleum products like gasoline, diesel fuel and home heating oil from refineries to consumers. These systems too have their vulnerabilities and are often prone to attack by terrorists and pirates. Regulations to promote the safe, environmentally sound, secure, and efficient marine transportation of petroleum and petroleum products are essential for energy transportation security.

IT-related Data Exchange

The security of the information is crucial to efficient functioning of a port since operations at a seaport depend heavily on the integrity of the information infrastructure. A modern marine oil terminal operation is dependent upon a central computer database to track energy transactions such as loading/ discharge, pipeline operations, and clearing customs and tanker traffic. The information infrastructure is vulnerable to disruption and interruption caused by cyber attack. These attacks are aimed at obtaining intelligence, disruption, at times financial gain, or even collecting information on law enforcement agencies. Information warfare attack by the terrorist and criminal groups at seaports and harbour is a reality and several groups are building capability and expertise in order to disrupt the energy infrastructure.

Natural Disasters

Tsunamis, hurricanes and earthquakes can severely disrupt energy supply chains. These may occur anywhere in the world and, if sufficiently severe, will affect the energy situation in all countries. For instance, Hurricane Katrina damaged the shipping channel as well as much of the U.S. oil and gas production and transportation infrastructure.[6] Fortunately, the December 2004 Indian Ocean tsunami did not affect the Malacca Straits. Otherwise the entire Asia-Pacific region and the East Coast of the United States would have suffered greatly from an extreme fuel shortage. Even cold weather can lead to fuel supply disruptions on an international basis.[7]

Geo-politics

The commercial realities of energy transportation are often ignored or misunderstood in the face of more exciting geo-political aspects, but they are no less important to a complete understanding of the problem. Gaining control over energy transport routes and key communications has always been an issue of utmost importance to world powers. This control helps provide certain rewards in establishing domination in various parts of the world. In modern times, world powers especially seek control over transport and energy communications, connecting sources of energy resources and consumer countries.

The Persian Gulf is a reservoir of the world's largest oil reserves and is a major incentive for the extra regional powers to become involved in the region's security. The region continues to be a theatre of strategic interactions between major global, political and economic powers and the regional states. Importantly, the world's leading oil producing countries are either politically unstable and/or at serious odds with the Western powers. Most of these countries are members of the Organization of Petroleum Exporting Countries (OPEC) and the OPEC countries produce about 40 per cent of the world's oil; they hold 80 per cent of proven global reserves, and 85 per cent of these reserves are in the Middle East.[8]

Economic Impact from Disruption of Supply Chains

The world's reliance on gulf oil is irrevocable despite prospects of newer and attractive sources. And the bulk of this oil must transit through the Strait of Hormuz, Suez Canal, Malacca Straits and the sea lanes in the Indian Ocean. In the Indian Ocean region, economic and security interests impact in a concentrated form.

There are bound to be a range of economic costs resulting from disruption of energy supply chains. The eight-year Iran-Iraq war produced 543 attacks on ships with approximately 200 merchant sailors killed. More than 80 ships sank or were declared beyond repair leading to a monetary loss of more than US$2 billion in direct losses to cargo and hulls.[9] This caused worldwide insurance rates to increase by 200 per cent resulting in the hike of oil prices from US$13 to US$31 per barrel. The net loss to the world economy was estimated to be US$200 billion.[10]

A study for the period 1968–79, covering 200 countries, found that a doubling of the number of terrorist incidents would lead to decreased bilateral trade between targeted economies of some 6 per cent.[11] Similarly, *Fortune* magazine of 18 February 2002 noted that "the impact on US supply chains due to increased inventories, border closures, increased lead times and other changes and security measures resulting from the events of September 11, 2001 is estimated at US$150 billion a year".[12] Disruption at U.S. West Coast ports would result in a 0.4 per cent reduction of nominal GDP in a number of Asian economies and the impact on Hong Kong, Malaysia and Singapore was estimated to be as high as 1.1 per cent of nominal GDP.[13] It will be important to note that the 9/11 attacks against the World Trade Centre (WTC) resulted in US$19 billion in insured property losses and an estimated economic loss of up to US$90 billion in 2001.[14]

Insurance costs are a critical issue. For instance, the Lloyd's Market Association's Joint War Committee (JWC) has declared the Straits of Malacca and twenty other maritime areas in West Asia and Africa as highly prone to piracy, war, strikes, terrorism and related perils. The JWC decisions are the fallout of a report that warns of an Al Qaeda attack on a "significant maritime target", with fears that Al Qaeda could exploit piracy in the Malacca Straits to attack ships. It took Malaysia, Singapore and Indonesia two years to convince the JWC that the piracy attacks in the Malacca Strait had reduced drastically and it was unfair to declare the straits a zone of high risk to shipping. The JWC has now decided to delete the Malacca Straits from its list of twenty areas worldwide that it deemed as security threats to shipping.[15]

Similarly, insurance underwriters had declared Sri Lanka a war risk zone following the attack on Colombo International Airport in 2001, which led to the destruction of several commercial aircraft. Shipping companies had to pay extra for Sri Lankan imports and exports to cover vessel calls at Colombo.[16] After suffering for almost one year, the Sri Lankan government had to request global insurance giant Lloyds of London to engage in a security audit of Colombo, Galle and Trincomalee ports, and the Bandaranayake international airport.

Premiums were tripled for ships calling at ports in Yemen after the 2002 terrorist attack on the French oil tanker *Limburg* off the Yemeni coast. This forced many vessels to cancel Yemen from their schedules or divert to ports in neighbouring states.[17] For a typical supertanker carrying about two million barrels of oil, the rate rose to US$450,000 a trip from US$150,000, adding about US15 cents a barrel to the delivered cost of the oil — and that is just for the ship; the cargo is insured separately.[18]

More recently, war risk premiums for merchant ships visiting Israeli and Lebanon ports had been raised because of the conflict and naval blockade of Lebanese ports.[19] Both Lebanon and Israel were placed on the Lloyd's Market Joint War Committee list of risky areas for merchant shipping that were prone to war, strikes, terrorism and related perils. Meanwhile, several foreign multinational shipping companies including Italy's Mediterranean Shipping Company SA (MSC), COSCO Shipping Co. Ltd., China Shipping Group and Grimaldi Group had diverted their ships to the port of Ashdod or to nearby ports.[20]

Geo-strategic Significance of Bay of Bengal

The Bay of Bengal region is geo-strategically important to Bangladesh, Myanmar, Thailand, Malaysia, Singapore, Indonesia, Sri Lanka and India. It connects the vital sea route between the Indian Ocean and the Pacific Ocean. The Malacca Straits is witness to heavy maritime traffic, and on an average 200 ships transit every day through this strategic choke point. The marshalling point for the mercantile traffic entering or leaving the straits lies in the Bay of Bengal. Strategically, the Andaman and Nicobar Islands are located at the heart of the Bay of Bengal and are of considerable significance and relevance to India's security. The islands occupy a commanding position and lie astride the sea lanes of communication (SLOC) through the Malacca Straits and hold the key to the "Eastern Gate" to the Pacific.

The Bay of Bengal is also home to two emerging strategic waterways. The Sethusamudram Canal Project (SSCP) between southern India and Sri Lanka and the Isthmus of Kra in southern Thailand. These waterways have been dubbed as Asia's Panama Canal and debated by respective governments for quite some time.

The SSCP project, as and when it reaches fruition, will result in a canal that will reduce transit times by 36 hours for ships transiting from the Arabian Sea to the Bay of Bengal and vice versa. The coastal vessels will save over 400 nautical miles in terms of distance. At the same time, it will help minor ports along the passage to grow resulting in economic growth. Thirteen minor ports in Tamil Nadu will benefit from the project.[21] It will also help the Indian port of Tuticorin to emerge as a competitor to the Sri Lankan port of Colombo as a major transshipment hub, particularly container cargo.

From a geo-strategic perspective, the sea lane transiting through the Indian Ocean will pass through it. This will add to traffic density bringing

Figure 9.1
Geo-strategic Significance of Bay of Bengal

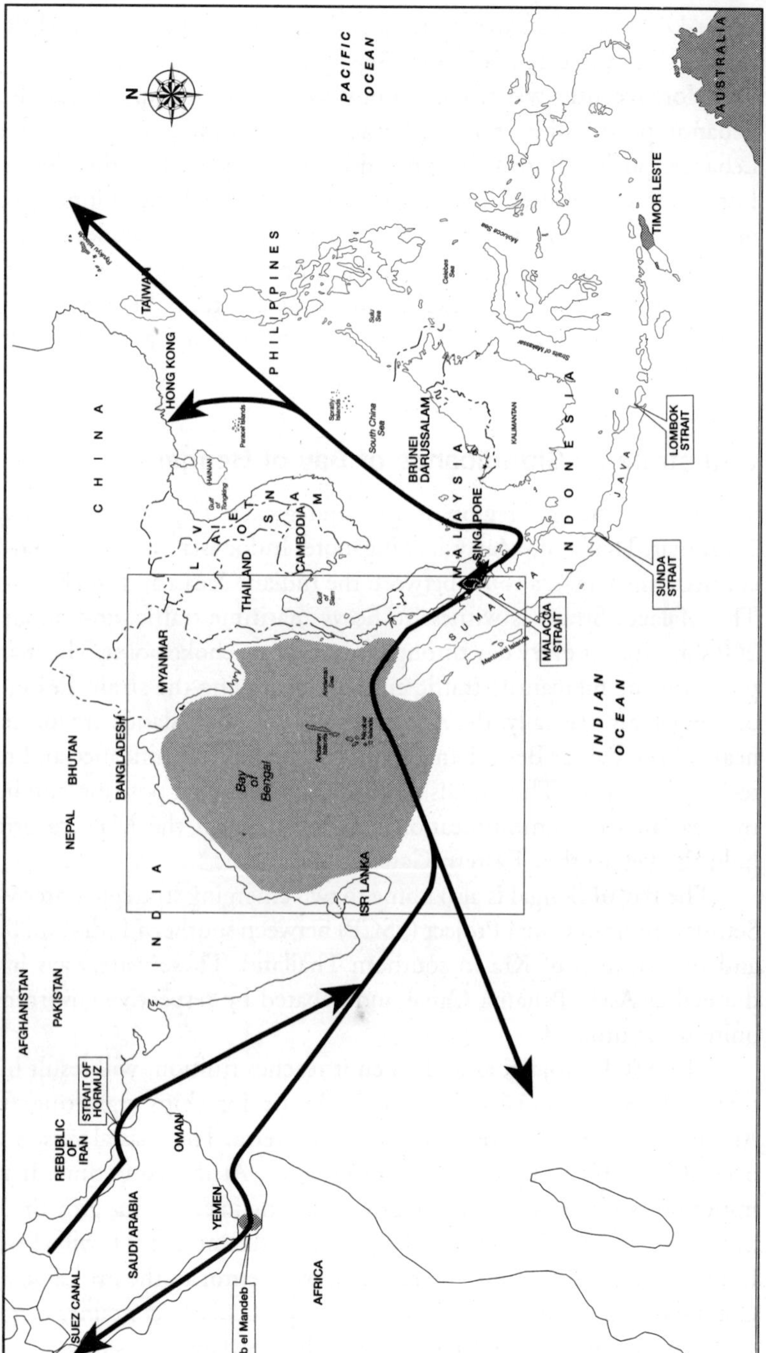

Figure 9.2
Sea Lanes in Bay of Bengal

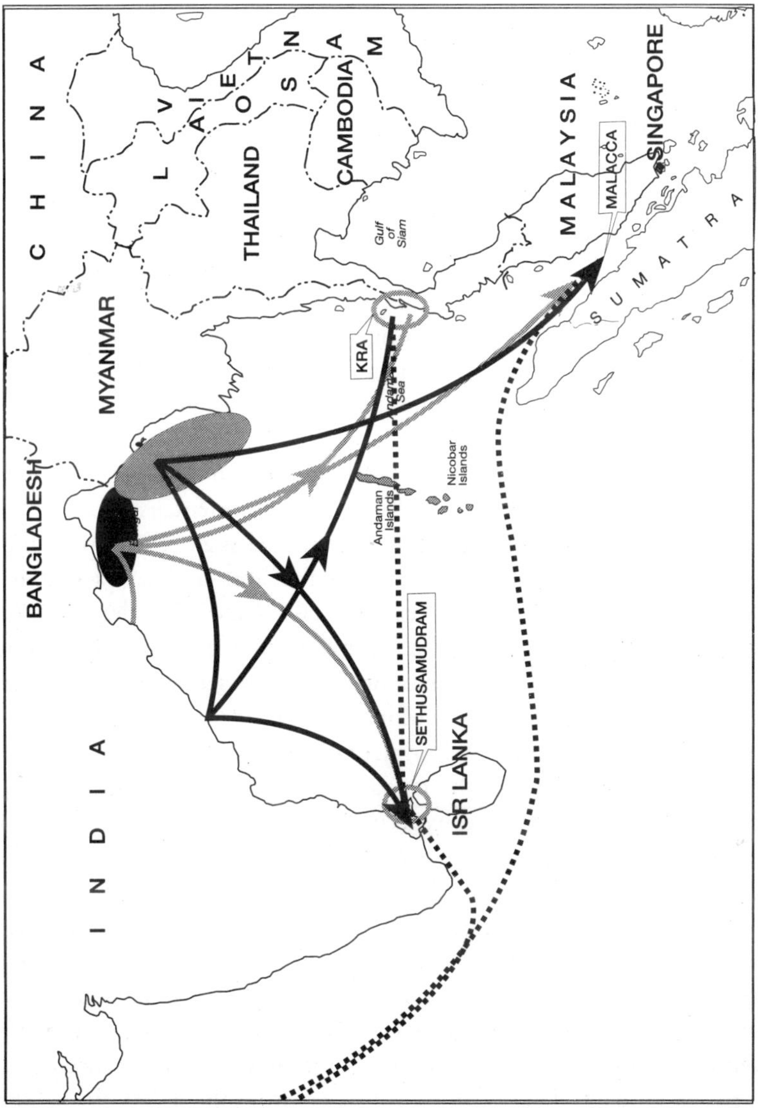

with it the attendant problems of shipping that can be much to the discomfort of both India and Sri Lanka. Given that market forces look at cost cutting by following the shortest route, and the density of traffic of smaller ships through Sethusamudram Canal, for the environmentalists, the threat of sea pollution will be important.

As far as the Isthmus of Kra is concerned, it is an ambitious plan to dig a canal across southern Thailand to link the Bay of Bengal to the Gulf of Thailand and provide a sea lane linking the Indian and Pacific Ocean trade routes.[22] The Kra Canal will reduce the time and cost of East-West shipping by bypassing the Straits of Malacca and Singapore, the world's busiest waterway. This project would drastically alter the maritime, trade and economic landscapes of the Bay of Bengal littorals and perhaps the Asia-Pacific region. Like the SSCP, the Kra Canal in Thailand has been a subject of intense debate and discussion. Discussions relating to environmental and economic benefits have surfaced — along with the adverse economic impact it will pose to Malacca Straits littorals. The canal will allow long-haul shipping to bypass the Straits of Malacca and cut their journey by at least 1,000 kilometres.

There are several economic benefits that can be derived by linking the SSCP and the Kra Canal, but for the environmentalists, the threat of sea pollution will be important. Then there is the issue of the impact of the canal on the fragile ecosystem built around the flora and fauna in the Gulf of Mannar, and the adjacent sea areas of the Kra Canal. The density of the traffic will also have an impact on the fishing grounds on either side of the canal.

Given these geo-strategic-economic-environmental conditions, a maritime contingency, be it in the form of maritime accident, piracy attack, pollution, illegal activity at sea, environmental degradation or for that matter a catastrophic disaster like the tsunami can quickly turn into a global event both in economic and security terms for the Bay of Bengal littorals. This has direct security implications for maritime states of the region and those that use these waters.

Energy experts point out that both Bangladesh and Myanmar are sitting over a gas lake that has the potential to provide the much-needed energy requirements of Asia, in particular that of China and India, and are engaged in drawing out routes of pipelines to transport this gas to their hinterland that remain poorly developed.[23] Some reserves have also been discovered in the Krishna-Godavri delta off the Andhra coast, Mahanadi basin off the Orrisa coast, Andaman and Nicobar Islands and the east Sri Lankan coast, but none of these discoveries are anywhere near the potential of the gas deposits along Bangladesh and Myanmar coast. Petroleum giants like Gas Authority of India Limited (GAIL) and Oil and Natural Gas Corporation (ONGC) of India and China National Petroleum Corp (CNPC), China and Daewoo of Korea, are actively engaged in exploration activities.[24]

It is evident that the main thrust towards using these energy resources in the Bay of Bengal will promote the construction of marine infrastructure, building of newer and larger drilling platforms, gas storage facilities, underwater pipelines, and improved facilities at harbours and ports among the littorals, that is, Sri Lanka, India, Bangladesh, Myanmar, Thailand, Malaysia, Singapore and Indonesia. There will also be demands for the creation of thoroughfares at sea that will greatly allow a reduction in existing transportation and an increase in the safety of navigation. It is in this context that the SSCP and the Kra Canal, the two mega maritime infrastructure projects in the Bay of Bengal, merit attention.

Today, the Bay of Bengal stands at a cross-road with huge potential for meeting the rising global demands for energy. Significantly, the SSCP and Kra Canal projects would drastically alter the maritime, trade and economic landscapes of the Bay of Bengal littorals and perhaps the Asia-Pacific region. As more gas and oil exploration takes place in the region, it will witness greater volumes of energy transportation traffic but would confront difficulties associated with overburdened ports and inter-modal links. However, as supply lines are shortened, stability and predictability of supplies will improve. Also, the short-sea nature of many of the trade lanes will add to the agility of the supply chain, which is not available in other areas. The shorter distance will also create the flexibility for vessels to make sailings on a more frequent basis, with more room for adjusting schedules as smaller vessel size facilitates port operations by not having to accommodate massive cargo volumes.

Maritime Disorder in the Bay of Bengal

There exists a robust relationship between energy transportation and security that is based on safe and secure waterways and seas. A significant downstream consequence of a terrorist attack on the energy transportation system would most definitely entail disruption of the supply chain resulting in a range of impacts on global economy, business continuity and economic loss. To that extent, the Bay of Bengal has its own share of piracy and terrorism that can disrupt the energy transportation system in the region.

Jaffna, Sri Lanka

Ethnic violence in Sri Lanka is now more than two decades old. It has been interspersed with political assassinations, talks on settlement of the dispute, ceasefire and peace initiatives and naval battles between the Sri Lankan Navy

(SLN) and the Liberation Tigers of Tamil Eelam (LTTE). Interestingly, what distinguishes the LTTE from the other separatist groups is its ability to exploit the sea to further its cause. It is perhaps the first time that a non-state actor is conducting maritime operations at such a large scale and has been able to execute a classical sea control in waters off Jaffna in the northeast of Sri Lanka. The LTTE also owns and operates a fleet of deep-sea going ships that have facilitated logistical support by way of regular supply of arms, ammunition and other materials. Today, the bulk of LTTE shipping is carried out off Southeast Asia.

There have been several incidents between the LTTE and the Sri Lankan and the Indian navies. A large number of Sri Lankan naval vessels have been destroyed by the LTTE using asymmetric strategies. These include the use of human torpedoes, speedboats as suicide weapons and encounter with guns and small arms. The LTTE remains active despite the ongoing peace talks with the Sri Lankan government.

On 14 June 2003, LTTE oil tanker *Shoshin* blew up and sank. According to the Sri Lanka Navy, warning shots were fired and the vessel failed to stop.[25] In the ensuing exchange, its twelve-member crew blasted the vessel and jumped off before it could be boarded. The fate of the crew was unknown and they are presumed dead. In response the Tamil Tiger rebels warned of "grave consequences" and noted that the navy had no authority to open fire. The Sri Lankan government had played down the consequences of this sea clash in a bid to dispel fears that the rebels might go back to the ethnic war, which has plagued the country for two decades.

The LTTE appears to have little mercy on innocent seafarers. Although waters off Sri Lanka have generally remained free from piracy, the northeastern waters have witnessed frequent acts of piracy. In one incident, a merchant vessel *MV Cordiality*, was captured and five Chinese crew killed allegedly by the LTTE near the port of Trincomalee.[26] LTTE rebel forces are also reported to hijack ships and boats of all sizes and kidnapping and killing crew members is a common practice. In August 1998, a Belize-flagged general cargo vessel *MV Princess Kash* was hijacked by LTTE rebels.[27] While on its way to Mullaitivu, a LTTE stronghold, the Sri Lankan Air Force bombed the vessel to prevent the ship's cargo from falling into the hands of the LTTE. The status of the twenty-two-crew members is still not known. Fifteen Chinese and two Sinhalese were feared killed on 20 March 2003 when a Chinese trawler *Fu Yuan Ya 225* was attacked by a suspected LTTE naval unit off the Mullaitivu coast of eastern Sri Lanka. Reportedly, the Indian and Sri Lankan navies have instituted a range of measures to step up surveillance to prevent the LTTE from smuggling arms across the narrow northern strait separating the two countries.

Chittagong, Bangladesh

Bangladesh has attracted attention due to the alleged presence of Islamic militant groups and the spectre of "militant Islamization". Media reports have been widespread with strong indications of Bangladesh as a "hotbed of radical Islam". Reportedly, some 150 men belonging to Taliban and Al Qaeda from Afghanistan had entered Bangladesh in December 2001 through Chittagong.[28] They were seen carrying boxes of ammunition and AK-47 assault rifles. The Bangladesh foreign secretary rejected the report as baseless. Earlier, in April 2001, the *Far Eastern Economic Review* ran a cover story depicting Bangladesh as a "cocoon of terror".

The Harkat-ul-Jihad-al-Islami (HuJI), a force of about 2,000 men of Bangladesh, is closely linked with the Al Qaeda. HuJI came into existence in 1992 and is believed to be an offshoot of a Pakistani group financially and ideologically supported by Osama bin Laden. Western intelligence officials believe that one Fazlul Rahman signed bin Laden's 23 February 1998 declaration of holy war on the United States on behalf of the Jihad Movement in Bangladesh. Reports also suggest that several young Muslim radicals from Malaysia and Indonesia are present in Cox's Bazar and Chittagong and maintain contacts with local Muslim groups. The *madrasahs* serve as meeting grounds for exporting terrorism. The presence of Al Qaeda and now of Jemaah Islamiah, a Southeast Asian Islamic militant group trained in sea-borne guerrilla tactics, has fuelled fears that Bangladesh could become a haven for militants of all nations.

Intelligence sources believe that more than two dozen notorious local underworld gangs are engaged in gun-running in the port city of Chittagong. Besides, there are several arms manufacturing workshops. Chittagong and Cox's Bazar are a major transit point for arms smuggling.[29] The Bangladesh Navy too seized 123 foreign-made firearms and 146 rounds of ammunition from the three offshore islands, Sandwip, Moheshkhali and Kutubdia. They also recovered a huge number of local-made firearms and unearthed thirty local arms manufacturing workshops from Moheshkhali and Kutubdia.[30]

More recently, on 2 April 2004, following a tip-off, nine truckloads of arms and ammunition were seized from the port of Chittagong.[31] Reportedly, the haul comprised two consignments;[32] one consignment originated from the port of Hong Kong and was essentially of Chinese origin and the second was loaded at Singapore and consisted of weapons of both Israeli and U.S. manufacture. The shipment originated in Hong Kong and was then transported through the Straits of Malacca to be transhipped in the Bay of Bengal to two trawlers, *Kazaddan* and *Amanat*, which ferried the weaponry to a jetty in the port of Chittagong. According to JIR's sources, the shipment involved two key insurgent movements from India's northeast — the United Liberation Front of Assam (ULFA) and the Isak-Muivah faction of the National Socialist Council of Nagaland (NSCN-IM), which since 1997 has been in protracted peace talks with the Indian government, held mostly in Bangkok.

The sea is the main route for illegal arms coming from various countries. The land borders also provide alternative routes. The LTTE gun trade route passes through the Bay of Bengal and Andaman Sea. Arms originating from Cambodia are loaded onto small fishing trawlers in the southern Thai port of Ranong. These vessels then transfer the consignment to larger vessels for onward passage to Sri Lanka. Small boats to Cox Bazar transport a part of the consignment. Several vessels engaged in gun-running have been captured in the region. In 1996, the Bangladesh authorities seized 600 rifles from a fishing trawler originating in Thailand.[33] In 1997, the Royal Thai Navy seized an arms shipment for the People's Liberation Army (Manipur) following a chase in the Andaman Sea off the port of Ranong.

According to the International Maritime Bureau's (IMB) Piracy Reporting Centre, Chittagong port is the "most dangerous port in the world" with the highest incidence of piracy reported in the first nine months of 2006. Piracy has been rampant in Bangladeshi seaports for several years now. In 2001, there were 25 reported incidents and in 2002, this figure reached 32 incidents. In 2004, the IMB had been singularly appreciative of the Bangladeshi efforts to curb piracy in their waters that witnessed a sharp decline from 58 incidents in 2003 to 17 in 2004. But since then, an upward trend has continued with 21 recorded incidents in 2005, and now 33 incidents in the first nine months of 2006.

The report also notes that "Violence and intimidation of crew continues to be a hallmark of these attacks, with many of the pirates armed with guns and knives." Piracy is rampant in Bangladesh seaports and this has forced foreign shipping companies to impose additional charges for discharging cargo in these ports resulting in higher costs for the export and import of goods. These ports have been labelled "vulnerable and insecure" by foreign ships. The Bangladeshi authorities are conscious of this tarnished image of their ports but have not made any significant progress in containing this problem.

Malacca Straits

Although there is no reported incident of maritime terrorism attack in the Straits of Malacca, several plots have been unearthed that point to the fact that terrorist groups had plans to undertake attacks against maritime shipping. For instance, plans by a group of fifteen Islamic militants belonging to the Jemaah Islamiah, with links to the Al Qaeda, were discovered by the Singapore authorities in December 2001. The plans were indeed very ambitious and included attack on U.S. naval vessels entering/leaving ports in the northeastern shores of Singapore. There was another plan to attack American military service personnel travelling in a bus.[34] The Singapore government confirmed the plans and released videotape that featured how U.S. Navy vessels would be destroyed in a special "kill zone". Further, the topographic maps captured revealed that the group had good operational plans and targeting data and the attack was to be carried by using explosives-loaded small craft when ships were in shallow waters. Further, a bicycle carrying explosives would be used to attack the bus carrying military personnel between the naval base hosting U.S. Navy vessels and a train station. The U.S. Navy ships regularly call at Singapore ports for rest, recuperation and logistic support and the Changi naval base is large enough to provide even maintenance, repairs and dry-docking facilities to U.S. naval vessels including aircraft carriers.

Piracy in the Straits of Malacca (eleven attacks in 2006)[35] continues to top the list of threats posed to energy supply chains. The annual piracy report published by the International Maritime Bureau (IMB) highlights the inability of Malacca Straits littorals, particularly Indonesia (fifty attacks in 2006),[36] to control sea piracy in their waters. Many of these attacks were serious and involved vessels being fired upon and crew kidnapped for ransom.

The Gerakan Aceh Merdeka (GAM) or Free Aceh Movement, a separatist rebel group in Indonesia, too had been active in engaging in acts of piracy and terrorism in the Straits of Malacca.[37] GAM is strategically located astride the sea lane that serves as the umbilical cord to the Asia-Pacific and is vital for the economic well-being of the region. But the 2004 Indian Ocean tsunami had a major impact on the capability of GAM rebels who lost most of their maritime capability to undertake smuggling arms and hijacking ships.

In response, the littoral countries Singapore, Indonesia, Malaysia and Thailand have instituted the "Eye in the Sky" (EIS) initiative that entails coordinated air patrols over the Malacca Straits. Under the initiatives, maritime aircraft patrol the straits to detect and deter acts of piracy and transnational criminal activities in the straits. The maritime air surveillance and reconnaissance operations involving flight profile, pre-flight administration, operation centres, monitoring and action agencies and communication. Each flight involves a combined mission patrol team on board, a mission commander-in-charge of the safe conduct of the mission and the after-flight report, and observers from each participating nation. The EIS has resulted in considerable reduction in piracy-related incidents in the Straits of Malacca.

Concluding Remarks

Although the terrorist attacks of 11 September 2001 did not involve energy infrastructure, the attacks highlighted the fact that energy transportation systems present themselves as an attractive and vulnerable terrorist target. Several studies have reinforced the fact that there would be grave consequences for the global economy from an energy transport disruption. Energy-related infrastructure is perhaps the most difficult security challenge that exists within a nation's infrastructure. Consequence at one system of the energy infrastructure may multiply into multiple consequences throughout the transportation system.

Likewise, a safe and efficient transportation system is critical to domestic and international business. Any disturbance of an effective energy supply chain due to a terrorist or a piracy attack would have a significant impact on the competitiveness of nearby regions, with expected losses to local and regional economies.

It is evident that energy transportation systems such as ports and supply chains present themselves as potent targets which can be destroyed, incapacitated, or exploited. Therefore it is important to understand the strategic objectives of terrorists, what kind of targets they would choose and for what purpose. These are indeed very complex issues and in the past few years, several government and industry initiatives have been introduced to improve the security of the energy infrastructure. However, there still remain concerns over the vulnerability of supply chain continuity. What is perhaps needed is a comprehensive analysis to uncover risks to the energy transport enterprise and detail mitigation options for management.

NOTES

1 B. Raman, "Al Qaeda Attack on Saudi Oil Facility Fails", International Terrorism Monitor: Paper no. 27, available at <http://www.saag.org/papers18/paper1710.html>. This advice to his followers not to attack the oil wealth continued till December 2004, when bin Laden revised his earlier orders and called for attacks even on the oil wealth of the Arab world in order to disrupt the economies of the Western countries.

2 Cited in "Oil Markets At Risk From Terror Hit: Experts", available at <http://www.turkishpress.com/news.asp?id=122256>.

3 Joshua Sinai, "Terrorist Threats against Chemical Facilities", Powerpoint presentation available at <http://wwwnew.towson.edu/outreach/eeol/chemicalsecurity/downloads/sinai_presentation.pdf#search='The%20terrorist%20threat%20joshua%20sinai>.

4 Statement of Representative Ed Royce Chairman, Sub-committee on International Terrorism and Non-proliferation "Terrorist Threats to Energy Security", 27 July 2005, available at <http://wwwc.house.gov/international_relations/109/roy072705.pdf>.

5 "Attacks on Iraqi Pipelines, Oil Installations, and Oil Personnel", available at <http://www.iags.org/iraqpipelinewatch.htm>.

6 Herbert W. Cooper, "Addressing Energy Supply Vulnerabilities" available at <http://www.Redorbit.com>. On 30 August, the day after the storm (by which time 645 platforms and 90 rigs had been evacuated) 1,428,000 bbl/d of oil (95 per cent of the Gulf of Mexico's daily production) and 8.798 million cubic ft/d of gas (88 per cent of the Gulf of Mexico's daily production) were shut. Two weeks later, 841,000 bbl/d of oil (56 per cent of the Gulf of Mexico's daily production) and 3,383 million cubic ft/d of gas (34 per cent of the Gulf of Mexico's daily production) remained shut. One month later, on 24 September, Hurricane Rita struck Louisiana, leading to the shut-in of additional oil and gas production. As of 29 December, 411,000 bbl/d of oil (27 per cent of the Gulf of Mexico's daily production) and 1,954 million cubic ft/d of gas (20 per cent of the Gulf of Mexico's daily production) remained shut.

7 For example, in mid-January 2005, when temperatures in Russia and Eastern Europe fell to –20°F to –30°F, the coldest since 1927, demand for gas naturally rose. Attempting to cope with its own internal needs and weather-related production difficulties, Russia had to reduce its exports to various European countries by 5–20 per cent.

8 "The Geopolitics of Oil", available at <http://www.iags.org/oiltransport.html>.

9 Reynolds B. Peele, "The Importance of Maritime Chokepoints" available at <http://www.carlisle.army.mil/usawc/Parameters/97summer/peele.htm>

10 Ibid.

11 Nitsch, V. and Schumacher, D., (2002) "Terrorism and Trade", paper for workshop on *The Economic Consequences of Global Terrorism* (DIW-German Institute for Economic Research, Berlin, June 2000) on 24–26 November at Sophia-Antipolis (Nice), France, cited in P.H. Barnes and R. Oloruntoba, "Assurance of Security in Maritime Supply Chains: Conceptual Issues of Vulnerability and Crisis Management", in the *Journal of International Management* 11, no. 4 (2005).

12 Ibid.

13 Ibid.

14 Ibid.

15 Kang Siew Li, Hamidah Atan and Farrah Naz Karim, "Lloyd's Takes Malacca Strait Off High-risk List ", *Business Times*, Malaysia, 9 August 2006.
16 Nirupama Subramanian, "Terror at Katunayake", *Frontline* 18, no. 16 (4–17 August 2001).
17 "Growing Vulnerability of Seaports from Terror Attacks, to Protect Ports while Allowing Global Flow of Trade is a New Challenge", *Viewpoint* — Institute of Southeast Asian Studies, available at <www.iseas.edu.sg/viewpoint>.
18 "Threats to Oil Transport" available at <http://www.iags.org/oiltransport.html>.
19 "Ship War Risk Surcharge Criticized by Israeli Government", 30 July 2006, available at <http://www.port2port.com/Index.asp?ArticleID=991& CategoryID=43.
20 "Haifa Port: Estimated Revenue Loss of NIS 30 million", available at <http:// www.port2port.com/Index.asp?ArticleID=989&CategoryID=43>.
21 Raghunath Rau, "Root Canal for Palk Bay", available at <http://www. hardnewsmedia.com/nov2004/waterways.php>.
22 Nazery Khalid, "Proposed Kra Canal Project: Potential Effects on Malaysian Ports and the Shipping Sector and their Implications", available at <www. mima.gov.my>.
23 Anand Kumar, "India-Myanmar Gas Pipeline: Disentangled at Last ", Paper no. 1822, available at <http://www.saag.org/papers19/paper1822.html>.
24 Ibid.
25 For more details, see Vijay Sakhuja, "Will LTTE Give Peace a Chance?" at <http://www.ipcs.org>.
26 Xinhua (Beijing), "Report on Ship Attack in Sri Lanka", FBIS, 11 September 1997.
27 Rohan Gunaratna, "Trends in Maritime Terrorism — The Sri Lanka Case", *Lanka Outlook* (Autumn 1998), p. 13.
28 Alex Perry "Bangladesh: Al-Qaeda's New Safe Haven?" at <http://www.hvk.org/ articles/1002/128.html.31990.VINCLUDEFIX>.
29 See "Terrorists get weapons from the underworld" at <http://www.matamat.com/ fullstory.php?gd=19&cd=2003-09-09>.
30 Ibid.
31 No reliable list of the seized weapons has been made public. However, the shipment — altogether worth an estimated US$4.5–7 million — is known to have included around 2,000 automatic and semi-automatic weapons, among them 1,290 Type 56-1/Type 56-2 Kalashnikov-type assault rifles; 150 T-69 rocket propelled grenade (RPG) launchers; quantities of 40mm RPG ammunition; 25,000 hand-grenades; and 1.8m rounds of small-arms ammunition.
32 Anthony Davis, "New Details Emerge on Bangladesh Arms Haul", at <Dak Bangla Intelligence Scan.mht>.
33 Muhammad Shahedul Anam Khan, "Linkage Between Arms Trafficking and the Drug Trade in South Asia", in Jayanth Dhanapala, *Small Arms Control Old Weapons, New Issues* (Vermont; Ashgate Publishing Ltd, 1999), pp. 266–67.

34 "Singapore Says Terror Ring Planned Attacks on Americans", *Los Angeles Times*, 12 January 2002. The terror cell, which called itself Jemaah Islamiah, had been reportedly operating in Singapore for years and many of its cadres had travelled to Afghanistan for weapons training in camps run by Osama bin Laden's Al Qaeda network. Singapore Defence Minister Tony Tan said that the terrorists had planned to blow up embassies and military installations. Also see <http://www.pakistanlink.com/headlines/Jan/08/07.html>.

35 ICC International Maritime Bureau, "Piracy and Armed Robbery Against Ships Annual Report 1 January–31 December 2006", p. 6.

36 Ibid.

37 For more details, see Vijay Sakhuja, "Terrorism or Freedom Struggle: The Free Aceh Movement", Article no. 929, 19 December 2002, available at <http://www.ipcs.org>.

10

Ethical Business Practice or Camouflage? Energy and Mining Companies and Corporate Social Responsibility

Andrew Symon

The Bay of Bengal region appears set to emerge as an important new oil and natural gas producing province. Major new discoveries have been made, mainly offshore, in eastern India, Bangladesh and western Myanmar. Development raises many issues for governments. One of the most important, but sometimes overlooked, in concerns over energy supply and security and then the euphoria that comes with new discoveries and their economic and commercial allure, is how to best manage the social and environmental impacts of petroleum development. Governments clearly have responsibility to ensure that oil and gas projects in their midst — upstream extraction, midstream pipelines and downstream processing — do deliver real benefits to local regions as well as the overall country, and do not harm them through social and environmental damage. This should also be seen to be vital in ensuring the long-run success of a project. What then is the role of corporations? They too must show responsibility in this regard — and again it is something in their commercial self-interest. There is a strong case then for a partnership between the corporate sector, central and local governments and local communities to deal with these wider dimensions of petroleum development.

The extractive industries — petroleum and mining — are burdened by often damaging stereotypes of their attitudes towards such issues. Record profits being declared by major international oil and mining companies as a result of high commodity prices are fuelling the old stereotypes about these corporate giants. Here, some say, is evidence again of behemoths selfishly and ruthlessly going about their business, extracting finite resources around the globe, especially from the developing world, with little care for the consequences of their operations on local communities and environments. In Bolivia, such fears about foreign oil companies have brought down governments and in late 2005 helped propel Evo Morales to office as Bolivia's new president, promising he would nationalize the country's petroleum industry.

The transnational oil and mining groups, with profits exceeding the gross domestic product (GDP) of some countries, are often seen as laws unto themselves, prepared to make deals with corrupt governments in the developing world and influence powerful Western governments to achieve their goals. This sort of image is common fodder in press reports, magazine articles, books and movies. Such an unscrupulous U.S. oil company is at the centre of the plot of the recent American movie, *Syriannna*, actor-director George Clooney's fictionalized story inspired by the biography of a former CIA agent in the Middle East. And in the case of a recently published critical look at AngloDutch oil company, Shell, by journalists, Ian Cummins and John Beasant, there is no hiding behind fiction as underlined by its provocative title, *Shell Shock: The Secrets and Spin of an Oil Giant.*[1]

But tarring all international oil and mining companies with this sort of brush is unfair. Certainly there are elements of truth. And the record of the industries is hardly faultless, both historically and current. But I would argue that the prevailing position among major companies now is that they truly do want to mitigate adverse social and environmental impacts of their operations. They want to be seen as beneficial for host countries and communities. What is termed "corporate social responsibility (CSR)" is seen to be in the company's own self-interest as far as ensuring a project is successful commercially over the long term; that the company can secure other business in a country; that it can meet concerns of shareholders and investors; prevent damaging public criticism and scandal; and avoid possible legal actions both in its home and host countries.

Companies that may have had bad records often have come to reform themselves as they realize that it is to their greater benefit. Of course, this may not be a sudden Pauline-like conversion. Rather they may have been forced into this position by public pressure and new laws and regulations. And not every company remains blemish free. But at the same time, there is also a more positive impetus for good practices stemming from the character and professionalism of good companies and their staff. They care about what they do and want to leave positive legacies. As tough and ambitious as some oilmen and miners may be, they should not all be typecast as resource buccaneers plundering foreign seas and lands.

What Does Corporate Social Responsibility Mean?

Before looking at examples and experiences in the Southeast Asia and the overlapping Bay of Bengal region, we need to ask just what do we exactly mean by corporate social responsibility (CSR)? Does it mean companies simply meeting and conforming to government laws and regulations in areas ranging from taxation through to employee wages and conditions, safety and environmental standards — as they indeed should? Or is it about companies going beyond prevailing laws and regulations to initiate additional programmes that benefit communities around them? In countries where the corporate, labour and environmental and safety regulations are under-developed and/or poorly enforced and prone to corruption, the temptations and challenges for companies are great. Even where a company is not taking advantage of the situation, simply conforming to existing conditions can mean that the company falls well short of what may be expected of it elsewhere. Yet the company can lead by example and follow best practice standards. And in these situations, how far should a company also concern itself with encouraging better government policy and regulations?

This chapter considers both petroleum and mining industries as they share many common issues and themes as far as CSR matters are concerned. They are both non-sustainable industries from an environmental perspective. Ultimately, oil and natural gas, coal and minerals are finite resources. They also have similar economic and political impacts on countries, governments and communities and give rise to similar issues. The resource extractive industries, petroleum and mining, feature some of the greatest concerns over CSR issues. This reflects the extent to which petroleum and mining become entangled in broader issues affecting countries as well as the particular environmental and community impacts in the area of their operations.

Politics, Economics and Government Policies

The political and economic impacts of petroleum and mining companies on a country can be enormous. Resources extraction can trigger strong nationalist sentiment where the leading companies are foreign owned and controlled. Such reaction has a long history. There are few other areas of the economy where fears that foreigners are exploiting the country can be more pronounced.

An example from the Bay of Bengal region is the long-standing opposition in Bangladesh against natural gas exports to east India. While foreign petroleum companies operating the candidate fields, Chevron (formerly Unocal before the latter was taken over by fellow U.S. company, Chevron, in 2005), Shell and Cairn Energy of the United Kingdom all argue that there is abundant gas available for pipeline export and this would benefit Bangladesh, they also argue there is plenty also for Bangladesh's own needs. They are supported by the World Bank and Asian Development Bank. But the government says it is not convinced, reflecting popular suspicions about foreign company motives. The government says that proven gas reserves are not high enough, that gas development should anyway be concentrated in Bangladesh, and any exports should be of value-added content from gas processing, for example, electricity generated by gas or fertilizer manufactured from gas.

A country with a booming resource sector attracting petroleum or mining companies after big discoveries have been made, can find that other industries in agriculture and manufacturing — either export oriented or facing international competition (that is, the other parts of the traded sector) — are made much less competitive as a result of appreciating exchange rates and inflation brought about by the high resource exports. There may be high unemployment outside the resources industries — which, being capital intensive, do not in any case employ directly large volumes of labour, especially after the construction phase.

Resource prices may also turn out to be very volatile with economy-wide upheavals caused by sudden falls, loss of export income, falling exchange rates and a consequent exodus of overseas capital. Resource booms can be especially fatal for poorer developing countries where the modern economic sector is small — outside of the mineral or petroleum industry — and much of the population is reliant on semi-traditional agriculture. A new resources industry can overwhelm an economy. But the dangers are not exclusive to developing countries as the Netherlands found in the late 1960s and early 1970s when North Sea gas was first produced and exported. The economy was upset by sudden rise in exports which resulted in exchange rate appreciation, inflation and the squeezing out of other industries. This gave rise to the economists' term for such a plight — the "Dutch Disease".

In the Bay of Bengal region, Bangladesh and Myanmar, two of the poorest and least developed countries in the world, are especially vulnerable to adverse economic effects of possible resources booms. Both could potentially produce large volumes of natural gas for export. As noted above, Bangladesh could be a large exporter to India. Myanmar, which already exports to Thailand from offshore fields in the southeast, could possibly export from recently discovered offshore fields in the west, piped to India, or shipped there and elsewhere as liquefied natural gas. India also enjoys significant new oil discoveries, but the size of the Indian economy will blanket distortions.

Resource booms are a bonanza for governments, giving them large revenues through royalties, production sharing agreements, and taxes. This does give them the opportunity for wise long-term investments in infrastructure, health and education. But revenues can also be wasted through bad economic management and, worse, as seen in many parts of the world, frittered away through corruption and personal aggrandizement among government leaders, bureaucrats and the military.

Of course, whatever one may think of politicians and bureaucrats, not in every country would one expect them to stash away public funds into Swiss bank accounts. But the danger of poor management remains. Fluctuating resources prices inevitably make those government budgets overly reliant on resource rents vulnerable. A solution is to dedicate a good proportion of resource rents to a long-term investment fund which can provide for long-term investment and development capital for future generations. The rest may be used to support annual recurrent spending. Reinforcing this policy is the very nature of petroleum and mining. Given that they are not ultimately sustainable activities, it makes sense that at least some of the current revenue be earmarked for the future and to support hopefully sustainable activities of long-term benefit. This reasoning is applied by quite a number of developed and developing countries enjoying large resource revenues as a proportion of total revenues. Designated funds operate in Norway, the state of Alaska in the United States, Alberta in Canada, Chile, Venezuela, Botswana, Kuwait, Oman, Iran, Azerbaijan, and Kazakhstan. In the Asia region, the new state of Timor Leste, is also setting up a fund for mainly natural gas revenue from Timor. While these policy decisions are the province of governments, they should also concern petroleum and mining companies. Better management of resource revenues in turn means a more positive political and economic environment for their operations.

Petroleum and mining operations can also lead to, or exacerbate, conflicts between central governments and provinces. Local communities may feel that the central government is taking all the riches from petroleum and mining operations in their midst and not giving them a fair share. As a result, petroleum and mining companies can find themselves in the midst of tensions and conflict between regions and central governments. Much depends then on how well government resource revenues flow back to the local regions. If the central government is not providing adequate local services and benefits, the resources companies may be seen by local communities as being in league with a detested government and become the target of their wrath. This is the case for Shell and foreign oil services companies in Nigeria where expatriate workers face virtually constant threat of kidnapping by militants championing a better demand for communities in the Niger delta. Similarly, it was the case a few years ago in Aceh in Indonesia's northern Sumatra. U.S. company, ExxonMobil, which operates gas fields supplying the Arun liquefied natural gas plant, was targeted and attacked several times by Acehenese separatists.

Some Corporate Case Studies

Experience shows that business will be difficult or even come to grief if a company does not pay attention to the wider social and environmental impact of its operations and the political and economic context in which it finds itself in any country. A good example in Southeast Asia is the operations of U.S. copper and gold miner, Freeport, in Indonesia, where, in Papua, it operates one of the world's largest mines. Freeport now suffers because of its association with the corruption and cronyism of the Suharto years and human rights abuses of the military. Freeport's story is well documented by Denise Leith in her Ph.D. study and later book, *The Politics of Power, Freeport in Suharto's Indonesia.*[2] Since this book was published, further allegations have been made that Freeport has improperly paid millions of dollars of payments to the Indonesian military. The Indonesian government also has threatened to take legal action against Freeport if it does not improve its environmental practices.

Another example in Indonesia is the Anglo Australian miner, Rio Tinto. In the early 1990s, Rio Tinto's Kelian gold mine in East Kalimantan on the island of Borneo allegedly polluted rivers, forced diversion of watercourses and resulted in bitter relations between the miners and local Dayak peoples. After the resignation of President Suharto in 1998, Indonesian and international condemnation led to Rio Tinto agreeing in 2001 to provide substantial compensation to local people and to put in place new community and environment programmes. Mediators of the agreement included Indonesia's National Human Rights Commissioner, Asamara Nagagan and Australian Federal Court Judge, Justice Marcus Einfeld.

All this may be avoided if good practice is followed to begin with. U.K. petroleum company, British Petroleum (BP), is one company operating in Indonesia that has taken heed of Freeport's experience. Developing large gas fields and liquefaction plant in the Bird's Head area of Papua, the US$5 billion Tangguh project, BP has set up an independent monitoring panel of prominent international and Indonesian figures to check that the project's environmental impact is acceptable and the effect on local communities is positive. The panel's reports and BP responses are published on BP's website thus, BP argues, making the project transparent and publicly accountable.[3]

Good practice can be simple enough to talk about in mission statements. But putting it into place effectively over the long term is often not an easy task. Resources projects, especially in the developing world, or where they impact on indigenous communities in the developed world, can be very tough. Even with the best wills in the world in the companies, governments and local communities, they are prone to enormous political and social difficulties. The big companies, technologically sophisticated and wealthy, are operating in often remote areas among poor, if not marginalized communities. Their cultures may be worlds away from those of the companies and their staff. Misunderstandings and conflicts easily arise. All faults and failings do not rest simply with the oil or mining company. Often they are seen as fair game for extortion of money and material by government officials, military, and local communities. Environmentally, as the search for resources pushes companies into new frontiers, so they are more likely to affect hitherto untouched natural environments.

A Cautionary Tale

An example of the difficulties that may be encountered are the experiences of U.S. gold miner Newmont in Indonesia. Claims were launched in 2004 against Newmont, the world's second largest gold mining company, for alleged damage to local community health from pollution from its now closed gold operations in north Sulawesi. A long criminal trial resulted, but finally concluded in favour of Newmont in April 2007.[4]

Allegations against Newmont from a group of villagers and NGOs surfaced in the latter part of 2004 after the Minahasa mine in Manado

Province on the northeast coast of the island of Sulawesi was being closed down due to the end of the economic life of the deposit. They claimed that the mine's tailings disposal via a pipeline into Buyat Bay had caused mercury poisoning of the waters. This, they said, had resulted in sickness among local people and the death of one baby girl. Their complaints led to police investigations of Newmont to the point where, in September 2004, police arrested six employees of Newmont, including the president director of the Minahasa mine, Richard Ness. They were kept in jail for thirty-two days in the same prison shared by terrorists who had attacked the Australian embassy in Jakarta.

In December 2005, a Jakarta court declared the police investigation illegal. Nevertheless, criminal charges were pressed by the authorities as a result of the complaints and hence the current court case against Newmont and Ness himself for criminal negligence. He faced the possibility a jail sentence if convicted. But he and Newmont were acquitted in April 2007.

The weight of scientific evidence and testimony by government officials would seem certainly to have been in Newmont's favour. The World Health Organization (WHO), the Commonwealth Scientific and Industrial Research Organization of Australia, the Minamata Institute of Japan, and the Indonesian Ministry of Health found no mercury or arsenic contamination. The WHO says that small traces of mercury in the nearby estuaries are attributable to local mining efforts, not to Newmont.

Only a report by the Indonesian police found unsafe levels of contamination.

The court case continued despite Newmont and the Indonesian government agreeing in February 2006 to settle a separate civil suit launched by the Ministry of Environment. The ministry lodged the civil case in 2005, seeking damages of US$133 million. Newmont paid US$30 million in the settlement. Newmont itself continues to operate in Indonesia, principally the major copper and gold mine, Batu Hijau, on the island of Sumbawa in eastern Indonesia. This is Asia's second largest in operation after Freeport's Grasberg operation in Indonesian Papua, which in turn is one of the largest in the world. Batu Hijau, which began operating in 2000, has not been embroiled in any Minahasa-like conflict and in fact is being held up as an exemplary project by the Indonesian government. In August 2005, Newmont was granted a second "Green Award" by the environment ministry.

Newmont's story illustrates just how prone to controversy resources projects can be. But there are plenty of others where the benefits of being a good corporate citizen are clear.

Chevron in Bangladesh

One current project in South Asia also illustrating the importance multinational companies place on demonstrating their sensitivity to the wider dimensions of their development is Chevron's Bibiyana gas field in northeast Bangladesh in Habiganj District. Chevron began commercial production in March 2007 of what it describes as a "world class field" and what is set to become the country's largest single source of natural gas.

The project is very important to Bangladesh in meeting growing gas for power generation. But development has been a slow process. The field was originally operated by fellow U.S. company, Unocal, which in turn was acquired by Chevron in 2005. The project has been slowed by various commercial contractual and regulatory uncertainties and delays by the government in dispensing land compensation to local people.

Suspicion remains also in public minds and within government towards the presence of large foreign petroleum companies in Bangladesh. This manifested itself in opposition towards the argument by Unocal and Shell a few years ago, that it made best sense for the country to take advantage of its significant gas reserves by exporting gas by pipeline to India. But this was met with widespread and often emotional opposition in Bangladesh with opponents arguing that Bangladesh ran the risk of exporting resources it would need later for its own development. Those who would profit, they claimed, would be the foreign companies.

Chevron's Bibiyana field is geared for local markets, however, with output contracted to the state-owned PetroBangla. And to build goodwill towards the company, the U.S. major has invested in community development programmes such as animal husbandry training for local families and has improved the sanitation for 2,700 households. Chevron has also emphasized local content, both in terms of local employees and local supplies within a 5 kilometre radius of Bibiyana. About 5,500 local workers were trained and most of the time more than 2,000 were working during the construction phase.

Shareholder and Invest or Scrutiny

Companies, especially the large listed Western companies, also are forced to demonstrate appropriate social and environmental standards and in some cases political behaviour because of the demands of shareholders and financiers. Premier Oil of the United Kingdom pulled out of Myanmar in 2002 and its operating interest in the offshore Yetagun gas field in the Gulf of Martaban, because of pressure from investors as well as non-government organizations

(NGOs) and the U.K. government, who believed that it should not be operating in the country given the human rights abuses of its military government. This field, together with the neighbouring offshore Yadana field operated by France's Total, supplies about 25 per cent of Thailand's natural gas supply via pipeline. Premier sold its interests to the Malaysian state oil and gas company, Petronas. Just prior to Premier's decision, eight leading U.K. institutional funds managing of the order of US$800 million in investment declared that they had grave concerns about countries with operations or business relations in Myanmar.

Investor and financier concerns, as well as those of the general public, have resulted in large listed companies providing reports of their social and environmental practices alongside of their traditional financial reports and balance sheets. In the United Kingdom, 70 of the top 100 British companies produce such reports. There is pressure for this sort of reporting to be mandatory in the United Kingdom as well as in various jurisdictions in Continental Europe. And it is not simply a matter of putting out reports and information on websites. Companies find it very difficult to raise offshore project finance from Western and Japanese sources unless they can assure lenders of that there will not be social reaction or environmental damage that will put the project at commercial risk.

Some may suggest that large listed Western companies pay more attention to these questions than smaller non-listed companies because of the greater scrutiny of shareholders concerned about such things and the wider public on their operations. There is also argument that non-Western companies generally pay less attention to social and environmental issues. This may also be an unfair stereotype. In fact, it is often used as an argument by Western companies who wish or do operate in countries whose governments are criticized by human rights and democracy activists. They say that if they are not there, other non-Western companies will take their places without their sensitivities as far as bringing about benefits to local communities and protecting the environment.

In any case, as more Asian-based resources companies seek Western finance and list on Western stock exchanges, so will they face greater scrutiny of their operations. An interesting example in this regard is China's largest state oil company, the China National Petroleum Corp (CNPC). CNPC's overseas spearhead is its Hong Kong and New York listed subsidiary, PetroChina. But in the case of the group's operations in the Sudan and Myanmar — both places whose regimes are severely criticized in the West for human rights abuses — CNPC operates as CNPC, that is, it is the unlisted parent, not the listed subsidiary, operating in the Sudan and Myanmar.

CNPC thus escapes any reporting requirement from these exchanges. Nevertheless, there has been some market censoring of PetroChina, with several institutional investors, including those of prominent U.S. universities, Harvard and Yale, deciding in 2005 to divest from PetroChina, citing CNPC's position in the Sudan as the reason.

Do Petroleum and Mining Industries Differ?

Petroleum and mining industries may also exhibit different propensities towards CSR. This is argued by American geographer, Jared Diamond, in his book, *Collapse: How Societies Choose to Fail or Succeed*.[5] Mining generally disturbs more of an area than does oil and gas extraction. Processing of ore on site often is also more environmentally hazardous because of the chemicals involved and the toxic waste produced. Much oil and gas extraction also takes place offshore — as in the case of much of the Bay of Bengal region, for example, the very promising new oil discoveries in deepwater off the central east coast of India — thereby reducing operational disturbance of communities.

On the other hand, even where the upstream impact may be minimal, petroleum production may be complemented by long distance pipelines on land which may need to be carefully planned to avoid adverse environmental and community impacts. An example here is the gas pipeline from offshore fields in Myanmar to Thailand. Construction of the overland section in the late 1990s from the Thai border to power plants at Ratchaburi, west of Thailand was challenged by community and NGO groups because it was cutting through the edge of a national park, forcing the government to accommodate their concerns.

Furthermore, while offshore petroleum production may be benign as far as environmental and community disturbance are concerned, it may result in onshore processing in the form of oil refining and/or petrochemical production that can have serious implications in both respects. India's memories of the terrible Union Carbide Bhopal chemical pesticide factory explosion and subsequent poisoning of surrounding communities in Madhya Pradesh in 1984 should give rise to great concerns as far as how downstream petroleum processing is managed. While Bhopal was not a petro-based chemical plant, it nevertheless points to the toxic dangers of any complex chemical manufacturing plant, including those based on petrochemicals. And to the extent that the Bay of Bengal does become a larger upstream petroleum province, then inevitably there will be plans for downstream processing of both crude oil and natural gas to produce oil products, fertilizer and petrochemicals.

Diamond also argues that industry economics and corporate culture are often more conducive to favourable CSR practices in the petroleum industry than the mining industry. Petroleum profits over the long run are higher and more predictable than those in mining, making it easier for corporations to fund social and environmental programmes. Large petroleum groups also usually have more of a public profile and reputation to protect and enhance as a result of their retail activities. BP sells petrol at thousands of outlets around the world. But copper and gold are not stamped with BHP, Rio Tinto or Newmont logos.

Contrary Argument: The Business of Business is Business

Having put the case for corporate social responsibility as good business practice, I should also set it against contrary argument that it is not, in fact, a proper or sensible function of a company to concern itself with social and environmental matters beyond what is required by government law and regulation. In other words, the view here is the social function of companies to focus on the job of making profits for shareholders, paying its employees and suppliers and paying taxes to governments — not to take on social roles that really belong to governments and civil organizations.

This may work in a theoretical textbook world, and perhaps in institutionally and economically mature countries, but not in developing countries, especially the poorer ones where petroleum and mining companies commonly operate. Here, the ability of governments to provide services to communities is often limited, at best. In any case, in the developed world, in North America, Europe, Australia or Japan, demands on companies to show wider social and environmental responsibility in their operations are very great. This cannot be better demonstrated than by the pressures on companies to respond appropriately to greenhouse gas emission, global warming and the threat of violent climate change.

Petroleum and mining projects are prone to social and political challenges and difficulties that companies cannot simply ignore. To gain community acceptance of the project in their midst, companies must show that they can provide social benefit and not cause unacceptable environmental damage. It also makes sense as far as self interest is concerned, to assist community development as a means of helping to support a project economically through local employees and supplies and services. All this may be required by terms of their operating agreements with central and provincial governments. But even where this is not the case, if communities are alienated, eventually it will result in government actions, even if in the short term the company is operating where governments show a lack of interest or even care little about the local context. Eventually, these things will come back to haunt companies.

But the dilemma for companies is just how far they should go in providing education, health, small-scale industry development and infrastructure (roads, ports and airports). They argue they are not, after all, alternative governments, although that may be in effect the expectation of local communities. Indeed historically, the transformation of foreign trading companies in Asia and Africa into proxy local governments in the eighteenth and nineteenth centuries in order to secure their commercial position was a key reason for the emergence of Western colonial control in these parts of the world. The host country government clearly has many responsibilities and cannot simply be a passive rent taker.

The Extractive Industries Transparency Initiative

The role of major companies in the petroleum and mining industries in developing countries is clearly intertwined then with critical and wider questions and issues to do with governance and economic development. This is recognized by the Extractive Industries Transparency Initiative (EITI),[6] first proposed by U.K. Prime Minister, Tony Blair in 2002. This features a coalition of governments, investors, companies and NGOs, supported by multilateral and bilateral agencies such as the World Bank and the International Monetary Fund. Both corporate and government practices are monitored by the EITI and reforms proposed and pursued. The initiative argues for complementary policies and actions by both companies and governments. As the chief executive officer of U.S. gold miner, Newmont, and chairman of the International Council on Mining and Metals, Wayne Murdy, writes:

> The international mining industry recognises that secure access to natural resources depends on environmentally and socially sustainable business practices. However, these are not solely under the control of mining companies. Enhancing the impact of mining on development requires joint action and new forms of partnership between governments, companies, civil society and international development agencies.[7]

More than twenty countries in Africa, South America and Central Asia with large petroleum and/or mining industries are already members. However, there are no member governments from East and South Asia apart from Timor Leste. Nevertheless, Asia will feel the impact of EITI initiatives as the World Bank and other agencies incorporate EITI principles and guidelines in their programmes assisting countries in these regions. Member companies are all Western: Amerada Hess, Anglo American, Areva, Barrick Gold, BG group, BHP Billiton, BP, Burren Energy, ChevronTexaco, Eni, ExxonMobil, Lonmin, Marathon, Newmont, NorskHydro, Repsol YPF, Rio Tinto, Shell, Statoil, Talisman Energy, Total, Woodside, Xstrata. Almost all of these have interests in Southeast Asia and several in South Asia.

At the government level, CSR matters are more the task of individual governments working with the companies operating in their countries. The EITI initiative does provide guidelines for governments in developing and implementing policy. The role of regional government forums, such as the Association of Southeast Asian Nations (ASEAN), the South Asian Association for Regional Cooperation (SAARC) and the 1997-formed Bangladesh, India, Myanmar, Sri Lanka, Thailand Economic Cooperation group (BIMSTEC), is probably more limited to promoting and supporting good practice and exchange of expertise and information between governments. The social and environmental dimensions of petroleum and mineral development have been recognized to some degree in meetings of energy and resources development related ministers and officials. Perhaps one area where they could focus attention, is to ensure that the desire to attract investment in petroleum and mining does not lead to a competition that pushes government standards and requirements downwards.

Conclusion

To conclude, there is now a vast literature about CSR from academic sources through to NGOs, business councils and development assistance agencies. Conferences on the subject seem a dime a dozen. They all echo a common argument: ethical corporate policy is consistent with self-interest and good business. Long-term business interests for investors and managers are best served by being good corporate citizens. Yet it is still true that not all companies are virtuous. And there must always be suspicion that talk of CSR is simply camouflage. But in an age of instant communications, CNN, Internet and e-mail, companies cannot easily hide unacceptable damages caused by their operations from the scrutiny of activists, NGOs, the media, and governments.

Not all the onus rests on the companies. Governments face a long list of policy and programme tasks to complement petroleum and mining company performance. Along with specific mining and petroleum industry laws and regulations that of course include safety and environmental standards, there must also be appropriate macroeconomic, tax and budgetary policies and good central-provincial relations and regional development planning.

NOTES

1 Ian Cummins and John Beasant, *Shell Shock: The Secrets and Spin of an Oil Giant* (Edinburgh: Mainstream Publishing, 2005).
2 Denise Leith, *The Politics of Power, Freeport in Suharto's Indonesia* (Honolulu: University of Hawaii Press, 2003), *passim.*
3 See <http://www.bp.com/sectiongenericarticle.do?categoryId=9004751&contentId=7008791>.
4 Donald Greenlees, "Indonesia Clears U.S. Mining Giant of Pollution", *International Herald Tribune*, 24 April 2007.
5 Jared Diamond, *Collapse: How Societies Choose to fail or Succeed* (New York: Penguin 2006), pp. 441–68.
6 See <http://www.eitransparency.org>.
7 Wayne Murdy, "Steps that can Make Mining a Global Force for Good", *Financial Times* (U.K.), 25 August 2006.

11

Sustainable and Renewable Energy: Scenarios for the Future

Christophe Bongars

Renewables represent less than 2 per cent of the global power generation capacity — excluding large hydro, also known as "new renewables" — and are projected to reach a 6 per cent capacity by year 2030.

With average growth rates per year of more than 30 per cent for solar photovoltaic (PV) and over 20 per cent for wind power over the last five years, the renewable energy industry has come of age. As for bio-fuels, a recent report from McKinsey and Company concludes that much of the projected growth in industrial biotechnology — a US$77 billion industry in value within the chemical sector, counting products made from bio-based feed stocks or through fermentation or enzymatic conversion — is attributable to bio-fuels (ethanol and bio-diesel) as production is rapidly increasing to meet demand.

Conservative estimates show that, at the current rate of growth, the total renewables output (combined with biomass and bio-fuels) equivalent to only 2 per cent of the primary energy mix worldwide today, will at least double in the next twenty-five years.

Figure 11.1
Installed Renewable Power Generation Capacity (excluding large hydro) in GW

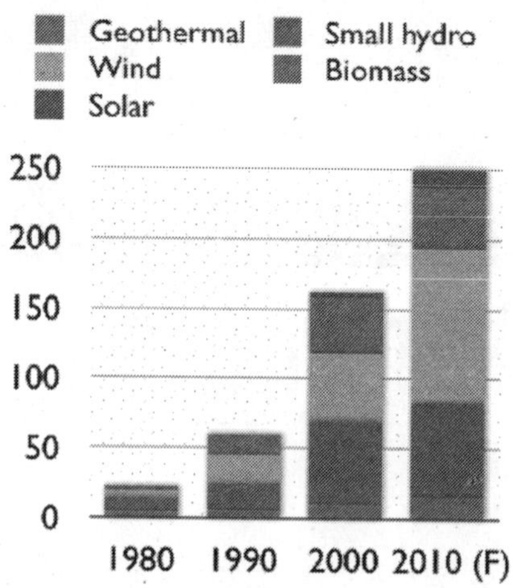

Main countries of installation: United States, Europe (Germany, France, Netherlands, Denmark*, Spain), China, India, Japan, etc. depending on RE policies.*23% grid-connected wind power, the highest in the world!

Sources: IEA, REN21 and Renewable Energy World.

Why is this Important to Us?

At the turn of the century, energy security has become the number one priority around the world. Every country is attempting to mitigate its reliance on limited and unstable primary energy sources. Due to the rapid economic growth of its two developing giants — China and India — and with a combined growth of more than 3.2 per cent per year — twice the world's average — the Asia-Pacific region surpasses the rest of the world in terms of energy demand. With half the projected global demand by year 2030, Asia-Pacific is central to this energy debate (source: Exxon Mobil tomorrow's energy report February 2006).

Will renewable energy shape the twenty-first century just like oil shaped the twentieth century world? The short answer is ... not quite: to meet this formidable energy challenge, conventional energy sources, including large hydro and nuclear power will continue occupying a large share of our near-term landscape. Despite its rapid start, new renewable energy alternatives have a long way to go before reaching mainstream and making a significant contribution to our global energy mix. Fossil fuels (coal, oil and gas) will remain the dominant source of energy of the century.

But there is more to it than numbers. Renewable energy has captured the world's attention and is making headlines — from high level institutions and governments, all the way to corporations, the academia and local communities — because it addresses two of the most formidable challenges of our time: climate change and human development goals. Public opinions are powerful agents of change: the combined effect of high oil prices and the support of adequate government policies, have truly hoisted the renewable energy industry to new levels.

Whichever side you are on — the UN Framework Convention on Climate Change (the Kyoto Protocol) or the Asia-Pacific Partnership for Clean Development and Climate (AP6) — the consensus is that climate change is a real threat to our common future. Recent media coverage such as "The Heat is On" (*The Economist*, September 2006) and the acclaimed documentary *An Inconvenient Truth* (Al Gore, July 2006), are calls for action and bring the debate from closed circles of government officials, scientists and experts, to the general public.

Furthermore, it has been recognized by governments and multilateral agencies throughout the world that not only a cleaner but also more decentralized ("distributed") approach to energy services, would better serve the needs of rural communities and remote (off-grid) energy users. The implementation of the Clean Development Mechanism (CDM) under the Kyoto Protocol has undeniably contributed to these objectives (ADB, "Towards Cleaner Energy Use in Asia and the Pacific", June 2006).

Why Are Changes not Happening Faster?

Solar energy is the primary source of energy on the planet: as shown on Figure 11.2 below, all other sources of energy are derived from solar energy. Even the accumulation of fossil fuels in the Earth's crust over geological times, has been powered by the sun. Since the start of the industrial revolution in the mid-nineteenth century, human activity has grown exponentially and has driven an insatiable energy demand. By definition, depleting finite stocks of fossil energy is unsustainable. A century-and-a-half later, addressing energy security and climate change risks has become an imperative.

Since the early days of the industrial revolution, tapping into easily accessible and seemingly endless stocks of concentrated coal, then oil and gas, has been a straightforward approach. Yet, the move from solid fuels (wood, then coal), to liquid (oil) and then gas, requires increasingly complex man-made infrastructure. Today's oil and gas industry is shifting toward massive infrastructure projects to tap the least accessible oil reserves and still under-exploited natural gas fields. Such mega projects include gas transmission and gas-to-liquid (or GTL, to convert natural gas resources into liquid petroleum based fuels), mobilizing vast amounts of capital and human resources.

By comparison, the seemingly benign new renewable energy approach, faces a different challenge: the source of renewable energy is captured either directly through sunlight converted into electricity via a photovoltaic cell (PV cell), by absorption of its heat via a solar heater, or indirectly by capturing the energy contained in the natural cycle of water (hydro), meteorological conditions (wind) or biomass growth (plant photosynthesis and biological metabolism). What all these forms of energy have in common is that they are abundant and well distributed around the globe — save for arid areas where biomass is quasi-absent due to lack of water (see Figure 11.2 below).

All these renewable sources however are subject to natural cycles — day/night, seasons, meteorological conditions, climate, etc. — and in some cases require vast areas of land, as for bio-fuels plantations, for instance.

Figure 11.2
Solar Energy Is Our Primary Source of Energy

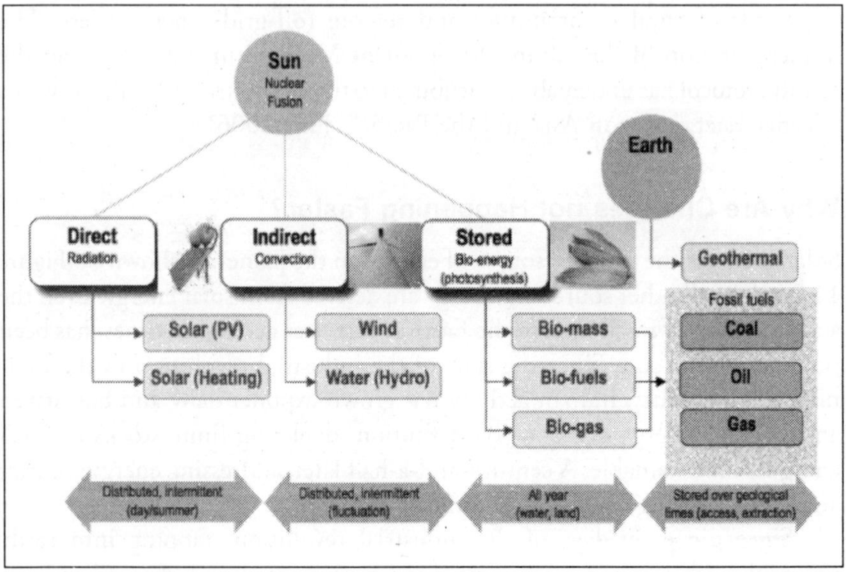

Source: SustainAsia.

Unlike fossil fuels, which are stored in certain geological formations in concentrated form, renewable energy sources are thinly distributed and subject to local fluctuations. By essence, the energy services delivered are intermittent. It is estimated, for instance, that wind turbines have an average capacity factor of 20–30 per cent only; this creates great technical challenges such as maintaining grid stability, as in Denmark where grid-connected wind power capacity goes as high as 23 per cent of the total power generation capacity.

Technologies have Barely Reached Mainstream...

All emerging technologies are facing the same challenges: miscalculating tomorrow's opportunity based on yesterday's knowledge has derailed many companies in fast-growing industries before, such as the IT industry. The comparison with the IT industry stops here as renewable energy technology is not "rocket science" and most of the technologies emerging now are streamlined version of yesteryears.

What has changed is the move towards mass production: the product scalability and cost efficiencies have shifted the entire industry from the R&D and small-scale demo plants to full commercial scale. Who would have predicted just five years ago that the solar PV industry's production bottleneck would be its ability to source Silicon wafers in competition with the chip making industry? Who would have guessed back then that among the top-tier renewable technologies manufacturers would be an Indian firm (Suzlon) for wind turbines? and a Chinese company (Suntech Power Holding, NASDAQ: STP) for PV cells?

The real issue is economic. Figure 11.3 is a schematic representation of the renewable energy electricity cost trends.[1] While in most countries tariffs of electricity produced by conventional means have crept up following the fuel cost trend, the cost of renewable energy generated electricity is dropping steadily. At some point in time, and given the right set of policies and local conditions, the two sets of curves are likely to collide. The "tipping point" occurs once this line is crossed and renewable energy becomes economically attractive: this is exactly what happened in the late 1990s in Europe. Lately, given the carbon credits provided under the Kyoto Protocol Clean Development Mechanism (CDM), the trend has expanded to developing countries too.

The secret, as for other emerging technologies, is in a virtuous cycle driven by economies of scale: as demand peaks up, encouraged by strong government policies and public support, the industry — including oil and gas giants who have always kept the pulse on these new energy alternatives —

Figure 11.3
Renewable Electricity Prices Trends

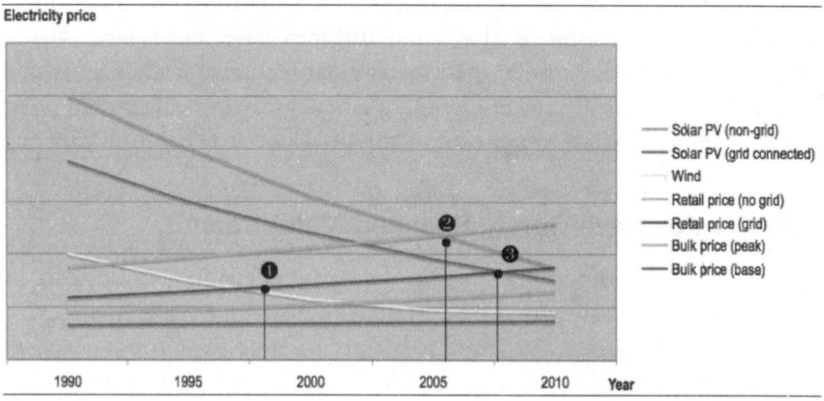

Source: SustainAsia.

is investing massively in the clean/renewable energy space. This in turns leads to further technological developments and cost efficiencies, etc.

According to Clean Edge, a U.S. based consultancy, the renewable energy technology market will be worth US$100 billion by 2014. Under the combined public support, market pull and R&D efforts, investments in clean technologies — and clean energy in particular — are starting to pay off.

Favourable Global Trends have Encouraged an Explosion of Projects in the Region

Most countries in the Bay of Bengal region have adopted favourable renewable energy policies and incentives in recent years, including feed-in tariffs or renewable portfolio standards, capital subsidies, grants or rebates, investment excise or other tax incentives. Other sophisticated measures already adopted in Japan and certain European countries, towards a fully distributed energy approach — such as two-way metering, which enables end users to become net exporter of excess electricity to the grid — are still a remote possibility in other parts of the world (see Figure 11.4).

A healthy pipeline of projects stimulated by carbon credits — the global demand for CER in developed countries who are signatories to the Kyoto Protocol, such as the European Union or Japan — public and private investments or loans, and transparent competitive bidding procedures, has lifted renewable energy projects to unprecedented levels.

Figure 11.4
Renewable Energy Policies (Asia)

Bay Of Bengal Countries

Country	RE Law since Year	Feed-in Tariff	Renewable port-folio standard	Capital subsidies, grants or rebates	Investment excise or other tax credits	Sales tax, energy tax, or VAT reduction	Tradable renewable energy certificates	Energy production payments or tax credits	Net metering (two-ways)	Public investment loans, or financing	Public competitive bidding	CER credits (Kyoto CDM)
Developed and transition countries												
Australia	2001		✔	✔			✔			✔		
Japan	2003	(*)	✔	✔			✔		✔	✔		
Korea	2003	✔		✔		✔						
New Zealand	2000			✔						✔		
Singapore				✔		✔						
Taiwan				✔		✔						
Developing countries												
Cambodia				✔								✔
China	2005	✔		✔	✔	✔				✔	✔	✔
India	2003	(*)	(*)	✔	✔	✔				✔	✔	✔
Indonesia	2002	✔										✔
Malaysia	2001	✔										✔
Philippines	2001				✔	✔				✔		✔
Sri Lanka		✔										✔
Thailand	2000	✔	✔	✔					✔			✔
Vietnam												✔

Source: REN21 report 2005 and SustainAsia.

With ninety-four registered CDM projects under the Kyoto Protocol, one third of a combined total of 299 registered CDM projects globally, India is leading the way and has become, *de facto*, the largest source of Certificates of Emission Reduction (CER or "carbon credits" as it is commonly referred to). China is not far behind and catching up fast with some of the largest GHG reduction projects to date (UNFCCC, September 2006).

India has become the champion of clean energy with an ambitious plan to meet its fast-growing energy demand: under the XI plan (2007–12), the Government of India is aiming to double its current renewable energy installed capacity from 6,000 MW (or a 5 per cent of the total capacity) today to over 11,000 MW, through additions of "non-conventional" energy sources. With a projected Total Power Demand of 157 GW in 2012 — which represents a doubling of its current demand every ten years — and in spite of a full deployment of India's huge hydroelectric potential (large and small), it is unlikely that additional renewable energy capacity will change its relative share of the overall power generation mix which will remain around 5 per cent. The Clean Development Mechanism under the Kyoto Protocol will of course contribute significantly to this additional renewable energy capacity: for ninety-four registered today, there are already over 319 projects approved by the Host Country Authority (HCA) in India — The National CDM Authority of India — so the current trend is likely to accelerate (Ministry of Power, Government of India).

Another knock-on effect of the deployment of renewable energy in the region is the possibility to electrify the most remote, and often poorest communities, by means of off-grid renewable energy solutions. Many experts and multilateral agencies, recognize that this distributed energy approach is key to break the isolation of such rural and under-privileged communities. Well-targeted energy schemes not only towards individual households ("one light for all" schemes do not necessarily lead to economic development), but also to power irrigation pump sets, cold chain applications, small and medium enterprises, local communities social, health and education services will save in infrastructure costs and empower further economic development.

Who will Benefit?

Besides the obvious public good delivered by clean and affordable energy to local governments and communities, it is interesting to analyse closely how the rise of the renewable energy industry will benefit other stakeholders in the private sector. In most developing countries, conventional energy infrastructure projects are highly regulated and driven by local governments. Due to the sheer size of capital required and the risks and complexity involved, such projects are traditionally funded by multilateral agencies and/or public private partnership schemes, through heavy-handed and top-down project financing structures.

By comparison, renewable energy projects are much smaller in size and driven mostly by local energy entrepreneurs, hence a traditional project finance model is ill-suited for such investments. Undeniably the CDM scheme has been a catalyst in the emergence of the renewable energy industry in developing countries. But CDM projects are only the tip of the iceberg of the market potential for commercial clean energy ventures: in order to leverage the full potential of this market, including energy efficiency and demand side management, now that the right set of pricing, regulatory policy framework and industrial capability is in place — thanks for a large part to the Kyoto efforts — the need for more creative, market-driven and localized financing schemes has become increasingly apparent.

One example of a possible scheme is shown in Figure 11.5. At first sight it looks like as a lighter version of a conventional project finance scheme.

Figure 11.5
Generic Financing/Risk Sharing Scheme SME Project (Commercial Basis)

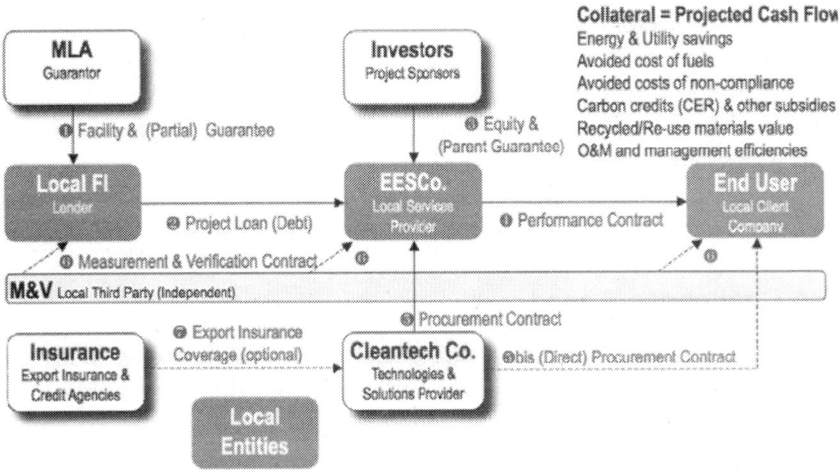

Source: SustainAsia, US Commercial Service (P2E2 scheme), IFC (World Bank).

However, there are several notable differences. First of all, since this scheme has to be closed on commercial terms between the various parties involved, clear financial benefits in the form of projected cash flows (including carbon credits and other incentives) and performances have to be agreed between the service/technology provider and the end user.

For the scheme to work efficiently, it is preferable that all contracting parties remain local and that any recourse under the relevant contracts be handled within one single jurisdiction. In such a scheme, the cash flow projections and binding contracts serve as collateral for a local financial institution (FI) to grant a project loan. The lender receives in turn the guarantee from a multilateral agency (MLA). A balanced allocation of risks versus returns, ensures that all parties shown in Figure 11.5 will benefit from the scheme.

Aimed at financing Pollution Prevention and Energy Efficiency projects (P2E2 projects) in the private sector between Hong Kong and China, this scheme has been actively promoted in Hong Kong under the U.S. China Commission on Commerce and Trade. It has received the full support of the HKSAR and China Governments under the China Closer Economic Partnership Arrangement (CEPA) and is being endorsed by multilateral agencies such as the Asian Development Bank (ADB) and the World Bank (IFC) as guarantors.

Released in June 2006, this P2E2 scheme has been unanimously welcomed by the private sector: nine commercial banks in Hong Kong are supporting it (Bank of China, Bank of East Asia, Citic Ka Wah Bank, Dah Sing Bank, DBS (Development Bank of Singapore), Hang Seng Bank, HSBC, Standard Chartered Bank and United Commercial Bank) on the debt part, as well as several specialized Investment Funds on the equity part.

This is just one example of the many possible market-driven funding schemes. Its principles could be easily extended to other jurisdictions.

The Challenges Ahead

The main challenge remains a diplomatic and a political one. With the United States and Australia opting out so far from the first round of the Kyoto Protocol, the next round will shape the future of the renewable energy industry, as well as climate change policies around the world. Public opinions, local communities and concerned industries have a great role to play in this global debate: given the present situation its outcome is very uncertain. On the economic side, any slowdown has the potential to derail the entire process for decades.

Renewable energy policies and incentives in isolation are not sufficient to resolve broader energy security issues: to be effective these should be subordinated to an overarching sustainable energy strategy, including broader social development, energy usage and demand patterns. Energy is the bedrock of any economy, therefore great resistance is to be expected from entrenched interests and lobbies in such a fundamental area.

In order to embrace the full extent of the rapid changes in our energy landscape, education and capacity-building is key: preparing the coming generations for the formidable task that lies ahead, is by far the greatest challenge of all. This requires strong leadership and vision from diverse constituencies as well as close cooperation efforts around the world.

NOTE

1 This schematic reflects global trends only in countries having adopted renewable energy policies. The figures shown here shall not be interpreted in absolute terms, as each country has specific pricing/incentive structure.

Index

N

T

Y